Lecture Notes in Computer Science

Commenced Publication in 1973
Founding and Former Series Editors:
Gerhard Goos, Juris Hartmanis, and Jan van Leeuwen

T0238272

Editorial Board

Theodor G. Wyeld   Sarah Kenderdine
Michael Docherty (Eds.)

Virtual Systems and Multimedia

13th International Conference, VSMM 2007
Brisbane, Australia, September 23-26, 2007
Revised Selected Papers

 Springer

Volume Editors

Theodor G. Wyeld
Swinburne University of Technology, Faculty of Life & Social Sciences
John Street, Hawthorn, Victoria, Australia, 3122
E-mail: twyeld@gmail.com

Sarah Kenderdine
Melbourne Museum, Special Projects
Carlton Gardens, Melbourne, Victoria, Australia, 3053
E-mail: skender@museum.vic.gov.au

Michael Docherty
Queensland University of Technology, Games and Interactive Entertainment
Creative Industries Precinct, Kelvin Grove, Queensland, Australia, 4059
E-mail: m.docherty@qut.edu.au

Library of Congress Control Number: 2008921920

CR Subject Classification (1998): H.5, H.4, H.3, I.2-4, J.4-5

LNCS Sublibrary: SL 3 – Information Systems and Application, incl. Internet/Web
and HCI

ISSN   0302-9743
ISBN-10   3-540-78565-5 Springer Berlin Heidelberg New York
ISBN-13   978-3-540-78565-1 Springer Berlin Heidelberg New York

Springer is a part of Springer Science+Business Media

springer.com

© Springer-Verlag Berlin Heidelberg 2008
Printed in Germany

Typesetting: Camera-ready by author, data conversion by Scientific Publishing Services, Chennai, India
Printed on acid-free paper   SPIN: 12238620   06/3180   5 4 3 2 1 0

Preface

The 13th International Conference on Virtual Systems and Multimedia was held in Brisbane, Australia in September 2007. This was the first time that VSMM was sited in Australia. The Australian conference theme reflected the country's cultural heritage, both recent and past – Exchange and Experience in Space and Place. Of the many papers submitted under this theme we were able to identify three core sub-themes: Virtual Heritage, Applied Technologies and Virtual Environments. With a truly international flavor, these sub-themes covered the diverse areas of heritage site and artifact reconstruction and analysis, Australian Aboriginal cultural heritage, training, notions of spirituality, human – computer interaction in virtual environments, 3D modelling, remote collaboration and virtual agents. This made for rich, varied and lively conference session debates.

Ninety-seven papers were submitted. Of these, 56 were accepted for inclusion in the general conference proceedings. Of these, 18 were further reviewed and selected for this Springer publication. The authors of these papers were invited to revise their papers following feedback from the conference before inclusion in this volume.

Many people contributed to the conference. We first wish to thank the Virtual Systems and Multimedia Society, who provided strong support to the whole process of the preparation of the conference. In particular, we would like to express our thanks to Takeo Ojika, Mario Santana Quintero and Hal Thwaites for their generous support and guidance.

We are grateful to Amanda Boland-Curran, Barbara Adkins, Laz Kastanis, Martin Lack and Jackie Lack for their hard work on the local arrangements. Last but not least, we would like to express our gratitude to all the contributors, reviewers and International Program Committee members, without whom the conference would not have been possible.

September 2007

Jeff Jones
James Hills
Hal Thwaites

Organization

Sponsor

Virtual Systems and Multimedia Society

Organizer

Queensland University of Technology, Australia
Australasian CRC for Interaction Design, Australia

Co-sponsors

Australasian CRC for Interaction Design, Australia
Creative Industries Precinct, QUT, Australia
Museum Victoria, Australia
VRSolutions, Australia
State Government of Queensland, Australia

With the Support of

The United Nations Educational, Scientific, and Cultural Organization's (UNESCO)
Culture Sector

Committee Listings

Executive Committee

Conference Chairs
Jeff Jones (Queensland University of Technology, Australia)
James Hills (Silicon Graphics, SGI, Australia)

Program Committee

Sarah Kenderdine (Museum Victoria, Australia)
Theodor Wyeld (Swinburne University of Technology, Australia)
Michael Docherty (Queensland University of Technology, Australia)

Organizing Committee

Amanda Boland-Curran (Australasian CRC for Interaction Design, Australia)
Barbara Adkins (Queensland University of Technology, Australia)
Laz Kastanis (Queensland University of Technology, Australia)
Martin Lack (Martin Lack & Associates Pty Ltd, Australia)
Jackie Lack (Martin Lack & Associates Pty Ltd, Australia)

Board of Directors, VSMM2007

David Bearman, ICHIM, Museum and Web
Ling Chen, Tsinghua University
Rand Eppich, Getty Conservation Institute
Maurizio Forte, CNR-ITABC Italy VHN
Bernard Frischer, The Institute for Advanced Technology in the Humanities
Bogumil Hausman, Embassy of Sweden
Ilona Heldad, Chalmers University of Technology
Elizabeth Jerem, Archaeolingua
Wang Jiaxin, Tsinghua University
Sarah Kenderdine, Museum Victoria
Hyungseok Kim, Miralab University of Geneva
Hyoung Gon Kim, KIST Korea
Brett Leavy, CyberDreaming, Australia
Zhigeng Pan, Xi'an Jiaotong University
Daniel Pletinckx, Visual Dimension bvba
Altion Simo, AIST, Japan DHRC, Tokyo
John Sutherland, University of Albertay
Yutaka Takase, CADCENTER
Jennifer Trant, ICHIM, Museum and Web
Susanne van Raalte, Vianova system
Krzysztof Walczak, The Poznan University of Economics
Hyun S. Yang, KAIST

International Review Committee

Albert Rizzo (USA)
Alfredo Andia (USA)
Altion Simo (Japan)
Amanda Oldroyd (USA)
Angelina Russo (Australia)
Angelo Beraldin (Canada)
Armin Grün (Switzerland)
Bernadette Flynn (Australia)
Bolchini Davide (Italy)
Charalampos Karagiannidis (Greece)
Daniel Thalmann (Switzerland)

Donald H. Sanders (USA)
Dora Constantinidis (Australia)
Edwin Blake (South Africa)
Ekaterina Prasolova-Førland (Norway)
Eric Champion (Australia)
Fiona Cameron (Australia)
Franca Garzotto (Italy)
Franco Niccolucci (Italy)
Franz Frischnaller (Germany)
Hal Thwaites (Malaysia)
Harald Kraemer (Switzerland)
Herman Neuckermans (Netherlands)
Hyun S. Yang (Korea)
Ilona Heldal (Switzerland)
Janice Affleck (Hong Kong)
Jan-Michael Frahm (USA)
Jeff Malpas (Australia)
Jeffrey T. Clark (USA)
Jim Cremer (USA)
Juan Barcelo (Spain)
Kati Geber (Canada)
Leonie Schaffer (USA)
Lewis Lancaster (USA)
Malcolm Pumpa (Australia)
Maria Economou (Greece)
Mario Santana (Belgium)
Mark Billinghurst (New Zealand)
Nadia Thalmann (Switzerland)
Nicoletta Diblas (Italy)
Olga De Troyer (Belgium)
Paul Bourke (Australia)
Rae Staseson (Canada)
Richard Beacham (UK)
Robert Sablatnig (Austria)
Roberto Scopigno (Italy)
Rodrigo Cury Paraizo (Brazil)
Ruzena Bajcsy (USA)
Sabry El-Hakim (Canada)
Sam Bucolo (Australia)
Sanjay Goel (USA)
Shaun Wilson (Australia)
Sofia Pescarin (Italy)
Susan Shazan (Israel)
Tim Hart (Italy)
Wolfgang Börner (Germany)
Xiangyu Wang (Australia)
Yehuda Kalay (USA)

Virtual Systems and Multimedia Society

Hal Thwaites (President)
Takeo Ojika (Honorary President)
Alonzo Addison (Vice President)
Robert Stone (Vice President)
Daniel Pletinckx (VSMM 2007 Conference Adviser)
Mario Santana Quintero (Executive Officer)

Table of Contents

Virtual Environment

Using a Dance Pad to Navigate through the Virtual Heritage Environment of Macquarie Lighthouse, Sydney

Eric Fassbender and Debbie Richards

Macquarie University, Computing Department, Division of Information and Communication
Sciences, Sydney, NSW, 2109, Australia,
eric@fassben.de, eric@ics.mq.edu.au,
richards@ics.mq.edu.au

Abstract. In this paper we look at the potential of a novel navigational interface, a dance pad, to allow users to intuitively explore a virtual heritage environment. An immersive Virtual Reality environment has been created to learn about the historical background of the Macquarie lighthouse in Sydney, Australia. Using the dance pad technology, we hoped to allow the users to literally step back in time and walk around the environment in whichever direction they chose. This paper introduces the Macquarie Lighthouse virtual heritage environment and the dance pad technology and describes its usage for navigation. We discuss the outcomes of a pilot study and note a number of current limitations of the technology. Future research directions in the field of intuitive Human-Computer-Interaction devices in virtual heritage projects are also presented.

Keywords: Virtual Heritage, Virtual-Immersive Environments, Virtual Reality, USB Dance Pad, Alternative HCI Input Devices.

1 Introduction

Educationalists have realised that game technology can improve learner engagement and motivation [1]. Also, games have even been employed to teach medical students [2]. In the *VirSchool* research project [3] we are currently focusing on bringing Australian history to life in an immersive Virtual Environment by using game technology. The project aims to take history off the dusty shelf by providing a positive and memorable experience that will encourage our heritage to be valued and thus passed on.

In the highly immersive CAVE-like (Cave Automatic Virtual Environment) environment that we are using in our virtual heritage project (see Figure 8), we wanted the users to be as immersively involved as possible without the restrictions of traditional input devices (i.e. cables or the need of a flat surface to operate a computer mouse, keyboard or joystick). Despite the existence of alternative input methods (e.g. the Footmouse [4] or data-gloves) the predominant navigational input device nowadays continues to be the computer mouse originally invented by Douglas Engelbart [5] back in the 1960s. While this input device certainly has benefits when working on typical office related tasks (word-processing, spreadsheets, etc.) it has

T.G. Wyeld, S. Kenderine, and M. Docherty (Eds.): VSMM 2007, LNCS 4820, pp. 1–12, 2008.
© Springer-Verlag Berlin Heidelberg 2008

limitations in regards to intuitiveness and freedom of movement. Hence, for our project, we were looking for a more intuitive navigational input device that allowed a more natural way of Human-Computer-Interaction. Others have pioneered this area of tangible interfaces. For example, Hiroshi Ishii and his tangible media research group at the MIT [6] used the Audiopad [7] or the Topobo [8] system to achieve "seamless interfaces between humans, digital information, and the physical environment" [6]. In this spirit, we investigated the use of human feet to navigate a player character (also called an Avatar) through the aforementioned virtual-immersive environment. A promising technology for this purpose appeared to be a dance pad, which we subsequently connected to a virtual heritage course.

Before describing the dance pad technology and a pilot study we conducted, we give a brief overview of the wider project context and the historical background of the Macquarie Lighthouse and the Virtual Reality technology that has been used to create the virtual heritage environment. We will discuss outcomes and restrictions of what we hoped would be an intuitive Human-Computer-Interaction (HCI) device. Finally, we will look at possible future research directions in the field of intuitive HCI devices in virtual heritage projects.

2 Background

Before we discuss the advantages and disadvantages of using a dance pad for navigational purposes, we will briefly explain the historical and technological backgrounds of our *VirSchool* virtual heritage project.

2.1 Historical Background

The Macquarie Lighthouse (See Figure 1) is the landmark icon of Macquarie University and, more importantly, it is Australia's first lighthouse (some even say it was the first lighthouse in the southern hemisphere [9] in [10]). It is situated on the South Head peninsula of Sydney's Port Jackson harbour entrance and the lighthouse that we are looking at today is the second lighthouse that was built in almost the same spot as the first lighthouse.

The history of the Macquarie Lighthouse begins with the colonisation of Australia and the arrival of the First Fleet in 1788. According to Casey and Lowe [10], a flagstaff was erected near the site where the lighthouse is located nowadays as early as 1790. The flagstaff's original purpose was to signal the arrival of a desperately awaited supply ship from England to the colonists, as well as indicating the harbour entrance to the incoming ship. In the years following the erection of the first flagstaff, the flagstaff was upgraded (1792), rebuilt (1797) and extended by a stone column (1790) and a fire beacon (between 1793 and 1805). On the 1st of January 1810 Colonel Lachlan Macquarie started his duty as Governor of New South Wales and in 1818 architect Francis Howard Greenway finished the construction of the first Macquarie Lighthouse. As early as 5 years after the end of the construction, repairs had to be conducted because parts of the building were falling apart. The causes for the decay were mostly attributed to the low quality of the sandstone and mortar.

Fig. 1. The Macquarie Lighthouse in Sydney, Source: [11]

Eventually, the deficiencies in construction were not tolerable any more and from 1880 to 1883 a second lighthouse was built only 4 metres behind the old lighthouse (which was subsequently demolished). After the power supply of the lighthouse had been changed from coal-gas to kerosene in 1909, the lighthouse was connected to the main city electrical power supply in 1933. The lighthouse was automated in 1976 and demanned in 1989. Despite being demanned, it is still operational and is nowadays operated and maintained by the "Australian Maritime Safety Authority"[1]. Public tours are organised by the "Sydney Harbour Federation Trust"[2].

2.2 Technological Background

To bring the history of the Macquarie Lighthouse to life we are creating a computer enhanced virtual reality course. For this purpose the course is set up in a 3-dimensional game-engine, which is run in a virtual-immersive environment. Figure 4 shows the Macquarie Lighthouse game mod (a modification of the original application) developed with 'The Elder Scrolls Construction Set' (TESCS)[3]. TESCS is a modding expansion for the game 'Elder Scrolls 4 – Oblivion'[4] and it allows the creation of complete virtual scenarios and supplies the developer with the necessary tools to design a virtual world in his or her own style.

In a first step, the landscape surrounding the Macquarie Lighthouse was modeled in TESCS. To achieve a high level of authenticity, the landscape was modeled by means of an accurate land survey supplied by the Sydney Harbour Federation Trust (See Figure 2). Afterwards, a 3d model of the Macquarie Lighthouse was created with 3d Studio Max[5] and then imported into TESCS. The 3d model was created based on copies of the original blueprints from 1883 (See Figure 3), also provided by the

---

[1] Australian Maritime Safety Authority: http://www.amsa.gov.au
[2] Sydney Harbour Federation Trust: http://www.harbourtrust.gov.au
[3] The Elder Scrolls Construction Set:
     http://www.elderscrolls.com/downloads/updates_utilities.htm
[4] Bethesda Softworks: http://www.elderscrolls.com/home/home.htm
[5] 3D Studio Max by Autodesk: http://www.autodesk.com

Fig. 2. The landscape surrounding the virtual Lighthouse was modeled as closely as possible to a land survey

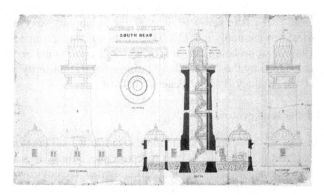

Fig. 3. The 3d model was created based on copies of the original blueprints from 1883

Fig. 4. A 3D Model of the Macquarie Lighthouse together with a virtual Avatar who is explaining the history of the lighthouse to the users

Sydney Harbour Federation Trust. Figure 4 shows the 3d model of the lighthouse on the landscape. The Avatar in the foreground is a fictitious descendant of the first lighthouse keeper, who is delivering the history of the lighthouse to the users.

3 Implementation of a USB Dance Pad into the Virtual Heritage Course

The Virtual Heritage environment has been created to narrate the story of the Macquarie Lighthouse and investigate the effect of different musical background stimuli on memory in a virtual-immersive environment. However, in the course of our research we were looking for new input methods to explore the described virtual-immersive environment more intuitively and we thought it would be more natural for users to use their feet to navigate a character through this environment. As a result, we investigated the usability of a dance pad as an input device.

Dance pads are typically used in dancing games, such as Konami's "Dance Dance Revolution"[6] or its open source equivalent "Stepmania"[7]. These games and the associated dance pads have a growing fanbase [12]. However, to the best of our knowledge the dance pads have not been used for much more than the aforementioned dancing games and we were interested to see the potential of such dance pads as input devices to explore virtual heritage environments. For this purpose a 'BNSUSA - Fusion' dance pad was purchased and connected to a PC (Personal Computer) which runs the Macquarie Lighthouse course in the Oblivion game engine. Normally, these dance pads are manufactured for use with XBox or Playstation gaming consoles and they are not suited for use with PC's. The dance pad we used in our tests was especially selected because it includes a USB (Universal Serial Bus) connector which is needed to operate the dance pad on a PC. This dance pad also comes with drivers for Windows XP. However, after connecting the dance pad to the PC it became obvious that the 'Oblivion' computer-game was not capable of being operated with the dance pad 'off-the-shelf'. Since Oblivion (the game engine we used to create and run the virtual heritage course) is designed to be played with either a computer-mouse **or** a gamecontroller (see Figure 5). If using a gamecontroller, the game expects the use of the two joysticks on the gamecontroller for movement and viewing. In our tests, the dance pad was recognized (as a gamecontroller) by the game but could only act as one such joystick, due to the design which basically consists of 4 arrow keys for forward, backward, left and right movement (See Figure 6). With this basic functionality it was possible to move in the respective directions when stepping on the arrow keys. However, the left and right movement was restricted to "strafing" which means side-stepping or shifting to the side with the viewpoint focused on the same view and always facing in the same direction. In contrast to this strafing, we wanted to be able to rotate/turn the character (and the view) when stepping on the left and right arrow keys. As mentioned, this turning command would normally be allocated to the second joystick on a gamecontroller but due to the fact that the dance pad can simulate only one such joystick, this functionality was not available instantaneously.

---

[6] http://www.musicineverydirection.com/
[7] http://www.stepmania.com/

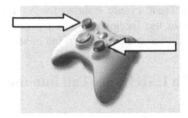

Fig. 5. Microsoft Xbox gamecontroller [8] normally used with games such as Oblivion

Fig. 6. The USB Dance Pad with the arrow keys for moving the character forward/backward and left/right within the virtual heritage environment

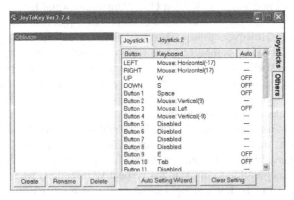

Fig. 7. Joy2Key, a Joystick/Mouse Emulator used to remap the arrow keys on a USB Dance Pad to keystrokes and mouse movements

Fortunately, Oblivion allows a mix of input devices to be used for interaction. For example, a computer mouse and a keyboard, or a keyboard and a joystick can be used simultaneously to execute commands in the game. Thus, the solution for the problem was to make the dance pad appear as two such input devices to Oblivion. The Y-axis

---

[8] http://www.xbox.com

would still be used as a joystick (for forward/backward movement) and the X-axis would be used as a computer mouse (rotation/turning of the character). For this purpose, a software program was used to remap the left and right arrow keys in order to emulate left and right mouse movements. In Figure 7 we can see the configuration screen of this software and in the right column we can see that the left and right button (the arrow keys on the dance pad) are allocated to negative and positive values of horizontal mouse movement. The software we used is called Joy2Key and for our tests, version 3.7.4 was used. The software can be downloaded and used free of charge [9].

4   A Dance Pad as a Navigational Input Device: A Pilot Test

Once the remapping of the arrow keys on the USB dance pad was completed, the feasibility of the dance pad as a navigational input device for our virtual heritage environment could be investigated. For this purpose, a pilot-test was conducted with 5 participants. Although the results reported here are of an empirical and experiential nature, we found that the reactions of the participants were overwhelmingly consistent and the results we found were quite unexpected. We further note that the number of participants involved in our pilot did not permit meaningful quantitative statistical analysis.

In Figure 8 we can see a user who is utilising the dance pad to navigate through the virtual-immersive environment and interact with the Avatar. When users first stepped on the dance pad the navigation through the environment was intuitively easy – a step forward/backward made the character walk forward/backward, a step to the left and right resulted in the first person character turning left and right. Unfortunately, this first impression of the intuitive use seemed to be the only beneficial aspect of the dance pad. Negative aspects were clearly showing the limits of the feasibility of this setup for virtual-immersive environments. The most obvious disadvantage was that people using this form of HCI (Human Computer Interaction) tend to be disoriented and their balance is affected by the virtual-immersive display system. The vertigo experienced in this virtual-immersive setup is sufficient to put users so much out of balance that they sway to the side. They have to put one of their feet out and step off the dance pad to avoid falling over. Even one long-time user of dance pads - with many months of experience with dancing games and dance pads as HCI input devices - stepped off the dance pad unintentionally in order to correct his position and regain his balance. The reason for this vertigo is very likely to be the result of a conflict between vision and our balance system. As Redfern *et al.* say in their article:

> "Visual conflicts can have powerful effects on balance. Moving visual environments can cause postural changes, disequilibrium, and motion sickness in healthy adults."[13]

We found that the vertigo could be partially overcome if a table to hold on to was placed in front of the participant, as shown in Figure 9. Chairs put to the left and right of the dance pad worked as stabilisers as well when held on to.

However, after the vertigo and balance issues were temporarily 'resolved' with a table or chairs, another problem became obvious. Although the basic functionality of

---

[9] http://www.electracode.com/4/joy2key/JoyToKey%20English%20Version.htm

Fig. 8. A user utilising a USB Dance Pad to steer towards an avatar (from first-person viewpoint) who explains the history of the Macquarie Lighthouse

Fig. 9. The same user, holding on to a table to avoid vertigo in the virtual-immersive environment

moving forward/backward and left/right could be realised with the dance pad, this form of navigation is not responsive enough (in terms of time needed to press buttons/keys) to maneuver comfortably in a virtual heritage environment. If for example, a user approached an avatar or an object and the user accidentally over-steered because the arrow key was activated for too long, then they had to change from one foot to the other in order to use the opposite arrow key with the other foot and reverse into the other direction to correct the previous over-steering. This change of direction takes a considerable amount of time and is not practical for extended use in virtual-immersive environments. As an example, in Figure 10 we can see the steps that are necessary to steer the virtual character. The black footprint represents the right foot and the checkered footprint represents the left foot. Pictures a-d in Figure 10 show the final position of the feet which navigate the character forward and left (Picture d). Pictures e and f-g show two alternative step sequences to change from the previous movement (forward and left indicated in Picture d) to forward and right (Picture h). While one might think that this change of direction would be a rather simple task, we were astonished at how complicated this was, at least over an extended period of time. The reason for this feeling of complexity is the amount of movement that is necessary to enter/transfer the movement commands into the system. When we compare the sequences to change the direction (Pictures a-h) to a gamecontroller (Figure 5) then we can see that the distance to get from one arrow to the opposite (e.g. left to right) is much higher for the legs and feet on a dance pad than for a thumb on a gamecontroller. Also, the momentum necessary to shift the weight from one side of the body to the other - in order to change feet - takes a considerable amount of time. Thus, the reaction time of the dance pad is rather slow when compared to traditional input devices (i.e. computer mouse, keyboard and joystick). To make up for this slow reaction time the users often ended up using the solution displayed in Pictures i-j, where the right foot would remain on the forward arrow and the left foot would press the right arrow key by moving it behind the right foot. Although this solution might improve reaction time, it is a rather awkward position, because one ends up with crossed-over legs. Understandably, this is not a very stable

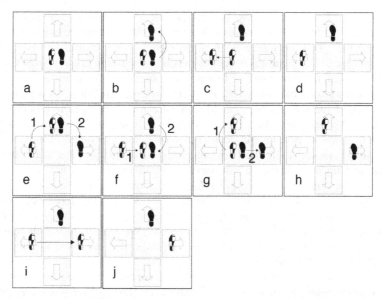

Fig. 10. The necessary steps to change from a forward and left movement (a-d) to a forward and right movement (e and f-h). Many steps are needed or one can end up in an unnatural position.

position, especially with the (albeit reduced) problem of vertigo in mind. A further problem with this form of navigation is that it lacks accuracy.

The On/Off characteristic of a digital signal (putting a foot Down/Up) makes it hard to steer precisely. For this reason it was often necessary to cautiously and repeatedly tap on the respective arrow key just very briefly, so that the digital signal was only activated for very short intervals. By using this tapping method the users were able to slowly approach the desired avatar/object, but it seems that this form of navigation would be ineffective for long-term use because it is too time-consuming and users get frustrated with the inaccuracy of this input method. An analog signal, which allows more precise steering, would be more beneficial for this purpose.

5 Conclusion

For our project we were looking at novel ways of navigating through virtual-immersive environments. After overcoming initial problems with the connection of the dance pad to the Macquarie Lighthouse virtual heritage course, we conducted tests to evaluate the usefulness of such a dance pad for navigational purposes. A pilot test was designed and conducted to give an initial indication of the feasibility of further experiments. The tests showed that the dance pad allowed movement and navigation within the environment, however, it was not the intuitive input device that we hoped it would be. During our tests we consistently encountered various problems, which included vertigo and balance issues, which forced participants to step off the dance pad. The tests also showed that a dance pad lags behind in regards to response time and steering accuracy compared to more traditional input devices like computer mouse, keyboard and joystick. The empirical evidence from this project shows that the possibilities for dance pads as navigational input devices are limited for the exploration of virtual heritage environments in a virtual-immersive environment.

Despite the appeal to engage our feet and thereby better utilize our body, as we do in driving a car or operating a sewing machine, it is interesting to consider past experiences with the footmouse or footmole [4], so named due to its larger size. In the footmouse the cursor can move left, right, up or down depending on which corner of the rubberized surface is depressed. Movement can be continued in this direction by continuing the pressure [14]. Dix et al [15] describe the footmouse more as a "isometric joystick" perhaps due to its limited method and range of movement. The limited information that can be found regarding its evaluation, usage and limitations are summed up as follows: "a rare device, the footmouse has not found common acceptance for obvious reasons" [15 p.65]. Unfortunately, the reasons are not given. We assume potentially having to remove one's shoes may have been an issue, however inaccuracy, lack of agility and familiarity of our feet with the required movements, are suspected to be the main reasons. We note that even though we use our feet to drive cars and operate sewing machines, they are used for stopping and starting, not for navigating.

From our tests we conclude, that in its current form a dance pad as an input device is more of a hindrance than an improvement in Human-Computer-Interaction. In order to foster learning in virtual heritage environments and improve intuitive interaction with a virtual environment, further tests and use-case scenarios of dance pads (i.e. how can they be used otherwise) would be beneficial. Also, it would be valuable to investigate the usefulness of additional input devices, like data gloves and 3d pointing devices in conjunction with foot-operated input devices.

6   Future Outlook

One such alternative use-case could be to use a gamecontroller for moving around in the environment and instead use the feet for other commands, which are not used as

Fig. 11. A Dance Pad with handle bars behind the users - as used in game parlours. Source[10] (Advertising removed)

---

[10] http://www.ddrgame.com/dance-dance-reovlution-am-energy-extreme2.html

frequently (e.g. to bring up menus, and inventory and maps). This is similar to the use of dedicated/preprogrammed buttons on a gamecontroller, which allow the gamer to shoot or jump, for example. Furthermore, to improve the usability of dance pads as input devices, it would be possible to use a handle bar behind the users like they are being used in game parlours (See Figure 11). This would greatly increase the stability of the users.

Acknowledgements

The authors would like to thank Brett Watson for his valuable input in regards to dance pads, Genevieve McArthur and Alexandra Frischen for their help with vertigo effects in virtual-immersive environments and Manolya Kavakli for her guidance and support. Furthermore, we want to thank Meredith Taylor for her help with the photos and John Porte and Iwan Kartiko for technical help. This project is partly funded by Australian Research Council Discovery Grant coded DP0558852 and Macquarie University Research Infrastructure Grant titled "Virtual Reality Engine". The main author is funded by iMURS (international Macquarie University Research Scholarship).

References

1. Bartles, R.: Designing Virtual Worlds. New Riders, Indianapolis (2003)
2. Roubidoux, M.A., Chapman, C.M., Piontek, M.E.: Development and evaluation of an interactive web-based breast imaging game for medical students. Academic Radiology 9(10), 1169–1178 (2002)
3. Fassbender, E., Richards, D., Kavakli, M.: Game engineering approach to the effect of music on learning in virtual-immersive environments. In: International Conference on Games Research and Development:CyberGames 2006, Western Australia (2006)
4. Greenstein, J., Arnaut, L.: Input Devices. In: Helander, M. (ed.) Handbook of Human-Computer Interaction, pp. 495–516. Elsevier, Amsterdam (1988)
5. Engelbart, D.C.: A Conceptual Framework for the Augmentation of Man's Intellect. In: Howerton, P.W., Weeks, D.C. (eds.) Vistas in Information Handling, vol. 1, pp. 1–29. Spartan Books, Washington (1963)
6. MIT, MIT Media Lab, Tangible Media Research Group, Website: (Last accessed: August 5, 2007) (2007), http://www.media.mit.edu/research/39
7. Patten, J., Recht, B., Ishii, H.: Interaction Techniques for Musical Performance with Tabletop Tangible Interfaces. In: Patten, J., Recht, B., Ishii, H. (eds.) ACE 2006, Advances in Computer Entertainment, Hollywood, California (2006)
8. Raffle, H.S., Yip, L., Ishii, H.: Robo Topobo: Improvisational Performance with Robotic Toys. In: SIGGRAPH 2006, Conference on Computer Graphics and Interactive Techniques, Boston, MA (2006)
9. Reid, From Dusk Till Dawn (1988)
10. Casey, M., Lowe, T.: Archaeological Assessment of Macquarie Lightstation South Head. In: Sydney Harbour Federation Trust, Sydney (2005)
11. LoA, Lighthouses of Australia Inc., (Last accessed: November 25, 2006) (2006), Website: http://www.lighthouse.net.au/

12. Phillips, A., Spilver, B.: Dance Dance Revolution Extreme 2 with Dance Pad. School Library Journal, Reed Business Information/ Reviews, 91–91 (2006)

13. Redfern, M.S., Yardley, L., Bronstein, A.M.: Visual influences on balance. Journal of Anxiety Disorders 15(1-2), 81–94 (2001)

14. Preece, J., et al.: Human-Computer Interaction. Addison Wesley, Harlow (1994)

15. Dix, A., et al.: Human- Computer Interaction, 2nd edn. Prentice-Hall, Harlow, England (1998)

3D City Model of the Ancient Hue, Vietnam; Reconstruction of the City Environment for the Cultural Heritage Identity Conservation

Fausto Pugnaloni[1], Giovanni Issini[1], and Nam Dang Minh[2]

[1] Polytechnic University of Marche, Department of Architecture Survey Drawing Urban Planning and History, Via Brecce Bianche 60100 Ancona
[2] Hue College of Sciences, Department of Architecture, Nguyen Street, Hue, Vietnam
{gioviss@gmail.com, minhdangnam@gmail.com}

Abstract. To have a correct knowledge and codification of their historic-cultural heritage, various Asiatic countries today present common problems. In particular the most urgent need is that of analyzing the heritage in order to be able to protect it and show it to better advantage without coming into conflict with the social transformations that are taking place in those countries. For this reason Virtual Reality is an instrument able to support this process. In the presented project the Italo-Vietnamese researching group has elaborated a 3D City Model of Hue, Vietnam. The object of this study is therefore an entire city that, in consideration of its existent cultural possessions, needed to undergo an all-over reconstruction in order to recreate a complete 3D environment. There are numerous possible applications from the model: Multimedia products, videos, render, together with a return of future projections of the city's development and monitoring of the urban evolution.

Keywords: Virtual environment, Cultural heritage defence.

1 Introduction

The paper describes the stages of the realization of the 3D Virtual Model of the ancient city of Hue in Vietnam, carried out by the united Italo-Vietnamese staff. The city of Hue is characterized by the presence of an immense cultural heritage still very little known at an international level. Vietnam, the country into which the research has been inserted, appears to the researchers' eyes as a country with new stimuli compared to the well-known European environments. In fact everybody knows that such a process of high economic growth and of social transformation, which is at present taking place in this country as in other Asian countries, may cause a rapid loss of the cultural roots of the population together with a loss of identity, especially among the new generations. In face of these types of problems common to the Last Developing Countries, Virtual Reality can play a fundamental role not only in reconstructing the image of the ancient environment and in witnessing it in the future, but also in supporting the choices of urban development that are at present taking

T.G. Wyeld, S. Kenderdine, and M. Docherty (Eds.): VSMM 2007, LNCS 4820, pp. 13–23, 2008.
© Springer-Verlag Berlin Heidelberg 2008

place. Starting from these general aims, research has verified that the documentary material of Hue's cultural heritage was already present and plentiful, even if it is mainly made up of orthogonal projections. This material, still very precise, has not however the power of being visible, interactive and easily accessible for the local and also foreign users who want to learn more about this city. Therefore research has created a Virtual Model of the city of Hue, fusing in a unique virtual environment three components: the landscape, the historic architecture and the residual urban texture.

In fact, as we shall see, the city of Hue is a Monumental City deeply harmonized with the natural ambient and the popular building industry, so a serious Visual Communication of this city must mould together the three elements in a unique representation.

2 Method and Stage of Work

The Virtual Model that has been carried out had the following aims:

- to reconstruct the all over image of the city of Hue, through the virtual reconstruction both of the areas still preserved or however existent, and of the areas destroyed by the bombing during the war against the United States
- to communicate in a simple and interactive way the quality of the cultural heritage of the city of Hue using a unique model of the city composed of 3d models of the monuments with a discreet detail level
- to create a virtual environment in which to experiment the planning solutions on both an urban and building scale
- to monitor the development of the city foreseen for the following twenty years both in terms of building expansion and in terms of safeguarding of the presence and recognition of the monumental system.

First Stage. The first step has been represented by the creation of the territory and of the water landscape that strongly characterizes the city. For this reason the method of virtual reconstruction was based on high resolution satellite imagery but also on elaborate autocad vectorial maps. This material has allowed us to re-create the territory, the waterways (rivers) and the slight mountainous reliefs that surround the city. The elaboration process was principally based on the use of the popular software AUTOCAD also chosen to be globally known and therefore to facilitate the long-distance work between the Italian staff and the Vietnamese staff. Secondly the work of the mapping of the land was carried out with the 3d STUDIO MAX software which allowed a precise placing of the high-resolution satellite imagery on the reconstructed portions of the territory. In this stage, it was plain that in spite of the good quality of the satellite imagery , it didn't have a clear definition such as to sustain a visualization of a virtual environment according to the scale of the building. Therefore the development of the model in a future stage foresees the insertion of digital photography areas carried out in portions.

Fig. 1. Satellitar view of the ancient Hue Citadel, Vietnam. It's possible to see the main walls, the canals and the Huogn River.

Second Stage. The second stage of the work concerned the creation of three-dimensional models of the monumental complexes of the city. The existent material was very heterogeneous and different methods were used to carry out the 3d models. The problem common to all the methods was to create the most agile models possible in terms of file dimensions since, at the moment of the joining up of the city model, there would result problems of the management of a very heavy model even for specially sophisticated machines such as those used by the two staffs. Therefore a compromise was reached among the detail levels of the 3d models, establishing some minimum standards relative to the dimensional reliability of the models, but the levels of detail were not carried out beyond a certain limit.

Generally speaking two methods of representation were used according to the presence of 2d reliable reliefs:

- 2d reliable relief: creation of a 3d model through software Autocad and mapping though 3D STUDIO MAX
- 2d non-reliable or inexistent relief: creation of points cloud through digital photographs (speditive photogrammetry) point elaboration through software PHOTOMODELER and mapping through software 3D STUDIO MAX.

The first method was used for the monuments that presented some reliefs, available thanks to the local institutions and found by the Vietnamese staff. In particular:

- four of the ten entrance doors of the ancient city (Sap Gate, etc)
- some portions of the town-wall of the historic city
- the Pale Blue Pagoda and the Literature Temple.

The second method has instead been used for the other monuments. In this sense the system of speditive photogrammetry has proved itself specially useful as it is based on some certain measures and on digital photographs taken in the appropriate way.

The photographic survey, using the techniques described above, was performed according to the following sequence:

- Photographic survey of the monuments and photograph cataloguing
- Identification of viewpoints on the photographs

- Image rendering using PhotoModeler software (generation of points cloud by the extracting of homologous points)
- Points cloud processing – generation of the wireframe model
- Creation of surfaces for the textures
- Scale definition by entering a known measurement.

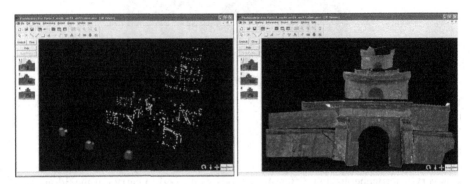

Fig. 2. Elaborations and mapping of surfaces. Clouds of points obtained from processing of digital images of monuments.

These methods of survey have proved to be particularly well suited for architectural heritage protection programmes, as detailed photographic surveys of monuments, encompassing all their portions, are sufficient for a faithful rendering. Overall, collecting sufficient information on a large number of buildings requires a few weeks for the on site work; processing can then be performed at a remote and shred online.

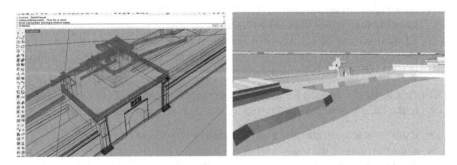

Fig. 3. Modelling of citadel rampards, walls and gates and modelling of landscape and transportation ways.

Third stage. In the third and last stage of the work the models, performed also by distinct persons who participated in the research project, have been assembled in order to extrapolate a total image of the city. This job has been carried out through the 3D STUDIO MAX software from which then, render, animations and films have been extrapolated for the representation and divulgation of the pre-war image of the city, in

Fig. 4. Mapping of citadel walls and gates. Mapping of earth trought elaboration of satellitar images.

which all the destroyed elements have been reconstructed in the Virtual Environment. Running parallel a Virtual Model of the City of Hue, that shows the state of present preservation of its monumental possessions has been created. In this stage the work of the mapping of the monuments, carried out thanks to a vast and complete photographic survey of all the city's monuments adjourned up to November 2005, has been especially important. The mapping of the 3D models through images, has been possible thanks to a work of photo-straightening of the same images by using TriDimetrix software. This software permitted the re-elaboration of the images eliminating the distortions caused by the instrument and the straightening and scaling of them thanks to the knowledge of a well-known measure and of some alignments.

The 3D City Model has been completed by the creation of a background of urban building, obtained through some elaborations of the available vectorial maps.

The detail level of the 3D City Model has therefore been tared according to the urban scale both for problems of the elaborating capacity of the available computers (that is often still more restrictive if carried out in the Last Developing Countries) and for the immense quantity of data to be elaborated. Also for this reason, we haven't gone, at least up to this moment, so far as introducing in the Visual Models elements of the completion of the virtual ambient such as the sound-effects typical of the city,

Fig. 5. 3D reconstruction of Sap Gate. The Gate has been mapped with texture obtained from elaboration of digital images.

the vegetation and lighting effects. However we must underline how the attained compromise has managed to satisfy the requirements we had initially aimed at. In particular the creation of the virtual city has allowed us to carry out Virtual simulations of project interventions concerning both the introduction of new building objects or the restoration of the existing ones, and plans of urban development.

3   The 3D City Model of Ancient Hue

The City of Hue presents one of the most significant examples of an eastern citadel in entire South-East Asia. The dimensions of the main town-wall, that enclosed the historic city, the imperial city and the forbidden city are already in themselves a significant datum: a square with a side of about 2,3 km and a perimeter, shaped by 24 ramparts, to be crossed passing through ten doors. The internal surface is of about 500 hectares subdivided into nine distinct areas by four main route axes.

The construction process of the citadel of Hue coincided with a historical period characterized by profound changes and innovations of the local culture due especially to the presence of French colonies, during the dynasties of Gia Long and Ming Mang (1802 – 1840). The city planting is based on the generating principles of Vietnamese tradition, in which the first kinds of fortified cities date back to 250 b. C. with the construction of the citadel of Co Loa near Hanoi. However the Vietnamese citadels had an identity of their own, made up of subsequent concentric town-walls, where the external ones adjusted themselves to the land with oval or circular forms, while the internal one, that enclosed the Emperor's palaces, was constituted by a rectangular plant. The massive walls were made up of compact earth covered with bricks or baked clay and might be even 25 meters thick.

Therefore the 3D City Model has, as a fundamental element, the town-wall system, which has been reconstructed thanks to the representation methods already illustrated above. The town-wall system is made up not only of the town-walls but also of the double order of artificial canals that surround them, which have also been represented. The rather accurate representation of the town-wall system has been fundamental since the city lives its equilibrium of development between what is "internal" to the citadel and is always changing and what is "external" that tends to grow and to dispel the dominant role of the ancient city.

The system of the Access Doors is also associated to the system of the town-walls: The Access Doors are set at each side of the quadrilateral and are 11 altogether, two for each normal side and five for the main side, the one against which the forbidden city leans, that according to eastern tradition is turned towards the South-East (or the South). The doors were, originally, all identical, except for the central door of the main side, the Ngo Mon Gate, which unconditionally represents the passage between the "external" world to the city and the "internal" one. During the period of the American bombing many doors underwent some substantial alterations. Some, such as the Nha Do Gate or the Huu Gate were completely destroyed and some of them have today been reconstructed. Others such as the Dong Ba Gate were altered to achieve shooting points in reinforced concrete which substituted the original turrets. Thanks to the model, there also appears clearly the collocation that the city and the monumental sites assume, as to the orography of the land and as to the water system.

The choice of the site in which to set the city and its orientation, which would dictate the orientation of the streets and both the real and popular residential buildings, was based on Feng-Shui and "Dich Ly" rules. Differently from the fortified Chinese cities orientated along the North-South axis (Beijing, Xi' An), the Citadel of Hue is set along a North-West South-East axis. The reasons that have led the "geomancers" (the preservers of Feng-Shui culture) to distinguish themselves with regard to the Chinese tradition are bound to the same physiognomy of the place. In fact Feng Shui and Dich Li indicate the screen, the water, the open surrounding space, the blue dragon and the white tiger as favourable elements in relationship with the building. To favour the simultaneous effectiveness of these elements the builders have therefore rotated the usual axis up to the direction that best allows the integrating of the water system represented by the river Huong, the isle on the left and the one on the right as the white tiger and the blue dragon respectively, Mount Ngu Binh with a screening function on the city. Nature itself has therefore defined the urban system of Hue. The 3D City Model shows these peculiar aspects of the city of Hue, suggesting general views, guided visits, cultural virtual routes of the city. The simplified reconstruction of the internal quarters and of those immediately external to the town-wall, permit one to perceive the evolution of the dwelling density that is being attained.

A significant experience of the employment of the 3d CITY Model in the field of control and monitoring of the architectonic and urban development has been carried out by inserting the project of four important poles for services which the united researching staff has planned in order to restore some crucial areas within the historic city to their recognizability. In fact the projects were to be inserted in correspondence with the four main axes that subdivide the surface of the citadel in nine blocks. In the builders' original design these points had to represent the passage points among internal areas associated to different meanings and to be clearly identifiable by whoever went through the city so as to maintain a precise orientation. Subsequently, owing to the intensifying speculative building presence, these points have lost their degree of both functional and symbolic recognizability. Therefore four projects of urban increase in value of theses areas have been elaborated, and controlled through continuous simulations and tests within the 3D City Model. This process has systematically harmonized the force relationship between empty and full spaces, masses and surfaces, in order to integrate the intervention to the existent architectonic urban system without creating discontinuity in the present urban system.

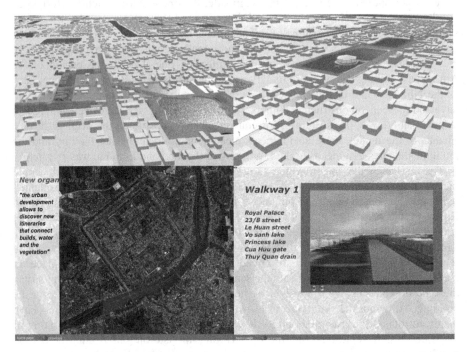

Fig. 6. Simulation of environmental impact of archictectural plan inside the Citadel. Proposal of urban planning of the monumental areas.

Another useful experience for testing the functionality of the 3D City Model was the one regarding the re-planning of the Mang Ca quarter set in the North-East quadrant of the citadel. In fact, along the internal tract of the road that connects the Trai Gate to the Chan Tay Gate, a quarter with a mixed residential-commercial destination is going to be reconstructed in the free area, presently occupied by the Army. Consequently the 3d model of the new quarter project has been inserted in the Virtual Environment.

These two experiences have therefore shown how the use of the 3D City Model for controlling and verifying the new projects or interventions of restoration is useful on two levels. For the active persons of the planning process, that is to say for managers, investors and architects to be helped in administering the transformations to integrate them with the present urban system. For the passive persons, that is to say the citizens who have the possibility of participating in the urban transformations with simple and effective communication instruments at their disposal such as multimedia products, films, render.

4 Multidisciplinary Contributions and Collaborations

In the work of realization of the 3D City Model of the city of Hue several competences have joined.

The international cooperation between Italy and Vietnam has consented the gathering together of different approaches to the reconstructing work.

In detail the work has been carried out by:

- Italian and Vietnamese architects, researchers and professional men who have performed the work of researching historical documents, the controlling operations of the mapping phase of the virtual model, software employees: Autocad 2004, Rinoceros, 3D STUDIO MAX 6.
- Designers and graphic computer experts who have accomplished the work of the creation of the 3D objects and also the elaboration and the retouching of the digital photographs to be applied on to the surfaces of the 3D objects. Software employees: Adobe Photoshop 6.0, Adobe Premiere, Photomodeler, TridiMetrix.
- Local Directors, Superintendents for the preservation of the heritage, who have put at everyone's disposal the bibliographic and cartographic material they had, about the monuments, and have verified the capacities of the 3D City Model of Hue in order to experiment the future urban developments.
- Designers have worked out of the 3D city Model, some multimedia products for the cultural and tourist promotion of the territory but also to present the new local urban plans of development and the transformation strategies of the 2000-2020 city. The Software used is Macromedia Flash.

5 Results

The 3D City Model of Hue, fairly precise, complete, in the initial stage of the models, of about 60% of the whole cultural heritage. Today the model being adjournable and modifiable, it has been adjourned so as to reach 73% of the represented heritage. Therefore there exists the possibility of definitely completing the work of modelling of the monuments within the next few years and of starting, for each of them, a process of adjournment of their degradation and preservation state. Nowadays the model is used as a data bank of the city's cultural heritage:

- The already experimented possibility of extrapolating, from the 3D city Model of Hue, several multimedia promotion products, such as for example, the Multimedia DVD "Hue Citadel Tomorrow", in which the city, its history and its monuments are presented, together with the plans and future development hypothesis, giving the user the possibility of viewing films of simulated insertion of the new projects and quarters.
- The Virtual laboratory for Hue's transformation, made up of the Italo-Vietnamese research group, is a fundamental instrument for controlling the extremely fast urban transformations and for monitoring the consequences on the environment, on the water system and on the cultural heritage.

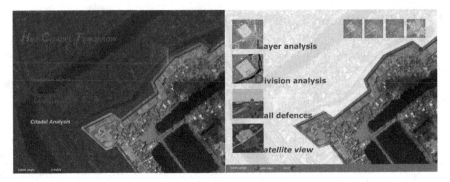

Fig. 7. Examples of multimedial products obtained from the 3D model, finalized to promote the Hue cultural heritage

6 Possibility of Future Development

Possibility of a future greater precision and insertion of a higher detail level on the monuments, sound effects of the environment, human activities and vegetation. This development is presently being carried out and is through time facilitated by the continuous adjourning of the modelling software and by the improving of informatics services. Development of a complete model to be publicly visited through internet with "Live" modalities for promoting the architectonic qualities of the city at a "global" target. Development of a website dedicated to professionals (architects, engineers, planners, etc.) where they can easily verify the impact of their project by inserting it into 3D City Model. Adapting and simplifying the model to share it on exploration software (Google Earth, visual Earth). Creation of a database of Vietnamese Architecture shared by the researching organizations and the local organizations that operate in the territory.

References

1. Debevec, P.: Modelling and rendering architecture from photographs, University of California, Berkley
2. Dang, N.B., PhuonG, N.V.:Traditional Vietnamese Architecture. Gioi Publishers
3. Pugnaloni, F., AA. VV.: Recreating the past-visualization and animation of cultural heritage. In: Conference acts isprs (2001)
4. Mariano, M.L., Fangi, G., Malinverni, E.S.: Rilievo fotogrammetrico speditivi per la creazione di database per i beni culturali: il caso delle porte monumentali della cittadella di hue. Polithecnic University of Marche (2004)
5. Martino, C., Fangi, G., Malinverni, E.S.: Rilievo fotogrammetrico speditivi per beni culturali e modellizzazione tridimensionale per applicazioni multimediali: il caso delle porte monumentali della cittadella di hue. Polithecnic University of Marche (2004)
6. Grossi., L., Fangi, G., Malinverni, E.S.: Tecniche di fotogrammetria architettonica speditive, il tempio di aizanoi (turchia) e la porta nord di hue (vietnam). Polithecnic University of Marche (2003)

7. AA.VV.: Masterplan of Sectors and National Programs in Vietnam to the year after 2000. Vietnamese Statistical Publishing House (1997)
8. Benevolo, L.: History of oriental town, Laterza (1989)
9. AA.VV.: Structural Studies, Repairs, and Maintenance of Heritage Architecture IX. In: Baldonado, M., Chang, C.-C.K., Gravano, L., Paepcke, A. (eds.) Conference acts, Malta 2005 (2005); The Stanford Digital Library Metadata Architecture. Int. J. Digit. Libr. 1, 108–121 (1997)

A Conversation on the Efficacies of the Game Engine to Address Notions of Sacred Space: The Digital Songlines Project and Transgressions of Sacredness

Theodor G. Wyeld[1,2], Patrick Crogan[3], and Brett Leavy[2,4]

[1] Swinburne University of Technology
[2] The Australasian CRC for Interaction Design (ACID)
[3] The University of Adelaide
[4] Cyberdreaming
twyeld@gmail.com, patrick.crogan@adelaide.edu.au,
brett@cyberdreaming.com.au

Abstract. The Digital Songlines (DSL) game engine is used as a vehicle for Indigenous Australian storytelling. Their storytelling is inextricably linked to the 'country' from which it emerges. The game engine provides a simulation of that country for embedding of the stories to be told. Much of the 'country' referred to is sacred. However, the fundamental underlying principles of three-dimensional reproduction of space in a 3D computer game (3DCG) defines all spaces as mathematically equal – there is no place for notions of sacred spaces. This presents a dilemma for those cultures that do not subscribe to the scientific notions of ontological certainty underpinning such mathematically modelled space. In the case of the DSL game engine, notions of the sacredness of the country modelled has been made explicit in order to highlight its importance for its physical-world corollary. Hence, this paper discusses notions of sacredness and its place in the simulational spaces of the DSL's 3DCG engine. It presents a series of dilemmas for the inclusion of sacred places in simulational spaces. It does not attempt to resolve these dilemmas, but rather to bring them into sharp relief with examples drawn from the DSL project experience. In so doing, it presents a new way of thinking through the significance of this issue for Western and non-Western use of the 3DCG in cultural heritage applications.

Keywords: Sacred Places, Sacredness, Uluru, Digital Songlines, 3D games, Cultural Heritage.

1 Introduction

3D Computer Game (3DCG) spatial simulation is unlike other forms of spatial simulation that are based on normative conventions of narrativised text – films, storybooks, theatre, and so on. 3DCG simulation introduces an interactivity with the spatial narrative not possible in other genres [2, 13]. Spatial narratives – the interaction with, navigation of, and cognitive inhabitation in space – mean different things to different cultures. Space itself as a concept has been redefined in many

T.G. Wyeld, S. Kenderdine, and M. Docherty (Eds.): VSMM 2007, LNCS 4820, pp. 24–34, 2008.

different ways over time and by different cultures. For Western culture, space was once finite and divided between heaven and earth. Many spaces were considered sacred. Sacred spaces are those spaces that defy the logic of scientific definition, of quantifiable space, such as, the space of religious worship (churches, synagogues, temples, and so on); the space demarcated as a place of socio-cultural importance related to historical events; the homes of celebrities, and so on. Sacred spaces are controlled spaces. Access to and representation of these spaces and what they contain and what can be seen from them is often subject to rules and regulations. Different cultures may define their own sacred spaces in different ways but similarly feel the need to control how that space can be accessed and how it is represented. While physical sacred spaces can be controlled by physical means, the modelling of space by 3DCG that may include sacred spaces has introduced a new method for experimenting with notions of the sacredness of such spaces – from forensic reconstructions, the virtual entering of ancient tombs, to re-enactments of historical events. Experimentation with the notion of sacred space predates the 3DCG. Notions of the sacredness of space were profoundly altered for the West during the European Renaissance. In the Renaissance, previously conceived notions of the duality of body and soul, and their place in space, were dismantled by the emergence of Nicholas of Cusa's 'universal ideal' among other methodologically scientific shifts in thinking. Following this, all space was knowable, testable, mathematically quantifiable, and by implication, reproducible [7]. The 3DCG is the latest manifestation of the apparent reproducibility of space. Although the 3DCG is utilised in many different ways other than reconstructing sacred spaces, sacred spaces, as part of a pre-Renaissance culture, are constantly eroded by technological innovation thus raising questions about the basis of their sacredness. As such, it is a topic worthy of investigation.

This paper discusses the place of sacredness in a 3D computer game engine. More specifically, the appropriation of a 3DCG as a storytelling vehicle for the telling of Indigenous Australian stories which, by their very nature, include spaces that are sacred. As such, they provide for the experimentation of notions of the sacredness of these spaces in a simulated environment. In turn, this presents a dilemma, as the opportunity for experimentation with these spaces in the context of a 3DCG is only possible as a product of the Western technological dismantling of notions of the sacredness of space. While this paper attempts to tease out the issues raised in these dilemmas, only a few can ever be addressed in full.

2 Simulational Spaces

3D computer game (3DCG) space provides a more active kind of participation with a virtual environment than the seemingly more controllable, passive participation with other media forms such as films, photography, theatre, storybook, and so on. 3DCGs are simulational spaces. They are different from these other conventional media forms, which are based on the reception and perception of existing narrativised texts; they are simulational spaces designed for interactivity [2, 13]. As such, users or, more precisely, 'inter-actors' can play out interactive narratives with simulated spaces with apparent impunity. Unlike in a film, photograph, theatre, storybook or other more conventionally *received* narrative, the game space allows new narratives to evolve through interaction with the space rather than the given narratives *per se*. For example, the interactor can experiment with a sacred space that might normally be censored from traditional media. That they are able to do this is a product of its underpinning technological ideology and faithful reconstruction of a universalised space, which includes sacred places as part of notions of holistic integrity which sees all spaces as equal in the modelling process.

Modelled space invites experimentation. As such, 3DCG simulational spaces are also spaces of the future [3]. They are about *what can be done*? with the spaces; experimental spaces; spaces for speculating on *what ifs*? In the Western sense of reducing reality to *knowns*, the spaces are simulations of the real. Within the scientific reductivist paradigm, experimentation does not raise questions of the sacredness of spaces. For, Western representations are abstractions of the real – metaphorically: this as that. However, for many cultures, abstraction and reality, subject and object, are often merged. Not all cultures subscribe to the Western scientific paradigm. Hence, representation may not be abstract. It may be more like re-presentation of the real. In this sense, the simulated spaces can be as sacred as their physical-world corollaries. This raises questions about how such spaces can retain their sacredness when re-presented in a 3DCG simulational space.

3   Transgressions of Sacredness in Simulational Space

Along with 3DCGs, *Second Life* [http://secondlife.com] is a simulational space experiment. As a massive multiuser platform with millions of users, and ostensibly a simulated 'other-world' social experiment, there are many opportunities to test notions of sacredness in *Second Life*. As in other media, opportunities arise to transgress normally respected notions of sacredness. A recent example of this is Tesltra's (the Australian national telecommunications company) use of a model of Uluru (a profoundly sacred rock, protected by its Indigenous custodians) on their *Second Life* 'island' without permission from the traditional owners [4]. Strict rules governing photographing, filming and viewing of rock paintings associated with Uluru have been in place since 1987, when control of the rock was handed back to the traditional owners. Although in Telstra's simulation of the rock, barriers were provided to prevent avatars walking over sacred sites, visitors can view other sacred sites around the rock normally controlled. Moreover, that the ire of the administrators of Uluru (on behalf of the traditional Anangu people) was raised by this act suggests that notions of sacredness do extend to simulational spaces, and that transgression of appropriate respect for how they are re-presented needs to be addressed in simulational spaces as it is in other media.

4   The Digital Songlines Simulational Space

The simulation of Indigenous Australian sacred spaces in 3D virtual environments is not only restricted to those insensitive to its affects. A group of researchers in Australia, working closely with rural and urban Indigenous Australians, have been developing the 3D game platform as a storytelling vehicle. The Digital Songlines

(DSL) digital storytelling project, funded by the Australasian Cooperative Research Centre for Interaction Design (ACID), has been developing protocols, methodologies and toolkits to facilitate the collection, education and sharing of Australian indigenous cultural heritage knowledge since 2004. The project explores the areas of effective and culturally sensitive, recording, content management and virtual reality delivery capabilities involving indigenous custodians, leaders and communities from around Australia. It investigates how players, in a serious gaming sense, can experience Indigenous cultural heritage in a high fidelity fashion with culturally appropriate interface tools. In the construction of the DSL simulated environments, many sacred spaces are re-presented. Where this differs with the Uluru transgression is that these sacred spaces are actively identified by their custodians as important parts of a larger story needing to be passed on to current and future generations. Yet, in turn, this raises questions of how this can be reconciled with the ability to transgress these spaces within the simulated environments by the uninitiated, or simply naiveté to its significance? The central charter for the construction of these simulational spaces is for the dissemination of cultural heritage knowledge. But, what sacrifice is being made in the transition to a world view (Western notions of universally accessible space) which is predicated on observable experimentation within these simulated spaces – some of which are sacred?

5 Simulational Space as Archive

In order to address the issue of transgressions of sacredness by the uninitiated, the DSL project involves a different kind of conditional engagement or encounter with the material contained. The DSL project uses its simulational spaces as active knowledge archives. This is different to traditional archiving (documents, photographs, video, film, audio, and so on). An archive is something that preserves and stores and provides access to things that are past. It's primary function is for the heritage and benefit of the people who come after. What the use of a 3DCG engine by the DSL team to create a simulational space provides is a digital platform that is dedicated to exploration and experimentation. This allows for active participation in the creation of contemporary stories contextually situated in their place of origin and access to historically sensitive stories often involving reconstructions of sacred sites. However, this sets up a tension between the possibility for futurist experimentation and traditional archiving, meaning the re-presentation of the knowledge recorded can often be too intrusive. The ability to control access and reproduction available to the traditional archive is foregone in favour of experimentation with the 'spaces' of the archive because the custodians of this knowledge consider it is too important not to be included. Of course much material can never be accessed, but many of the sacred sites included are simply considered too important to the authenticity of the stories to be told to be left out.

Added to this notion of the importance of the inclusion of sacred knowledge and spaces is the notion that archives often become a substitution for the thing they are trying to record or represent. The DSL project presents a different version of the same problem. The 'space' becomes the archive. DSE is a database which is activated by the spatialising engine that it uses. It becomes the simulational space for encountering those things it contains in terms of a different temporal orientation. The simulational spaces become a substitute in the archival sense for the real, and they also inform the real in terms of the possibility for experimenting with what is possible with those spaces that it simulates. It means interactors can do things that they could not necessarily do in the real. In time, these actions also become a substitute for the real: if most peoples' interaction with the spaces are in the virtual, what happens when they visit the physical and expect to have the same access rights as those in the virtual, and so on?

More than this, the past, present, and future are conflated in these worlds. The archive becomes the reality. Everything that is simulated, in any kind of archive, is a representation of that time. In this sense, anthropological work is always an interpretation. Hence, it becomes archival, 'the fact' of that period. Yet, each subsequent generation interprets this same archive in terms of their own contemporary understandings. Charles Mountford [11] is an anthropologist from the mid twentieth century who recorded Aboriginality in his time. He talks about his encounters with Aboriginal people and builds characters around them. Particular individual Aboriginal people are photographed in his books, for which there were few protocols for how this should be done at the time. Geoffrey Bardon [1] is another non-indigenous person working in close relationship to Aboriginal groups, recording their art and craft in the 1970s. He did establish some protocols, but these were more about what he was hoping to achieve than a consensual set of guides open to negotiation with the people he was trying to protect. The sheer number of books Bardon [1] produced, of beautifully illustrated works, represents an archive in itself. Some of the works recorded are the most important Aboriginal artworks in Australia because of Bardon's [1] meticulous recordings and the iconography captured in them. Many of these icons are not seen in today's paintings because they are considered too sacred (the early paintings Bardon [1] recorded were produced in an atmosphere of naivety about who would have access to them). Mountford and Bardon's recordings are only two examples of the many anthropological works that demonstrate the evolving need to establish protocols for dealing with notions of sacredness and in what forms it can or cannot be re-presented.

As an archiving project, DSL is faced with the same challenge of respecting the material it records. Where DSL differs from previous archival projects is both its emphasis on contemporary culture contextualised within its historical background and that each project is instigated by a member of the culture it purports to re-present. DSL has established a set of protocols that are open to negotiation with the Indigenous peoples engaged [see 6]. Yet, many compromises are confronted in its attempt to marry contemporary Aboriginal culture with traditional. The need to overcome these is paramount as the elders claim they are very worried that once they are gone their culture will go with them if it is not recorded. The younger generation they are trying to reach are more interested in playing computer games and engaging in mainstream culture to learn about their own heritage. Hence, in using the computer game as a platform, the elders are hoping to reach that generation using the same voice.

But, Indigenous Australian culture is very complex. It is not so easily reduced to the determinist confines of the 3DCG. Yet the very notion of simulation is to simplify the complex; to model phenomena in a manner that makes it more easily understood

[2]. As such, by its very nature, simulation is selective from the beginning, because there is only so much that it can support. In a similar manner, only so much can be retrieved from a regular search of archives, in terms of documentation, and the documents themselves are very selective. In the least, because they are interpretations of events and already large deductions of what could potentially be recorded or shown. The most expensive flight simulator in the world cannot perfectly model every facet of flight, but they can do it to a level of functional affectivity which is good enough for pilot training. Hence, the DSL project can only ever be a compromise. Whether it achieves its goals of preserving the important aspects of the cultural heritage it seeks to capture is open to interpretation. What makes the DSL project unique is its idiosyncratic use of the 3DCG format and game-play. Combined, these express the needs of its creators rather than the 3DCG *per se*. This alone assists in presenting the DSLs game engine as an authentic and meaningful platform for communicating Indigenous storytelling, and is recognised as such by the various Indigenous communities engaged in its production, despite the ongoing conundrum of the inclusion of sacred sites and what this means to notions of sacredness in an open simulational space that invites experimentation.

6   Idiosyncratic Simulational Space

Development of the DSL game engine is not alone in its use of idiosyncratic game formatting. The recent emergence of idiosyncratic games outlined by Stiegler [14] represent a counter challenge to the spread of simulational culture in general. They actively question what can be done with goals other than the mainstream commercial application, instrument training, or entertainment. The DSL project is an example of idiosyncratic use of a game engine to archive and reinvigorate cultural knowledge and practices.

DSL's use of the 3DCG engine as an archive is different from gaming in general because it engages the user in certain functions that are not related to game play but more like search functions. Yet the fact that it uses simulation of space, and that the whole game engine genre is built around this, also shows how space simulation is such a dominant model in our society [9, 12]. The navigation of space as traversed in the attainment of certain goals is, historically, a military position. In a military context, space becomes a trajectory, a series of trajectories to be overcome or navigated.

Hence, the challenge for DSL is to not trivialise certain parts of the culture that seem appealing and can be mapped onto contemporary non-Aboriginal culture simply because game engines are particularly good at specific types of game-play pursuits. The challenge for the DSL game engine is how to create authentic spaces and the game or role play in it. Should there be quests, and what can be learnt from those quests?, is of primary importance in terms of an educational outcome.

It is its localized (spatiotemporal) subjective interpretation, innovation, and adaptation or 'idiosyncraticity' that announces its peculiarly Australian Indigenous format and differentiates it from the more mainstream, historically militaristic games.

The legacy this represents comes from a merging of the need of the Indigenous peoples involved and what the game platform can provide. Yet, in terms of the standard game behaviours that it implicitly involves or encourages or assumes still come from the history of computer culture in general: militarily techno-scientific developments around the 1940s onwards .

The DSL project avoids much of the militaristic legacy of the 3DCG because the fundaments of the DSL database is highly contextualised landscapes rather than quests alone. These landscapes are described in affectionate terms by their Indigenous custodians as an entity: 'country'. Everything is built on this notion of 'country' as an entity. 'Country' manifests the ancestral beings in terms of the dreaming and they are uttered into existence through the telling of stories embedded in their simulated 'country'. The naming of the landscape features in 'country' brings them into existence and maintains their existence, but it also allows for change over time. It is not a linear excursion, it is disjunct in that one can wander around and find things which are both contextualised but approachable in many different ways.

For example, in the DSL's Vincent Serico World , one can stumble across one of his paintings relating to that part of 'country' one finds themselves in. The interactor can then right click and a screen pops up with his painting taking up most of the available interface (see figure 1). Sweeping the mouse cursor over the painting, the interactor notices hotspots. Clicking on one of these launches another popup with Vincent talking about that part of his painting and the stories behind it. There are also a series of small TV icons along the bottom of the frame that provide a linear sequence of voiceovers to follow. In a sense, the non-linear option most closely follows the nature of Indigenous storytelling; a story does not start at the beginning and end at the end, it can be entered at any point, and it can be changed and so on. In this manner, Serico's simulated world reflects some of those qualities. The TV icons are the Western abstracted symbolism announcing the audiovisual popups (which rely on one knowing what the symbol for a TV looks like), whereas the hotspots (although reliant on an abstract change in the type of cursor and pre-knowledge on what this change means) are more closely related to parts of the painting and the haptic method of story telling with paintings most familiar to Indigenous storytelling customs [see 1].

The addition of hotspots as an aside surprise found in Vincent Serico's World is also an emergent strategy of mainstream game construction for maintaining interest in a game. In a contemporary mainstream first person shooter game these aside interactivities are used so the player can discover secrets which are usually superfluous to game play, if the main objective of the level is to kill all the monsters and go to the next level. While this may be the main goal, the additional asides make the game space more interesting. However, the main trajectory design of the space is still about moving through it and eliminating the targets to get to the next level. In the DSL simulated world, on the other hand, in the absence of this main role-play trajectory, it is, instead, discovery of the asides that becomes the main goal. It is this tension between moving in and out of the mainstream trajectory to an activity function inside the space, that has moved it from being peripheral to central, that captures the interactors' imagination.

Fig. 1. Vincent Serico painting embedded in 3D game interface and 'country', near Carnarvon Gorge, South-West Queensland, Australia. (*Troopers*, Vincent Serico 2003, acrylic on canvas 60x103cm).

7 Permission to Visit Sacred Sites in a 3DCG

Vincent Serico's World contains sacred spaces (rock art, monolithic rock totem formations, waterholes and so on). Ordinarily, visitors are discouraged from touching, seeing, or interacting with their physical corollary. For example, one should not touch or deface the rock art or approach it without paying particular attention to seasons and so on. Similarly, one should not clamber to the top of a monolithic rock just because a view is available from there. And, one should not swim in a waterhole without the appropriate permission from the local tribal elders. All of these are possible in the Vincent Serico World. Hence, the simulational space is both referent to the real, a re-presentation of the real, and subject to the same notions of sacredness, but at the same time, immune to these strictures because there is an implied and explicit permission from the outset. In the DSL game levels, interactors are accepted as honorary members of the local clan who's 'country' is being visited. This is bestowed upon each game level by the clan elders of the re-presented country.

Nevertheless, where simulation in serious gaming and training is normally approached with a hypothetical future orientation – what can we do with this simulation? – and often little thought is given to what relationship the simulation has to the real, with the DSL game engine, it is both prospective and also archival. Hence, despite the clan elders' permission to explore their country, there still exists a tension between the simulational temporal engagements about what can be done with it and the sorts of historical preservation, hopes, and ambitions are expected of it in an archival manner by the elders who instigate it.

Thus, it remains both a challenge and an absolutely important thing to be doing. The use of a 3DCG engine provides the platform to support the essential character of Indigenous cultural practice – the emphasis on 'country' as all-sustaining, spiritually and physically. Yet, the restrictions of the 3DCG engine, when compared to the rich physical-world narratives possible, are symptomatic of the reductivist approach exemplified in the modelling paradigm and manifest by gaming culture in general. The rise of the visual over haptic that identifies Western culture [8] stems from the same renaissance concept of placing oneself outside the space and experimenting objectively on it. This reduction of the whole to things in isolation is anathema to Indigenous cultural practices hence presents yet another dilemma.

On the other hand, what the DSL project heralds is also a departure from this monism. The unfolding narratives embedded in their 'country' of origin sees the landscape as not a backdrop but as an active, central, participant in the storytelling. In this sense, the DSL project challenges the gaming norm through its idiosyncraticity. Its subscription to the current global paradigm, what Derrida [5] calls "globalatinisation", both supports and makes it possible to be counter to this visual monism [8]. Hence, the DSL project is not a departure from the gaming genre norm but rather a paradigm shift within the existing system. As such, it also offers a new way forward for idiosyncratic gaming. Here is a simulational space that reserves sacredness by providing access rights from the outset. One enters with an understanding that there are certain behaviours to be observed when engaging with the sacred spaces contained. In turn, a new respect and understanding about another culture's notions of sacredness are honoured.

According to those involved in the project the younger generation are losing their heritage to this global paradigm. They see the way to make them engage in their own culture again is within rather than outside this paradigm. By including sacred space in their reconstructed 'country' they are better able to engage the respect sought from the younger generation targeted. The global paradigm, that both provides the mechanism for their engagement and the impetus to challenge it, is not reinforced by the technology, rather it is co-constituted by mainstream media technology in general (in McLuhan's [10] sense). This is because media is increasingly the primary means by which the world is encountered. Hence, to the extent that the West's media technology dominates perception experience today, it is also important for any kind of project, not only projects dealing with Indigenous issues, but all kinds of artistic and other culturally important projects, to engage the mainstream technology to have their messages heard. The DSL project has done this by idiosyncratically altering the accepted norms, to temporalise their message in ways that highlight and counter what makes them different to the mainstream and promotes a basic characterisation of the Indigenous culture – the embedding of storytelling in its country of origin – and make this appealing to Indigenous and non-indigenous potential interactors alike.

8 Conclusion

This paper arose from a discussion between two of the authors following a public lecture demonstrating the DSL project and Vincent Serico's World (one of the many commissioned 3DCGs). In particular, the notion of sacredness in a simulational space was broached because of comments from the lecture about the apparent inappropriateness of climbing atop a large rock in Vincent Serico's World. This led to mention of the recent case regarding Telstra's insensitive use of Uluru as an icon to promote itself in *Second Life*. What differentiates the two examples was that Telstra did not have the appropriate permissions to use the sacred Uluru, whereas the DSL project has explicit permission to include sacred spaces in its 3D reconstructions of specific 'country'. Nevertheless, both rely on the exactitudinal nature of a mathematically constructed simulational space. However, such spaces fall outside the normally controllable strictures of what could be considered sacred. This announced our first dilemma: the mathematical reproduction of three-dimensional space being founded on universalising notions that do not value one type of space over another, hence there is supposedly no place for notions of sacredness in this model. Moreover, their open, holistic, and definable nature, encouraging experimentation, is anathema to notions of sacredness. This led to the second dilemma: not all cultures subscribe to the notion of a universal spatial construct. Indeed, Indigenous Australian culture, the culture at the centre of the DSL project, conflates subject and object such that representation becomes re-presentation, and thus the representation of sacred spaces in a 3DCG demands the same protection as its physical-world corollary. In turn, this led to our two further dilemmas, the tension between futurist experimentation inherent in the simulational spaces of the DSL project, and its aspirations as a spatial archive of sorts, and the *need* to use this technology to attain the 'voice' necessary to communicate an important message to a generation already familiar with gaming culture.

The last of these dilemmas unpacks into a conundrum: the DSL project is specifically tailored to use the features of the game engine to support the disjunct, non-linear, performative, character of Indigenous storytelling, yet it is also in direct competition with the global universalising paradigm that underpins the very same 3DCG technology that threatens to erode their culture. Despite and because of this, the Indigenous elders, along with the DSL project leaders, have made a paradigmatic shift within the system rather than reject it outright. This is manifest by the idiosyncratic approach to the construction of the DSL simulational spaces which at once talk to the generation targeted and communicate in a sensitive manner the sacredness of the messages contained. From this, a new genre of 'game as archive' has emerged – one which supports spatial narratives but makes no assumptions about the dismantling of its own sacredness due to the technology employed. We of the gaming fraternity could learn much from this approach about new ways to communicate the sacredness of some non-Indigenous sites!

Acknowledgements

This work is supported by ACID (the Australasian CRC for Interaction Design) established and supported under the Cooperative Research Centres Program through the Australian Government's Department of Education, Science and Training.

References

1. Bardon, G.: Papunya Tula: Art of the Western Desert, J.B. Books Australia (1999)
2. Frasca, G.: Simulation 101: Simulation Versus Representation. (Retrieved April 1, 2003), (2001) source
   http://www.jacaranda.org/frasca/weblog/articles/sim1/simulation101d.html
3. Frasca, G.: Simulation versus Narrative: Introduction to Ludology. In: Perron, B., Wolf, M.J.P. (eds.) The Video Game Theory Reader. Routledge, New York and London (2003)
4. Haines, L.: Telstra in Second Life 'Ayers Rock' kerfuffle: Aboriginal owners probe virtual Uluru, The Register (May 2007), source:
   http://www.theregister.co.uk/2007/05/25/uluru_kerfuffle/
5. Derrida, J.: Above All, No Journalists! In: de Vries, H., Weber, S. (eds.) Religion and Media, Stanford Univ. Press, Stanford (2001)
6. Leavy, B., Wyeld, T., Hills, J., Barker, C., Gard, S.: Digital Songlines: Digitising The Arts, Culture And Heritage Landscape Of Aboriginal Australia. In: Kalay, Y.E., Kvan, T., Affleck, J. (eds.) New Heritage: New Media and Cultural Heritage, Routledge, London (in press 2007)
7. Lefebvre, H.: The Production of Space. Blackwell, Oxford UK & Cambridge USA (1991)
8. Manovich, L.: 1993, The Mapping of Space: Perspective, Radar, and 3-D Computer Graphics (May 2000), source:
   http://jupiter.ucsd.edu/~manovich/text/mapping.html
9. Manovich, L.: The Language of New Media. The MIT Press, Massachusetts (2001)
10. McLuhan, M.: Essential McLuhan. In: McLuhan, E., Zingrone, F. (eds.), Routledge, London (1997)
11. Mountford, C.P.: The Aborigines and their country. Rigby, Adelaide (1969)
12. Virilio, P.: War and Cinema: The Logistics of Perception. Patrick Camiller (trans.). Verso, London (1989)
13. Ryan, M.-L.: Will New Media Produce New Narratives? In: Ryan, M.-L. (ed.) Narrative Across Media: The Languages of Storytelling, University of Nebraska Press, London (2004)
14. Stiegler, B.: Technics and Time 1: The Fault of Epimetheus. Richard Beardsworth and George Collins (trans.). Stanford University Press, Stanford (1994) (reprint 1998)

Digital Tools for Heritage Information Management and Protection: The Need of Training

Mario Santana-Quintero[1] and Alonzo C. Addison[2]

[1] R. Lemaire International Centre for Conservation, Katholieke Univeristeit Leuven,
kasteelpark Arenberg 1, B3001 Heverlee, Belgium
[2] UNESCO World Heritage Centre, 7, Place de Fontenoy, F-75352 Paris, France
mario.santana@asro.kuleuven.be, a.ddison@unesco.org

Abstract. This paper is aimed at demonstrating the need of training material for the design and deployment of cultural heritage resource information systems in management and protection. Heritage information plays an essential role in the adequate preparation, implementation and monitoring of conservation strategies. Good decisions in conservation are based on the information available and, in this sense, the use of information systems are needed for providing timely and relevant collection, storage, management and presentation of cultural heritage.

Keywords: architecture, cultural heritage, information systems, conservation, multimedia, recording, and documentation.

1 Introduction

This manuscript seeks to explore the need of guidelines for the design and deploy of digital tools directed at the global understanding of the significance of heritage sites and the threats affecting its integrity and for decision-making.

A digital system should be based on recording and managing indicators that are capable of providing information about the degree of impact to the site, providing potential stakeholders with a tool to be able to make decision about interventions aimed at protecting heritage effectively.

In addition, the development strategy should involve the consultation with stakeholders and users of the system, including operators and information providers. This will ensure an adequate deployment of a system that is both adapted to local needs to take care of cultural heritage.

1.1 Building a Heritage Information System: Dogmas

The preparation of heritage information systems often is confronted with dogmas preventing the definition of an adequate approach. Generally, these dogmas can be classified according to the following list:

1. The World Heritage dogma: all sites are considered worth of universal importance, lack of revision of the current international and national legal framework governing the operation of a system prevents the system designer

T.G. Wyeld, S. Kenderdine, and M. Docherty (Eds.): VSMM 2007, LNCS 4820, pp. 35–46, 2008.

to propose an approach that will improve institutional operations to protect heritage;

2. The 3D-4D dogma in completeness of information: usually system designers are confronted with an inadequate definition of level of recording: everything needs to be documented to the full extend, this prevents to understand the minimal requirements of a system to timely and effectively collect and manage information

3. The digital anastylosis: everything needs to be reconstructed virtually, this dogma is associated to dogma 2, this prevents effective heritage information assessment, we don't need to know exactly how a column is built to be able to protect it;

4. High tech provides more information of low tech: this dogma prevents the system designer to identify a effective and suitable approach, a misunderstanding about long and short term investment; as well, as capacity of the institution;

5. Scale vs the accuracy: this dogma prevents the designer to understand the need of a defined level of detail and the adequate assessment of existing information before deploying a system;

6. Re-inventing the wheel: this prevents not assessing and adopting standards and guidelines;

7. The heritage information specialist: this dogma prevents the designer to understand the need of multidisciplinary approach to designing and deploying a system.

1.2 Operability Issues

'After conservation intervention, documentation provides the basis for monitoring, management, and routine maintenance of a site, as well as a record for posterity' (Eppich, R. LeBlanc, F. 2006).

This statement clearly identifies the need of recording for posterity, in terms of heritage information system, this issue has not been developed consistently, the issue of preserving electronic data is a critical issue.

Longevity: deals with life expectancy in an average number of years of media, where heritage information systems is stored and disseminated, figure 1 shows the life expectancy of media in terms of years and this arises the issues of how ensuring data now stored in electronic media is preserve for the future, very little has been done in this field in relation with built heritage, however several initiatives in the field of library are currently developed, perhaps it is worthwhile to involve these groups in the discussion about media generated from inventories of built heritage (movable and immovable).

Compatibility: upgrading systems and addressing new needs is an expanding problem in the application of information systems, in this case the use of metadata to define data collected is crucial, since electronic equipment and software might constantly evolve in the future, upgrading should be an integral part of any strategy to deploy an information system.

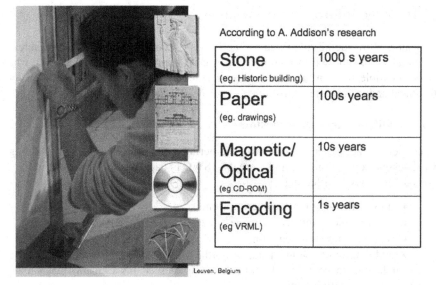

According to A. Addison's research

Stone (eg. Historic building)	1000 s years
Paper (eg. drawings)	100s years
Magnetic/ Optical (eg CD-ROM)	10s years
Encoding (eg VRML)	1s years

Leuven, Belgium

Fig. 1. Storage media longevity issues, according to Addison's approach

2   Heritage Information System's Objectives for Conservation

Cultural heritage is a unique and irreplaceable source of information. The heritage information acquired serves for the identification and classification of objects, for the development of adequate policies for its conservation and maintenance, as well as to promote identity and cultural tourism.

The objectives of a system should allow:

- Knowledge that permits the advance of understanding of the cultural heritage, its significant and integrity;
- Promote the interest and involvement of the people in the preservation of the heritage through the dissemination of acquired information;
- Permit informed decision for management and control of interventions changing the fabric of cultural heritage;
- Ensure that the maintenance and conservation of the heritage, related to its integrity (physical form, materials, construction, etc) and its historical and cultural significance.

Additionally, a system should also permit monitoring the following issues threatening the management of sites (Palumbo, G.):

- Demographic growth around and inside the site;
- Urban encroachment condition;
- Potential infrastructures development;
- Modifications of land-use;
- Lack of integrated planning;
- Lack of heritage surveys
- Lack of knowledge of condition and status of cultural heritage.

3 Heritage Information Indicators

Indicators allow identifying threats to heritage by recording variables or measures that potentially can supply information about what is happening in a heritage site, when it is not possible to monitor or measure every component of the environment due to technical and/or financial constraints.

3.1 Identifying Heritage Indicators

A convenient approach is to identify the heritage site issues by using the strengths, weaknesses, opportunities and threats (SWOT) approach. It should take into consideration issues affecting:

- Physical condition (weathering forms);
- Significance - Integrity – values;
- Interpretation – Perception;
- Other issues to be identified, according to the nature of the heritage site.

Usual factors to consider affecting heritage sites (Parks Canada) that should be considered when defining indicators:

- Development Pressures
- Environmental Pressures
- Natural Disasters and Preparedness
- Visitor/tourism Pressures
- Number of inhabitants within property, buffer zone
- Threat of armed-conflict

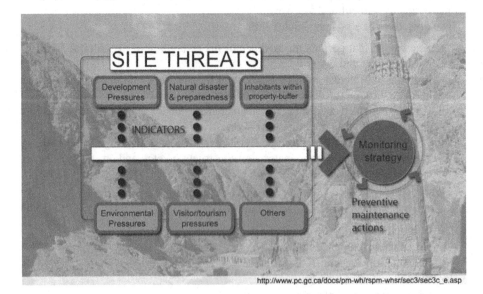

Fig. 2. Site threats in defining indicators, author based on Park Canada's approach

The evaluation of these threats and the corresponding indicators will allow to ensure a monitoring system, where a heritage information system will play a crucial role to record information about these indicators.

4 Types of Heritage Information Systems

The following Table, as being prepared as a guideline to the current practices in preparing Heritage information systems:

Table 1. Types of heritage information systems

Types	Pro's	Con's	Example
Paper inventories and catalogues	Easy to visualize and share	Difficult to retrieve information if not well indexed	http://www.nps.gov/hist ory/hdp/standards/CRG IS/paper.htm
Electronic databases	Interaction with other inventories is difficult	Indexing is easy	http://www.kikirpa.be/ www2/en/doc/docu.htm
Geographic Information Systems (GIS)	Data integration easy	Requires considerable input of mapping information	http://www.timemap.net
Online GIS with spatial imagery	Combines advantages of GIS with an intuitive and easy to understand «real» background		http://earth.google.com/

5 Defining a Baseline

Indicators, explained previously provide a guide to the issue to be recorded for the monitoring of the site, additionally to the indicators a the subsequent baseline definition involves a 'mapping effort'.

This mapping effort consists in prior to survey anything, to review and identify gaps in the existing information (documentation) on the site. This first assessment will allow estimate the degree of additional recording work required to prepare an adequate set of documents to mapped indicators.

The following checklist can be used as guideline to minimum requirements of information required to define the baseline:

- Identify site location (centroid, boundaries, elements and buffer zone);
- Identify and map evidences of criteria;
- Significance and integrity assessment;
- Risk assessment: threats and hazards associated to indicators;
- Administrative and management issues (current and passed mitigations);
- Other assessments.

Fig. 3. Defining the site baseline, author

6 Digital Sensors

Digital sensors to register, document and record cultural heritage, these can be classified according Addison's approach in the following categories:

- Visual (Still and video cameras)
- Dimensional (surveying, 3D scanning, photogrammetry, metrology, GPR)
- Locational (GPS, compass, ...)
- Environmental (thermal, acoustic, C14, ...)

Visual: technology capable of providing a visible impression of colour, shape and motion of a scene.

Dimensional: technology capable of providing a measure of spatial extent, with width, height, or length.

Locational: technology capable of providing the place where something is or could be located; a site, a location according to a national and/or international coordinate system (ex. UTM, longitude-Latitude, north orientation, etc).

Environmental: technology capable of providing information of potentially harmful factors originating in the environment, as well as, sensors providing 'dating' information, when a particular point or period of time at which something happened or existed.

6.1 Heritage Information: Sensors (Techniques) and Site Variables

The careful study of variables dealing with the characteristics of sites (resources) to be studied and mapped in a heritage information system and their direct relation with the technology (sensors) available at hand would allow to predict the timeframe, institutional impact and budget requirements for the capturing of the indicators providing information to the system (see figure 5).

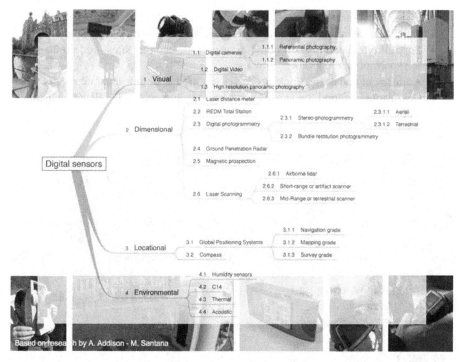

Fig. 4. Digital sensors in recording heritage information, based on Addison's approach

Heritage site variables:

- Accessibility (legal, environmental & physical): time available and constraints accessing the site to carry out the survey.
- Budget: available funds for the survey.
- Expected quality: scale and level of detail expected from the survey.
- Timing: available timeframe to carry out the survey.
- Expertise: capacity of your staff to operate, process the data obtained from the sensor
- Quantification: existence, extend and quality of metric survey data available of the building.
- Other variables: additional constraints appropriate to the physical, social and cultural location of the site
- Project information needs:
- Condition mapping, inventory, management/conservation plans.
- Cyclic monitoring requirements.

Sensor (technique) variables:

- Speed: time to record an indicator.
- Precision: accuracy factor of the capturing equipment.
- Measuring Range: reach of the tool, depends on distance and other environmental constraints.

- Field operability: constraints in relation to the fieldwork.
- Robustness: strength to extend adverse weather conditions and impact.
- Portability: capability of being transport to remote sites, requirements of transport, power and other factors.
- Adjustment and corrections: processes required to obtain accurate results.
- Occlusion: respond to shadows, obstacles, and material related constraints (reflectivity)
- Price: rental and/or purchase of the sensor.

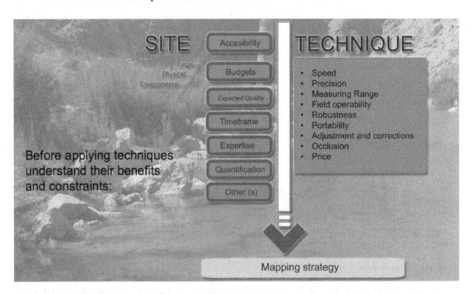

Fig. 5. Digital sensors and site variables in preparing a site baseline definition, author

7 Training: Heritage Information Capacity Building

Traditionally, heritage organizations assumed that the implementation of information system is unique to their organizations and this approach prevents them to allocate time to research to existing approaches, the issues affecting the adequate inventorying of cultural resources around the world is a global problem. Currently, several international initiatives have tackle this problem, allowing new approaches to be transmitted to experts and heritage organizations, among these experiences:

- UNESCO's World Heritage Centre Development of a World Heritage Information Management capacity in the Arab States: this project seek to address the need of information systems applied to the protection of WH sites in the Arab region, there were two seminars organized for experts;
- ICCROM's Athar courses: Documentation and Management of Heritage Sites in the Arab Region: courses about the role of information in site management, using role play exercises;
- World Monuments Fund – Getty Conservation Institute Iraq Cultural Heritage Initiative: the establishment of a heritage information system for rapid-

assessment of sites in Iraq, involving training courses in heritage information capturing, storing and management.

These experiences are focused in overcoming common issues in the utilization of heritage information systems, including:

- Lack of staff and institutional capacity and standards for collecting and referring information;
- Consistency in the identification and mapping of indicators for preventive strategies;
- Lack of long-term strategies to tackle longevity issues;
- Accessibility to technology
- Identification of funding
- Operational and institutional organization

Additionally, the CIPA's RecorDIM initiative has been seeking to produce training material for improving the consistency and use of standards for preparing heritage information systems.

7.1 Basic Guidelines

Currently, the following documents provide initial guide for the preparation of heritage information systems, it important to review them prior to start designing a system:

- ICOMOS Charter – Principles for the analysis, conservation and structural restoration of architectural heritage (ICOMOS 2003);
- ICOMOS Principles for the Recording of Monuments, Groups of Buildings and Sites (ICOMOS 1996);
- Council of Europe's Guidance on inventory and documentation of the cultural heritage (Council of Europe 2001);
- Council of Europe – Getty Information Institute's - The Core Data Index to Historic Buildings and Monuments of the Architectural Heritage (COE – GII 1998)
- Council of Europe – Getty Information Institute's - The International Core Standard for Archaeological Sites and Monuments (COE – GII 1998)

Although these documents provide a solid principles ground to start working, they do not provide strategic information about how to apply technology and adapt it to the institutional needs.

7.2 Proposals

In order to overcome the shortage of information on how to use documentation for heritage information practice, a number of guidelines are currently on the make, to assist in the preparation of heritage information system, including:

- ICOMOS resource manual on World Heritage Nomination fiels;
- RecorDIM's Information for Conservation (The Getty Conservation Institute);
- RecorDIM's Documentation for Conservation: Illustrated examples (The Getty Conservation Institute);

- RecorDIM's Documentation for Conservation: Metric Survey for Heritage Documentation: A manual for teaching Metric Survey Skills (English Heritage);
- EPOCH's heritage information scenarios (Addison – Santana).

8 Current Practices

Additionally to the manuals, the following table is a preliminary assessment of current practices under development around the world, where information systems have been deployed for heritage conservation:

Table 2. Current practices

Name	Information system objective	Accessibility	Link
UNESCO World Heritage Centre	Information system to disseminate information about sites enlisted on the World Heritage List and activities of UNESCO to promote and promote them	Accessibility levels deployed, rich information, limited spatial accessibility	http://whc.unesco.org
Monument Watch Flanders	A monitoring and maintenance system for the (Built) Cultural Heritage in the Flemish Region	Electronic, restricted access	http://www.monumente nwacht.be/
Monument damage diagnostic system (MDDS)	A decision support system for architects, conservators (prototype phase)	Local, not accessible yet online	n/a
Egyptian Antiquities Information System (EAIS)	GIS instrument for improved site protection and management for the safeguarding of the physical wellbeing and legal standing of each of Egypt's historical sites.	Local, not accessible yet online	http://www.eais.org.eg/
The Jordan Archaeological Database & Information System (JADIS)	Database of archaeological sites in Jordan, currently under review to approach the conservation of these sites	Currently under revision for upgrading, not accessible	Unofficial link: http://archaeology.asu.e du/Jordan/JADISGIS.ht m

It is important to mention the lack of good practices in this field, and the lack of public accessibility of these information systems.

9 Closing Remarks

Heritage information systems can play an important role to site managers in the planning process for allocating, managing, and applying for funding for the conservation of heritage sites.

Currently, the training gap in the preparation of these systems prevents managers to understand the utility and potential in their current work, capacity building should be a priority of international organizations providing training in developing countries around the world.

10 Future Work

Future training initiative should also adopt a stakeholders approach in the preparation of heritage information systems, as well as, the ideas of preventive maintenance approach, where information is collected to prepare baseline information of the site and to subsequently continuous record interventions carried out.

Acknowledgements

The authors wish to acknowledge and thank the support of the Raymond Lemaire International Centre for Conservation for this opportunity of supporting this short research.

In addition, we would like to thank the support to this paper from my friends at RecorDIM and CIPA. Special thanks to Bill Blake, Alonzo Addison, and Rand Eppich.

Finally, we would like to thank all those individuals and institutions that in one way or the other helped with the completion of this report.

References

1. Box, P.: GIS and Cultural Resource Managements: A manual for Heritage Managers. UNESCO, Bangkok (1999)
2. Clark, K.: Informed Conservation. English Heritage, London (2001)
3. Council of Europe, Guidance on Inventory and documentation of the cultural heritage, Council of Europe Publishing, Strasbourg (2001)
4. Eppich, R. LeBlanc, F.: Documenting our past for the future, Getty Conservation Institute (last reviewed June 19, 2007)
   http://www.getty.edu/conservation/publications/newsletters/20_3/feature.html
5. Gillings, M. Wise, A.: GIS Guide to Good Practice, AHDS Guides to Good Practice, (last reviewed June 19, 2007)
   http://ads.ahds.ac.uk/project/goodguides/gis/index.html
6. HABS/HAER/HALS, Preservation Architect, The Newsletter of The Historic Resources Committee, Washington (2006)
7. ICCROM's Athar programme: Documentation and Management of Heritage Sites in the Arab Region (last reviewed June 19, 2007)
   http://www.iccrom.org/eng/prog2006-07_en/08athar_en/archive_en/2006_12documentation_en.shtml
8. King, J. (ed.): Understanding Historic Buildings. English Heritage Publishing, Swindon, UK (2006)
9. Parks Canada Periodic Report on the Application of the World Heritage Convention (last reviewed June 19, 2007) http://www.pc.gc.ca/docs/pm-wh/rspm-whsr/sec3/sec3c_e.asp

10. Santana Quintero, M.: The Use of Three-dimensional Documentation and Dissemination Techniques in Studying Built Heritage. R. Lemaire International Centre for Conservation (KU Leuven), Leuven (2003)
11. Savage, S.: The Jordan Archaeological Database & Information System (JADIS) (last reviewed June 19, 2007) http://archaeology.asu.edu/Jordan/JADISGIS.htm
12. UNESCO's World Heritage Centre: Development of a World Heritage Information Management capacity in the Arab States (last reviewed June 19, 2007) http://whc.unesco.org/en/activities/58/
13. World Monuments Fund – Getty Conservation Institute Iraq Cultural Heritage Conservation Initiative (last reviewed June 19, 2007) http://www.getty.edu/conservation/field_projects/iraq/index.html
http://www.wmf.org/iraq.html

Beyond the Map: Issues in the Design of a Virtual 3D Knowledge Space for Aboriginal Knowledge

Malcolm Pumpa

Australian CRC for Interaction Design (ACID), Queensland University of Technology,
Australia
m.pumpa@qut.edu.au

Abstract. This paper examines the role of Virtual Reality technologies (in particular, the Digital Songlines Environment), in the expression of a sustainable Aboriginal landscape knowledge base. The effectiveness of these new kinds of knowledge practice is framed by their sustainability and how they complement existing cultural knowledge practices. These issues of sustainability and complementarity need to be addressed in the design and implementation of the VR product. This paper frames the process and product of Digital Songlines Environment as a performative, cross cultural knowledge space, which has the potential to negotiate the controversies between Western techno-science and Aboriginal knowledges. The twin themes of reflexive design and respectful cross cultural engagement and trust, are seen as imperatives for the process and product to align with the authenticity, ownership and purposes of Aboriginal knowledge traditions.

Keywords: Virtual Heritage, Design, Information Visualization, Cross cultural.

1 Introduction

This paper sets out to explore some issues in the design process of a 3D virtual world which aims to express and allow performance of Aboriginal knowledge practices. It draws on a project – the Digital Songlines Project that is currently being developed and operationalised within the Australian CRC for Interaction Design (ACID).

Although sophisticated in its look and feel and the technological investment which underlies it, the Digital Songlines Environment is nevertheless a representation of people, knowledge, artifacts and landscape, and the relationships between them. As with any representation, it works to render the heterogeneous expressions of reality in a more fixed, and singular mode. Yet, the paradigms of Aboriginal knowledge and knowledge practice which it aims to express are radically different to Western traditions. Digital Songlines Environment and all digital archiving projects are "boundary objects" between Aboriginal cultural knowledge and the Western techno-science that is utilised to express it.

As "boundary objects" they inhabit a boundary across the social, cultural and technological aspects of radically different knowledge traditions. They also do a particular kind of work in negotiating the controversies between knowledge traditions.

T.G. Wyeld, S. Kenderdine, and M. Docherty (Eds.): VSMM 2007, LNCS 4820, pp. 47–57, 2008.
© Springer-Verlag Berlin Heidelberg 2008

The explicit and reflective deployment of the controversies emerging from this project is integral to its authenticity and the role it might play as a new form in the ongoing process of Aboriginal knowledge production and transmission. The concept of the project as a new kind of performative knowledge space [1] based on heterogeneity and trust is explored and the consequences for the iterative design process are investigated.

2 Design as Translation and Transformation

The cultural stories of all cultures are aligned with the forms, materials, performances and paradigms that are authenticated and stabilised in that culture. [2] However, when a culture attempts to tell its cultural stories through the forms, materials and performances provided by another culture, there are unintended effects that need scrutiny. The telling of the cultural stories with new media forms becomes a process of innovation that involves a series of translations and transformations. Lucy Suchman [3] sees such technological innovations as not the creation of new discrete objects but the "cultural production of new forms of material practice." (p.9)

The process of design and implementation is enacted by a collective of actors both human and non-human, and becomes one of crossing the boundaries between the two cultures and deploying controversies and negotiating equivalences. Turnbull [1] asserts that this involves holding knowledges in tension. He argues that any account of cross cultural knowledge making describes "...the contingent processes of making assemblages and linkages, of creating spaces in which knowledge is possible" (p.552). This is ontological and epistemological work that negotiates what entities exist in the world and how we can know about them. It is also political work that is concerned with how particular views of the world become stabilised and accepted, how they exert influence and even come to dominate. At the same time, it forms of resistance and the emergence of new permutations of practice which act to incorporate the new form into existing networks of cultural learning.

Aboriginal knowledge traditions exist in a profoundly reciprocal relationship with Land. The role of the Land differs radically from Western notions of a passive backdrop for human cognition and exploitation. For Aboriginal knowledge, the landscape itself is simultaneously a physical space; a sentient collective of diverse entities, a meaning system and an historical, spatial visual record of all past events. Aboriginal knowledge practices are constructed in this reciprocity between people and Land, through a variety of performances and representations. Knowledge constructed in this way is locally authentic, specifically owned and has specific purposes. If we (both Aboriginal and non- Aboriginal workers) are to attempt to express these knowledge traditions and practices with the forms and materials of Western techno-science (such as 3D digital virtual worlds), we therefore need to design for authenticity, ownership and purpose in ways that are aligned with existing Aboriginal knowledge practices.

How precisely this work is done is problematic indeed. The technology of 3D virtual worlds is at the end of the long chain of techno-scientific development that historically has been involved in the collecting and archiving of Aboriginal knowledge traditions. This process is inherently heterogeneous and spatial and has involved people, technologies, sites and skills. It also inherently involves ontological and epistemological work of *symbolising, categorising, and representing* the various artifacts and performances of Aboriginal knowledges into forms and materials which Western science can accommodate into its established conventions and standards.

There are two important negative consequences of this ontological translation and transformation. First, there is a reduction of the diversity and richness of the ontologies of situated knowledges. Second, there is the long-term domination of a Western techno-scientific knowledge tradition with its claims of being able to authentically represent the ontological foundations and epistemological processes of diverse knowledge traditions, regardless of context. The result of such a process is inevitably a derivative form of knowledge that must be constantly evaluated with regard to its legitimacy. [4] At worst, this derivative form of knowledge risks being extracted, abstracted, and transformed from its oral, performative formats, dislocated from its place of origin and connection, and severed from its web of relationships with other entities in country. [5]

3   New Knowledge Spaces

It would seem to be a fact of history that knowledge practices change in accord with changes in knowledge technologies. The increasingly profound and widespread entanglement of social and technological practices suggests that this process will only become more powerful as time goes by. Various authors maintain that design is a culturally laden process [3; 6] yet, how can the design process of new media negotiate the two undesirable consequences stated above? That is, firstly, can we be reflexive and critical about the translation process, in order to make meaningful gains in avoiding the reduction and domination inherent in the use of techno-science, and the epistemological assumptions which underpin it? And secondly, how will it be judged that those gains have in fact been made?

These two threads are interwoven and integral to the design process of new media which seek to represent Aboriginal knowledge traditions. The actions of translation between Aboriginal knowledges and Western techno-science need to be critically examined and theorised, in order to arrive at representations which might be deemed to be capable of supporting, enabling and fitting in with a wider ecology of Aboriginal knowledge practices. As Victor Hart [7] maintains, "...there is a clear danger that digital tools and activities will supplant myths, rituals and learning about country from one's direct experience and immediate community" (p.53). In other words, the responsibility for judgements about the translations process and the resultant authenticity must always rely on Aboriginal knowledge custodians and their involvement in all aspects of the design process.

The design of such new media as Digital Songlines Environment can therefore be seen to be a process of translation which inhabits a boundary zone between two disparate knowledge traditions. When one of these knowledges is a hegemonic Western techno-science, then the major issue becomes the maintenance of plurality and equity of knowledges. Various authors [1; 8; 9] maintain that two moves are essential to address this issue. First, Western techno-science has to be de-privileged and framed as but one among many, partial, situated knowledge traditions. Its historical alliance with industrial capitalism has allowed it to be exported to all parts of the world and assume hegemonic proportions. Second, any theoretical treatment of the translation process into new media needs to align with the ontic and epistemic constructs of Aboriginal knowledge traditions.

These two moves have many profound effects on the design process. One consequence is that the traditional roles of user, designer and researcher are practically re-defined and aligned in terms of motivations, purposes and power relationships. The three roles are more practically seen as one role expressed differently in different situations. Also, alignment with Aboriginal ontologies requires recognition of a range of new entities and relationships with the Land as sentient organiser. In addition, alignment with Aboriginal epistemologies requires an embrace of spatialised narrative and improvisatory performance. This epistemic move allows a view of the innovation process as improvisatory performance, which goes beyond the dualism of subject and object, yet incorporates aspects of both in a way that allows for the heterogeneity of situated knowledges and temporal change. Such a new kind of performative knowledge space is a *boundary performance* which requires a move away from singular and de-contextualised representation. This allows any creation of new knowledge to be more effectively critiqued not merely on its cognitive and intellectual characteristics but on its *performances* and the sites of those performances.

The move away from singular representation towards spatial performances of knowledge offers some hope for the re-distribution of power and the maintenance of the plurality of knowledge traditions. As Turnbull [1] asserts, the history of cross-cultural knowledge production can be seen "…as a history of the contingent processes of making assemblages and linkages, of creating spaces in which knowledge is possible." (p.552) Hart [7] also argues that any sustainable expression of Aboriginal culture and identity must be built on a foundation of heterogeneous and complementary technological and traditional methods of knowledge storage.

Paradoxically, the tools of Western techno-science offer possibilities for Aboriginal knowledge traditions to halt the erosion of cultural knowledge, and the incursions by Western knowledge traditions. The viability and stabilisation of new kinds of knowledge spaces depend on two main components [1]. The first component is the heterogeneity of people, skills, local knowledge and technology (maps, visualisations, knowledge artifacts). Secondly, there is a negotiation of the social organisation of trust which allows disparate knowledge traditions to work together. Therefore, different kinds of cross cultural knowledge spaces are performed by different assemblages from the available collection of practices, people, technologies and theories. The process of assemblage is one of making connections and negotiating equivalences between heterogeneous components while simultaneously establishing a social order of trust and authority [1]. An essential part of this process is the establishment of a hierarchy that determines the priority of components (for example, negotiations need to determine the relative priority of the information and judgements of Aboriginal Elders, the requirements of design, and the limitations of computer code). This hierarchy of authority arises out of the social organisation of trust within a knowledge space and should be explicitly addressed in both design and implementation phases. Unless trust is born out of the respectful engagement of knowledge traditions, assemblages struggle to become stabilised.

New performative cross cultural knowledge spaces such as Digital Songlines Environment may start to look distinctly *unlike* the Western notion of information because they are heterogeneous assemblages of collective knowledge practices, trusted authority, spiritual values and local social and cultural organisation [1]. The integration of new knowledge spaces within existing knowledge ecologies provides opportunities for palimpsests and co-existing knowledge practices that more efficiently serve local interests and resist hegemonic knowledge politics. The performances of new cross-cultural knowledge spaces are more likely to make explicit the hidden assumptions of power and politics about subjects, objects and relations that is not feasible at a purely representational level. Such spaces allow knowledges to be mapped according to different ontological categories using different epistemological tools. As a result, the purposes and outcomes of knowledge spaces are more closely aligned to local requirements than the generic outcomes of progress and development so closely aligned to most Western techno-science innovation.

4   Knowledge Spaces as Subject and Object

If Digital Sonlines Environment is to perform as a new kind of knowledge space it must be both **object** (something we use to store and represent knowledge) and **subject** (something that causes people to do things and generates new forms of activity and performances). This has implications for what Digital Songlines Environment looks like and how it functions within the broader Aboriginal knowledge community.

Aboriginal knowledge practices are inextricably located in the sentient Land that is both subject and object. By their attachment to specific localities they are narratives that are spatial and performative. Just as the actual country changes from year to year, season to season, day to day, so these narratives and their enactments are not fixed. They are negotiated, improvisatory truth-testing performances that gather related entities in stabilisations that work for that place and time [9]. This sort of ontology based on heterogeneity, relationship and uncertainty is at odds with the ontology of a digital world such as Digital Songlines Environment, based on algorithm, data and logic structures. Thus, Digital Songlines Environment, as an entity based on discrete data, can never hope to be a self-contained presentation of the abundance and complexity of Aboriginal knowledge practices. The issues of authenticity, ownership and representation of knowledge practices are too heterogeneous and emergent for an entity based on discrete data to come to grips with.

It is only when Digital Songlines Environment is incorporated into that "radical complexity and interconnectedness" [9, p.5] that it can become a powerful actor in what John Law [10] terms an assemblage of methods that are used to present Aboriginal knowledge. Although Digital Songlines Environment is constrained by its genesis in data, three important characteristics of its design allow it to be incorporated more easily into collaborative knowledge testing in the actual world.

First, it represents a landscape, which although generated from discrete data allows two important performativities—embodiment and wayfinding. The user is immersed in a 3D environment which requires conscious locomotion or "walking country". The agency of the user is foregrounded in the choices made about where to go, where to stop, where to look. The landscape allows a sense of embodied wayfinding that can generate an almost infinite set of personal spatial narratives through the virtual country. Regardless of the number of informational data nodes in the world (which must always be finite), the possibilities of lines of travel between them are potentially infinite.

Second, the concept of a sentient landscape provides the metadata, relationships and narratives for cultural "objects" (artefacts, performances) to exist within. Inherent in this sentient landscape is the provision of the "law" which provides the semantics, logic, goals and possibilities for change within the virtual world. Aboriginal concepts of landscape and ontology are helpful because they provide explicit structure, boundaries and modes of action for both narrative and data objects. Although the structure may be explicit, it is not static. As Hart [7] states there is, "...a system of Indigenous landscape mapping which is an ongoing process of revelation, guided by customs and traditions, both old and new" (p.54). Located at the centre of this system is the sentient landscape. Hart explains that, "what has remained central is the means by which the land is spoken for, as against how land is spoken about." (p.54)

Digital game theorists, whether they are proponents of narrative or ludology, agree that the richness and power of digital game environments is dependent upon the design of the higher levels of epistemology and ideology within the game environment. Thus objects and events are not as influential as the rules which govern their appearance and the goals and rationale for interacting with them. Chris Crawford [11] asserts that, "... an essential task (of game design) is to envision a dramatic storyworld, not a storyline."(p.56).   The storyworld is made powerful by the designer's control which, "... is exercised through the rules of the gameworld rather than the events of the gameworld" (p.52). Similarly, Frasca [12] has elicited a corresponding typology of the requirements of powerful game design, which relies on 3 ideological levels. The first and weakest level deals with representation and events, the second and more powerful level deals with the manipulation rules or what the player can do in the game, with the final and most powerful level being that of goal rules or what the player must do to "win" (in the case of Digital Songlines what they must do to reveal knowledge contained in the sentient landscape).

The generation of spatial narratives by users enables the third characteristic of design, which is the "leaking" of performativity from the virtual world into the actual world. This connection with the actual world is accomplished by collaborative truth testing between users themselves and between users and significant others (e.g. Elders) who overlay the issues of authenticity, ownership and representation on the virtual world experiences of the users. This extension into the actual world is essential if the narratives generated by users are to be tested in terms of the relatedness of entities in actual country.

Like the relationship between people and country, any collaboration between virtual and actual worlds needs to be reciprocal. Users in the virtual world must collaboratively seek further truth testing from other humans and country in the actual world, in order to establish the relatedness of their virtual narratives. At the same time, the issues of authenticity, ownership and representation flood from the actual world into the design of the virtual world. Elders and Traditional Owners upon seeing the virtual world that presents their local country have made clear the deficiencies through comments such as "You got to make those stones smaller—that's important—the way you got them now, they are too big to walk over like that—they are smaller—about like this." The absences in the virtual world are ruled equally by authenticity and ownership—some places cannot be presented, some must be skirted around— "I can't tell about that place"; "I can't speak for that place. Only (name of Elder) can talk for that".

This porosity between the virtual and actual world places Digital Songlines Environment as a *'telling object'* within a network of relations that perform Aboriginal knowledge. In the process of leaking between the virtual and actual worlds, Digital Songlines Environment becomes also a *'telling subject'* that exists as both the stimulus to collaboration and a collaborator in the continued performance of, and connection to, an actual sentient world. It is through this process of ongoing negotiations and improvised performances back and forth between virtual and actual worlds that ontological priorities and epistemological processes are reaffirmed by performances within the existing knowledge ecology. Barbara Flynn [13], building upon Lefebvres' [14] work, asserts that reconciling mental and real space allows spatiality to become a dynamic category that requires overlapping modes of engagement. A dialectical rather than a causal relationship operates between the experiential, the perceptual and the imaginary, and this links players in the virtual world to the historical, social and cultural of the actual world.

As a "telling subject" Digital Songlines Environment has to be both *porous and fluid*. That is, it needs to be able to be easily adapted to local knowledge ecologies and new performance situations. Information needs to be easily put in to the virtual world and accessed in culturally appropriate ways. Being fluid means that it can change the way it is used in different contexts, for example, in schools, family groups, community groups. It must still address the issues of authenticity, purpose and ownership. Basically, these processes act to reduce the gap between designer and user so that Aboriginal people are involved in all aspects of planning and design.

This relationship serves to promote the social organization of trust, necessary for the stabilization of new knowledge spaces. The performativity of the Digital Songlines Environment is enhanced by the intended development of a ToolKit interface which enables local community groups to add and delete various forms of media content from the 3D environment. Local groups can choose which forms and performances of knowledge they wish to put into the 3D virtual world and can modify this content to suit different iterations for different user groups, catering to cultural requirements of gender, clan, and age. This flexibility that can be added to the basic 3D virtual landscape allows for local control and foregrounds the role of local Aboriginal people as users, designers and researchers in an ongoing improvisatory performance that is the evolving knowledge space.

5   The Role of Design in Knowledge Spaces

The complex nature of advanced information technologies such as virtual reality means that any new product is necessarily the result of a team of people with different skills working with a variety of technologies usually in a variety of sites. This complexity of skills, people, technologies and sites means that the work of design is about "bringing it all together". Increasingly, new technological artifacts are being seen not as passive objects which are acted upon by users as subjects. Rather they are conceptualized as one link in a chain of performances which link designers and users. The production process is not separate from its precursors or how the completed object is configured in practice and in context. Correlated with this move to performance is the re-evaluating of both what counts as innovation in techno-science, and the separation of the roles and socio-cultural knowledges of designers and users. Consequently, systems development can be seen not as the creation of new discrete objects but, "… it is increasingly also one of animating and finding subjectivity in technical artifacts." [3, p.2]

All these new forms of material practice are dependent on a re-negotiation of both the relations of production and the relations of use. This involves the production process diminishing the conceptual and practical distance between designer and user and integrating new objects into the existing contextual ecology of knowledge practices. Suchman [3] maintains that this sort of design should attempt, "…to bring developing objects out into the environment of their intended use, such that their appropriability into those environments becomes a central criterion of adequacy for their design." (p.9) Rather than isolate the production of a new object in controlled conditions and test it without reference to situation, there is the move to *integrate* it in to the heterogeneous hybrid collectives and working practices of specific environments. The standardized, de-contextualized, universality of the "one size fits all" ICT application is replaced with a situated, partial object. This new kind of object arises out of working with existing collectives and practices that are largely determined by users and their situations. As Barry [15] argues, this is true innovation because it is associated with opening up questions and possibilities and the importance of technological innovation, "…not in the artifacts themselves but in the arrangements with activities and entities within which artifacts are situated, and might be situated in the future." (p.6)

6 Implications for Design

There are important implications for the role of designers, the nature of the design process, and the role of research from this move towards situated, collective practice. The first implication is a move away from the figure of the "heroic designer" to throw light upon the ongoing practices of socio-material configuration and re-configuration in use. Suchman [3] maintains that the development of useful systems requires developers to cross boundaries and not stand outside, locating themselves in the process, creating situations that allow for the meeting of different partial knowledges. To do this is to identify and be responsible for their participation in the translations and boundaries that are mediated by new technologies. Local networks need to be mapped and located within extended and global networks. Also, the control and judgement of the design process is deferred to an extended set of actors who are both designers and users. As Aanestad [16] emphasizes, the ongoing work of design takes place in the worksite by actors who must use the new technological artifacts to accomplish daily work tasks, rather than by inventors and designers in research and development facilities.

Secondly, any design process needs to move away from being a de-contextualized, commodity based, self-referential assembly line model, that is primarily concerned with standardized, homogeneous production. The consequences of such a design model are the invisibility of economic and organizational imperatives and assumptions of the neutrality of technological systems. Van der velden [7] asserts the design of information technologies contributes to the *visibility or invisibility* of different forms of knowledge by dividing between what can be digitized (commodities, artifacts) and what cannot be digitized (social relationships and processes), and the use of categories and forms which are chosen to organize and represent these knowledges. She states that, "The technology that produces digital connectivity also produces the non-existence of people and their stories, the fabric of the social nature of knowledge."(p.3)

The recognition of the design of the technological artifact as a boundary performance requires a move to a "located accountability" [3, p.6] which is built upon partial, locatable and critical knowledges. In these kinds of knowledges our objectivity is constructed by the collective knowledge of specific locations, rather than the singularity of a de-contextualized, standardized development environment, "...that can be stabilized and cut loose from the sites of their production long enough to be exported en masse to the sites of their use." [3, p.5]

Thus design work becomes a "view from somewhere" [3, p.5] that recognizes both the visible and invisible work involved in the design process; understands the transformations engendered by technology designed at a distance (physically, culturally) from its point of use, and it values heterogeneity that is achieved through integration with existing practices rather than by the domination of standardised homogeneous artifacts.

The third implication is that the role of research and theoretical critique is tied more closely to design and development. The recognition of partial, situated and owned knowledges such as Aboriginal knowledges requires critical analyses and alternative imaginings of the politics and power accompanying the production of technological artifacts which represent them. Yet, such critical analyses and imaginings can only be entered into after, "...progressively closer, more detailed inquiries in to the elaborate structures and intricate dynamics that comprise technical systems." [3, p.4] These detailed inquiries need to be sensitive to a number of central propositions in Feminist research. First, the concept of knowledges as partial, situated and performative. Second, the need to make explicit the visible and invisible labours required to stabilize socio-technical assemblages, and, also, the importance of the relations and symmetries between persons and things, which give rise to boundaries that are not fixed and given, but enacted locally within existing networks of practice.

Analyses informed by such propositions give rise to questions which address issues about the design process such as responsibility, power, and judgements about authenticity and effectiveness. They orientate research, "...towards the politics of difference combined with forms of constructive engagement aimed at more just distributions of symbolic and economic reward." [17, p.6] As imaginaries of alternatives of distribution of power and rewards, they call into question what truly counts as innovation both in techno-science endeavour and in representation of cultural knowledge practices. As critical analysis of taken for granted labour and technology in the innovation process, they act to de-centre sites of innovation from singular persons, places and things to engage with such innovations as multiple acts of everyday activity and the actions of actors at various scales.

In distributing these practices more widely, the value of innovation itself may be questioned as reproductive of specific Western cultural values and historical processes. Also called into question is the alignment of socio-technical innovation with the motivations, purposes and outcomes in terms of politics and everyday life for the wider range of actors, at the core of which are Aboriginal people as generators and users of knowledge.

Therefore any research approach needs to look at how such innovations have political consequences for Aborigines, in terms of possibilities that are truly available to them, the visibility of their contributions, and the control over ownership, authenticity and judgement that is afforded to them.

7 Conclusion

Visualisation of non-Western concepts of space as a sentient landscape, together with culturally specific embodiment and navigation, supported by spatialised narratives, provides a compelling manifestation of Aboriginal cultural presence in the virtual world. Flexibility of productions of iterations that fit into local, situated knowledges, allow a reframing from digital object to improvisatory collective performance. Linkages and relationships between the virtual world and the actual world mean that meaningful cultural learning can occur in different ways for different users, Aboriginal and non-Aboriginal in different settings. Different ways of representing landscape in the world lead to "dissonance" or "interference" [8] which are productive ways of holding knowledge in tension for learners, and make explicit the differences and assumptions of different knowledge traditions. Such interference acts both to prevent the collapsing of cultural difference into sameness, and also to promote the understanding of the differences that cultural knowledges construct. This is useful for both indigenous and non-indigenous learners.

Using 3D virtual reality technology for archiving and representing Aboriginal knowledge traditions allows a double move from representation to performance and also from object to subject. Overlap of experience in virtual and actual worlds leads to new kinds of performances of knowledge production. When such new performances are incorporated into existing Aboriginal knowledge ecologies, knowledge performance is extended into a knowledge space, built on heterogeneity and the social organisation of trust. Such a heterogeneous socio-technical collective may work to produce a sustainable hybrid of technological and traditional processes by which the complexity of Aboriginal landscape knowledge may be expressed into the future.[7] How, where and if this happens, remains to be seen, but the development of Virtual Reality 3D artifacts such as Digital Songlines, has at the very least brought into sharp focus the controversies of theoretical design, the examination of roles of all actors, and the importance of judgements by Aboriginal owners.

References

1. Turnbull, D.: Reframing Science and Other Local Knowledge Traditions. Futures 29(6), 551–562 (1997)
2. Huggins, J.: Keynote address. In: The Deadly Directions Conference-AIATSIS Conference, Canberra (2005)
3. Suchman, L.: Located Accountabilities in Technology Production, published by the Centre for Science Studies, Lancaster University, Lancaster LA1 4YN, UK (2000), http://www.comp.lancs.ac.uk/sociology/papers/ Suchman-Located-Accountabilities.pdf
4. Langton, M., Ma Rhea, Z.: Traditional Indigenous Biodiversity-related Knowledge. In M. N. Nakata, M. Langton (Eds.): Australian Indigenous knowledge and libraries. Canberra: State Library of New South Wales. Australian Institute of Aboriginal and Torres Strait Islander Studies. University of Technology, Jumbunna Indigenous House of Learning, Sydney (2005)
5. Nakata, M.: Australian indigenous knowledge and libraries. In: Nakata, M.N., Langton, M. (eds.) Australian Indigenous knowledge and libraries. Canberra: State Library of New South Wales. Australian Institute of Aboriginal and Torres Strait Islander Studies. University of Technology, Jumbunna Indigenous House of Learning, Sydney (2005)
6. van der Velden, M.: Invisiblity and the Ethics of Digitalisation. Designing So As Not To Hurt Others. Charles Darwin University, Darwin, Australia (2005), http://www. cdu.edu.au/centres/ik/pdf/MvdV_paper1.pdf
7. Hart, V.: Mapping Aboriginality. In: Investigating Queensland's Cultural Landscapes: Contested Terrains. Report 1: Setting the Theoretical Scene, pp. 49-64. Queensland University of Technology, Brisbane (2001)
8. Verran, H.: Software for Educating Aboriginal Children about Place, for Education and Technology: Critical Perspectives and Possible Futures. In: Kritt, D.W., Winegar, L.T. (eds.) , Lexington Books, Rowan and Littlefield (2006), http://www.cdu.edu.au/centres/ik/pdf/HRV_for_Kritt_WinegarFI NAL4-06.pdf
9. Christie, M.: Computer Databases and Aboriginal Knowledge, in International Journal of Learning in Social Contexts Number 1, 4–12 (2005)
10. Law, J.: After Method: mess in social science research. Routledge, London New York (2004)
11. Crawford, C.: Interactive Storytelling in The video game theory reader. Wolf, M.J.P., Perron, B. (eds.) , Routledge, New York, London (2003)
12. Frasca, G.: Simulation versus Narrative: Introduction to Ludology in The video game theory reader. Wolf, M.J.P., Perron, B. (eds.) , Routledge, New York, London (2003)
13. Flynn, B.: Games as Inhabited Places. Media International Australia 110, 52–61 (2004)
14. Lefebvre, H.: The Production of Space. Blackwell, Cambridge, MA (1994)
15. Barry, A.: Invention and Inertia. Cambridge Anthropology 21 (1999)
16. Aanestad, M.: The camera as an actor: Design-in-use of Telemedicine Infrastructure in Surgery. Computer-Supported Cooperative Work (CSCW) 12, 1–20 (2003)
17. Suchman, L.: Agencies in Technology Design: Feminist Reconfigurations in Gendered Innovations in Science and Engineering. In: Schiebinger, L. (ed.) Stanford University Press, Stanford (2003)

The Irreducible Ensemble: Place-Hampi

Sarah Kenderdine

Special Projects, Museum Victoria, Carlton Gardens, Melbourne, Australia 3053
skenderdine@museum.vic.gov.au

Abstract. This discussion examines several philosophical considerations (*phenomenology*, *embodiment*, *corpothetics* and *mediation*) which form powerful interlocking arguments, whose qualities are prerequisites for building *presence* and *place* in virtual heritage landscapes. The discourse draws upon Interpretive Archaeology and Interpretive Archaeological Systems theory and it is in Symmetrical Archaeology theory that we find a basis for complex emergent narratives in immersive virtual environments. Firmly rooted in praxis, the argument explores these issues through research associated with applications from the Place-Hampi project. Place-Hampi is an embodied theatre of participation in the drama of Hindu mythology focused at the most significant archaeological, historical and sacred locations of the World Heritage site Vijayanagara (Hampi), South India. Through the Advanced Visualization Interactive Environment a translation of spatial potential is enacted in Place-Hampi where participants are able to transform myths into the drama of a co-evolutionary narrative by their actions within the virtual landscape and through the creation of a virtual heritage embodiment of a real world dynamic. Place-Hampi restores *symmetry* to the autonomy of interactions within virtual heritage and allows machine and human entities to make narrative sense of each other's actions (as an *entanglement of people-things* cf Bruno Latour).

Keywords: co-evolutionary narrative; omnistereoscopic panoramas; virtual heritage; autonomous agency; Hampi; Indian mythology; Symmetrical Archaeology.

It is about conditions of possibility, the immanent relation between theory and practice . . . and a resolute belief . . . in the concrete potential of transdisciplinary. . .[1]

1 Introduction

Interpretive virtual heritage has emerged from a period of increasingly sophisticated digital model making and creation of navigable landscapes of pictorially rendered objects—to begin critical examination into the meaning of representations of space

---

[1] Organized Networks: Media Theory, Creative Labour, New Institutions by Ned Rossiter, reviewed by Geoff Cox <http://www.leonardo.info/reviews/jun2007/organ_cox.html> NAi, Rotterdam (2006).

T.G. Wyeld, S. Kenderdine, and M. Docherty (Eds.): VSMM 2007, LNCS 4820, pp. 58–72, 2008.
© Springer-Verlag Berlin Heidelberg 2008

and place, in its endeavors to facilitate dynamic inter-actor participation and cultural learning (e.g. various authors [6], [13], [15], [32], [14]). Practitioners must resolve a complex mix of HCI issues to generate for participants the hermeneutic, symbolic and epistemological meanings found in readings of real archaeological and cultural landscapes. As the discussion below will demonstrate, the malleable real-time nature of virtual environments and their associated visual, sonic and algorithmic technologies offer powerful tools for mediating tangible, intangible and abstract aspects of heritage landscapes—offering the opportunity for both embodied experiences and, new narrative engagement.

Fig. 1. Place-Hampi: augmented stereoscopic panoramic exhibition, Lille3000, France © Kenderdine and Shaw, 2006

The purpose of this paper is to articulate the relationship between the theoretical positions in Interpretive (e.g. [41], [42]) and Symmetrical Archaeology [46], [47], [48], [50], [51] collectively encompassing phenomenology, embodiment, corpothetics and mediation and, the interactive augmented stereographic panoramic exhibits from the Place-Hampi project. Place-Hampi is an embodied theatre of participation in the drama of Hindu mythology focused at the most significant archaeological, historical and sacred locations of the World Heritage site Vijayanagara (Hampi), South India. Stage one of the research (Demonstrator One, see Fig. 1.) premiered at the Opera House in Lille, France in October 2006 as part of a three-month arts and cultural festival celebrating France-India year[2]. For a full description of this work refer to prior publications [20], [21], [30].

---

[2] The work is now on tour in Europe and Asia/Pacific 2006-2008 including: *Lille3000*, Opera House; *Berliner Festspiele, Vom Funken zum Pixel*, Martin-Gropius-Bau; *Panorama Festival*, ZKM, Center for Art and Media Karlsruhe; *New Light on Hampi*, Museum Victoria.

In stage two of the research (Demonstrator Two) described below, the principal technical innovations are in the use of a unique multi user omnistereographic immersive environment (the Advanced Visualization Interactive Environment (AVIE) at iCinema Centre, UNSW [1]), and in real-time *co-evolving* narrative formulation. This discussion explores the affordances of the immersive technologies for both Demonstrator One and Two that find appropriate counterparts in the theoretical discourse observed in aforementioned positions in archaeological philosophy.

Periodically virtual heritage practitioners call to our attention the divergence between praxis in the discipline and the theoretical basis of New Museology, New Archaeology, Interpretive Archaeology and heritage discourse in general [6], [9] [14], [35]. These observations offer a counterpoint to the technological determinism prevalent in the discipline observed by Monod and Klein in analysis of the European Union Digicult Report 2002 [26], [27], where an increasing number of tools solve scientific problems for tangible heritage but are found to be inadequate for addressing the needs of interpretation of intangible and abstract aspects, indeed the phenomenological encounter between object/place/space—for a larger audience[3]. Fundamental dysfunction in the discipline itself is noted by Joseph Reeves who states "archaeological theory and scientific methodology have often been seen as the two sides of an archaeological coin. Rarely do the two disciplines meet...." [31]. Further "...attempts to marry archaeology theory and scientific practice in any useful sense are often clumsy affairs, usually consisting of a "theory bit" and an unrelated "science bit"" [31]. The inability of virtual heritage to address the wider conceptual arguments leads Neil Silberman to suggest "...we should (therefore) resist overstating the potential contribution of Digital Heritage to the wider social processes of re-creating and the understanding the past" [35].

In a longer-term vision statement Silberman concludes:

> ...the Future of Heritage requires forms and modalities of recording, analysis, interpretation, and public dissemination that go far beyond those already available. The watchwords are place, network, memory, identity, and communication. Obviously technology can and will provide the context and tools for these new approaches to heritage. From a strictly Cultural Heritage perspective, the big changes to be anticipated in the next ten years or so are unlikely to be about automation but rather about systemic changes in the way our heritage is categorized, protected, and interpreted [36: 20].

Interpreted is a keyword for the following discussion which will examine both Interpretive Archeology as a basis for immersive environment design, and Symmetrical Archaeology, in which *interpretation* is re-formulated as *meditation* allowing for the co-evolution of a narrative between people and things.

----

[3] In the European Union the bias observed in ICT CH may have been a direct result of the structure of funding—as acutely observed by the latest EPOCH Research Framework Report, David Arnold, Guntram Geser, D 2.11 Research Agenda, 17th January (2007). EPOCH proposed the Use-inspired Basic Research – "Pasteur's Quadrant" in the latest finding of their report to help redirect some of the research funding strategies to address the complex and inter-disciplinary nature of CH work that spans from basic research in computer science through to the applied work in cultural heritage organizations and by archaeological scientists.

2 Interpretive Archaeology (and Systems)

Within archaeology, Interpretive Archaeology is a trend well defined by Christopher Tilley [41], [42] and Julian Thomas [38], [39], [40] among others over the last fifteen years. In relation to this are the principles of hermeneutics, phenomenology, re-enactment, and embodiment. This framework has the particular archaeological aim of understanding the past through providing learning experiences and interpretation in a never-ending process of making sense. Interpretation is always in flux, and never final because more can always be said or learned. Interpretation is always historically situated and therefore changes through time (refer also to the hermeneutic spiral)[4] [2].

Drawing together theory from Interpretive Archaeology and from Interpretive Information Systems, Monod and Klein [26], [27] proposed a research framework for the interpretation of archaeological landscapes that could be considered useful for emerging design practice in virtual and augmented reality environments of these spaces/places. The core of their framework for building virtual heritage applications encompassed Re-enactment; Embodiment; Context; Self Projection; Possibilities of Being; Historical Self; Inquiring Being; Universality of Uniqueness. This framework was a seminal attempt to integrate both the theoretical and practical aspects of e-heritage research which appears to have been largely ignored by the virtual heritage community. My purpose here is to re-examine more closely some of the key philosophical principles that underlie the aforementioned criteria for interpretation as defined by Interpretive Archaeology (and Systems), and then to extend these to include the defining principles found in Symmetrical Archaeology.

3 Phenomenology and Archaeology

In archaeology, phenomenological discourse provides a philosophy that emphasizes the interpretation of the human experience [41], [42]. Merleau Ponty, whose

---

[4] Contemporary hermeneutics was given a new basis through phenomenology by Heidegger, who saw understanding as constitutive of human existence, and thus a phenomenology of human existence is a phenomenology of understanding. Hermeneutics considers that to understanding is not something as given but is always subject to pre-judgment. If this prejudice is modified in an interpretive encounter, it forms a new basis of the next engagement, and so on: this is the hermeneutic spiral. Appreciating hermeneutics as a living tradition is fundamentally a matter of perceiving a moving horizon, engaging a strand of dialogue that is an on-going re-articulation of the dynamically historical nature of all human thought. Refer also, Hodder, I.: The Archaeological Process. An Introduction, Oxford, (1999). Thomas, J.: The Great Dark Book. Archaeology, Experience, and Interpretation, In J. Bintliff (ed.) A Companion To Archaeology, Oxford, (2004): 21-36. Don Ihde promotes a material hermeneutics as a hermeneutics which "gives things voices where there had been silence, and brings to sight that which was invisible." Such a hermeneutics in natural science can best be illustrated by its imaging practices. The objects of this visual hermeneutics were not texts nor linguistic phenomena, but things which came into vision through instrumental magnifications, allowing perception to go where it had not gone before. One could also say that a visual hermeneutics is a perceptual hermeneutics with a perception which while including texts, goes beyond texts. Extracted from <http://humanitieslab.stanford.edu/Symmetry/746> last accessed 3 August 2007.

pioneering work on embodiment was constitutive of the existential philosophy, tells us that the meaning of experience is found in the synthesis of the subjective and objective aspects. Phenomenology simultaneously analyzes and describes consciousness, while also searching for understandings of 'space', 'time' and the world in non-cognitive terms, or as they are lived through embodiment. Phenomenological 'influence' recognized in conjunction with the study of landscape and other 'lived spaces'.

Tilley demonstrates the manner in which a phenomenological perspective, in which the past is understood and interpreted from a sensuous human scale, as opposed to an abstract analytical gaze, can provide a radically different way of thinking through the past in the present, and shed new light on old monuments. Tilley maintains that the body is continually improvising its relationship towards things because it not a closed mechanical system, constantly opening itself out to the world as it moves through it [41: 10]. From a phenomenological point of view the analytical approach in archaeology is rejected. "...the qualities of a thing, in fact, may tell us far more about it than any measurement of its geometrical properties. Descriptive accounts are fundamentally ambiguous and open-ended" [41: 10].

The body carries time into the experience of place and landscape. Any moment of lived experience is thus orientated by and towards the past, a fusion of the two. Past and present fold upon each other. The past influences the present and the present rearticulates that past. [41: 12]

4 The Irreducible Ensemble

The historical sense involves a perception, not only of the pastness of the past but of its presence[5]

Tilley incorporates a discussion of synaethesia and the "fusion of the senses" in a bodily relationship with place and landscape. "In the actual practice as opposed to the representation, of a person's encounter with landscape and place, the senses are always involved in a dynamic intertwining" [41: 16]. Merleau Ponty articulates the veracity of perception—that our vision 'goes to the things themselves' [25: 15] through the process of inhabiting the world as lived bodies. In the active sensorial participation or interplay with ones surroundings objects are attributed with anthropomorphic or animistic qualities. Natural objects, trees, stones, mountains and artifacts are regarded as being alive or having a soul and reciprocate in each others existence. Merleau Ponty's philosophy is effectively a modern Western exposition of animistic and totemic thought in which essences of persons and things are intertwined through embodied mind in which perception in a worldly event governed by participation rather than a disembodied mental image [41: 10-12].

The notion of the importance of the sensory and phenomenological engagement in an irreducible ensemble with the world has been a nexus of interest for many inter-disciplinary researchers including not only archaeology (see also Shanks, 1992 [33];

---

[5] Eliot, T.: Tradition and the individual talent. In F. Kernode (ed) Selected Prose of T.S. Eliot. London, Faber and Faber (1975).

Pearson and Shanks 2001 [28]) but anthropology (e.g. Howes, 2005 [16]) cultural geography (in the exploration of space and place (e.g. Tuan [43], [44], [45] Casey [7], [8]); architecture (e.g. Bruno 2002 [5] and film (e.g. Schoback 2005 [35]) among many others.

Suffice to say here that there ample discourse to situate the body at the forefront of immersive virtual heritage research as a space of phenomenological encounter. Further more, if in fact embodiment is the experience of the world through all the senses of the body, then narrative strategies privileging one sense over the other, or emphasizing certain aspects over others, prove to be unequal to the task of embodied representation. Embodiment explodes narrative and other traditional modes of representation [3].

5 Symmetrical Archaeology

Until meaning is left entangled within a mixture encompassing the material it remains asymmetrical. In other words, meaning must be reconfigured within heterogeneous networks comprised of collectivities of humans, materials, media and other companion species—only then will it acquire symmetry [23].

For Witmore, Webmoor, and others [46], [47], [48], [50], [51] the embrace of the Interpretive Archaeology framework is *asymmetrical*[6]. Interpretive Archaeology, they emphasize, weighs in favor of interpersonal functionality, at the expense of saying anything about the things of the past. For example, Julian Thomas recently concluded that "interpretation is a circle that we cannot escape (Gadamer 1975: 235)" [38]. This over-emphasis of the processes of making sense means we are simply left with increasing numbers of interpretations and as a result distance ourselves from material objects and materiality. Archaeology is after all the "discipline of things" (cf Olsen 2003) [51].

In the reformulation of post-processural archaeology then, Symmetrical Archaeology reconfigures a host of basic dualisms – such as past/present, subject/object, meaning/referent, representation/represented. Witmore asks "what if we were to treat things and people symmetrically?" [51: 10]. Furthermore, the current form of archaeological transformation, inscription and interpretation will "...never encompass locality, materiality, multiplicity or experience" [48]. In Symmetrical Archaeology rather than nature and society poised across from each other on a horizontal axis, nature-society is seen as a complex *entanglement of people-things* (cf Latour) [46]. Human beings are not "detached and singular intentional agents, but rather always are implicated in complex socio-technical assemblages" [46]. It is in this discourse that we find constructs that support co-evolutionary narrative between machine agents and human participants—a core research component in the Place-Hampi project.

---

[6] Christopher Witmore, while hoping to address the multiplicity of embodied experience from an archaeological standpoint, points out that the term *embodiment* itself implies a modernist duality of the Cartesian mind-body dichotomy. Phenomenology also is often subject to the same critique for its asymmetrical embrace of subjectivity (cf Latour 1993) Witmore, C.L.: Four Archaeological Engagements with Place: Mediating Bodily Experience through Peripatetic Video. The Visual Anthropology Review 20(2) (2004): 69.

5.1 Meditation

Whereas vision is a distancing sense, hearing is one of Alliance [49: 282]

Witmore suggests that *mediation* of the archaeological source "…as doing something fundamentally different from the semiotically-limited notion of representation in conventional scholarly forms of documentation and inscription"[7]. Mediation, for archaeology, occurs across a series of transformations between material presence and media. Mediation allows one to contemplate ways of transforming aspects of the material past while at the same time bringing forth something of the locality, multiplicity, and materiality left behind with conventional processes of documentation and inscription. Mediation is a process that allows us to attain richer and fuller translations of bodily experience and materiality that are "located, multi-textured, reflexive, sensory, and polysemous" [51].

Typically in archaeology, the sensory prosthesis tends to be entirely visual. The destructive process of transformation from the archaeological source relies on a host of technologies (e.g. theodolites, tapes, GPS, cameras, scanners etc) to produce maps, plans, diagrams, illustrations, catalogues and text. This (visual) perspective has allowed for a high degree of consistency and standardization to the discipline. However this record has great paucity and it has been acknowledged for example that auditory importance of landscape needs to be represented. This has only recently been the focus of archaeological investigation and documentation. *Sound* is itself highly transient much more so than the visual record [50: 272]. As Wolfgang Welsch comments "…the mode of being of the visible and audible is fundamentally different. The visible persist in time, the audible, however vanishes in time. Vision is concerned with the constant enduring being, audition, on the other hand, with the fleeting, transient, the event-like" [50: 272]. As Witmore points out however, while sound is transient it is also *re-current*[8]. Furthermore, "while the past does percolate through its material traces and memory, it can also do so through the liveness of performance and physical re-enactment" [50: 272]. It is the performative encounter with audible and visual landscape in a narrative exchange with and between people—that directs the research in Place-Hampi.

5.2 Co-action and Narrative

As previously argued [20] concepts of digital narrative applied in new media remain predominantly uni-modal while virtual heritage researchers continue to understand virtual heritage narrative as a derivative of conventional notions of virtual reality and cultural memory, lacking an understanding of the complex multi-dimensional quality of digital and cultural processes. Modelled on mimetic theory, they theorize narrative in spatial terms as simulation [4] and recovery [37]. These uni-modal formulations

---

[7] With each step in the archaeological process, from excavating a trench profile, drawing building phase sections, taking photographs, sampling, measuring, narrating, etc. we lose "locality, particularity, materiality, multiplicity, and continuity"—aspects of the material world—yet we gain "compatibility, standardization, text, calculation, circulation, and relative universality"—qualities of documentation (Latour 1999:47, in Witmore, 2004).

[8] Witmore, 2004, in summation of theorists Kaye, 2000; Lopex y Royo, 2005; Pearson and Shanks, 2001.

flatten narrative into a one dimensional ready-made object ignoring the multi-dimensional dynamics involved in a narrative generated through the interchange between ontologically divergent human and machine entities. Mediation on the other hand is a mode of engagement, which takes us beyond narrative, for scholarly narrative obfuscates the multiplicity of material presence. Critically, mediation calls attention to the co-action of what are conventionally split apart - subject and object - in accounts of representation. In this regard, mediation symmetrically shifts the 'burden of knowing', of knowledge claims in archaeology, away from a subject(archaeologists)-society pole representing inert reality out there [48]. "Mediation (re)balances claims to know the world by excavating beneath representation as conventionally understood, and provides both an ontology of the co-creation of people-things and an epistemology not encumbered by the subject-world gap…"[47].

6 Place-Hampi

Through the affordances of new technologies in AVIE, Place Hampi is able to transcend the common interpretive frameworks to become a site of mediation, an entanglement of people-things from the past and present occupation of the site. Place-Hampi is comprised of high resolution augmented stereoscopic panoramas (captured with the analog Seitz stereo Roundshot camera; imaged based modeling is used to derive geometry of the scenes) and surrounded by a rich aural field (derived from on-site ambisonic recordings and selected compositions by Dr L. Subramanian), and permits an unprecedented level of viewer co-presence in a narrative-discovery of a cultural landscape[9]. The research addresses the sensorium through a combination of immersive kinesthetic, and visual and sonic strategies. The discussion below embraces both the embodied corporeal aesthetics of place and its transformation through an assemblage of technologies (algorithmic software, immersive omnistereo environment architecture, and real-time animations).

6.1 Technologies of AVIE Architecture

The AVIE screen is a 10m diameter cylinder, 3.6m high and with an 80cm doorway (Fig 2a). The dimensions provide a vertical field of view of 40° for a centrally located viewer. 12 SXGA+ projectors with 1:1 throw are mounted in pairs so as to illuminate the entire cylinder, resulting in a total circumferential resolution of ~ 8000 pixels. A cluster of six dual Xeon Windows PC's is used to drive the 12 projectors. The system includes 24 high-quality loud speakers, distributed evenly around the top and bottom screen, provide real-time spatial audio [24].

Twelve infra-red cameras, distributed at various locations overhead, provide coverage of the entire AVIE arena. Twenty infra-red flood lights provide illumination.

---

[9] A large interdisciplinary team of professionals including south Indian art historical and archaeological scholars, Indian classical Carnatic composers and Indian artists and animators, classical Indian dancers, computer engineers, and museum and media arts specialists, contributed to Place-Hampi.

From this data the systems tracks individuals proximity to the screen, distribution in space, when people come in to contact with one another and estimated head position. Hand gesture information can also be tracked (Fig 2b) [24].

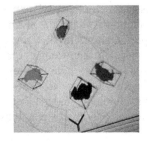

Fig. 2a. AVIE © iCinema Centre 2007

Fig. 2b. Voxel models built from tracking software in AVIE © iCinema Centre 2007

Stereoscopy is a powerful means of enhancing immersion. Conventional stereo projection demands that a viewer's position and orientation accurately match the position and orientation from which the imagery was rendered or captured (achieved through tracking users head position in real time). On the other hand omnistereo, assumes a view point at the centre of the cylinder and a view direction perpendicular to the screen surface. This method produces perceptually correct stereoscopic depth over the full 360° viewing circle and provides all viewers a valid stereo image.[10]

In Place-Hampi a translation of the spatial potential is enacted whereby participants in AVIE are able to transform the myths of place into the drama of a co-evolving narrative by their actions within the virtual landscape and through the creation of a virtual heritage embodiment of the real world dynamic. The transactional performance schemata are based on the types of narratives that are commonplace in Indian mythology and to phenomenon in the contemporary landscape. This conversation (envisaged by pilgrims to the site) between mythological characters and devotional site is integrated into the system design and well demonstrated in Demonstrator One of the project. The following section will briefly re-state the basis for corpothetic resonance however the reader is referred to the larger discussion for a full understanding [21].

6.2 Seeing and Being Seen

Hampi today continues to be an active pilgrim site, not simply an historic place. Information derived from the examination of diverse scopic regimes in historical and contemporary Indian iconography has been used to guide the aesthetic decisions of

---

[10] Omnistereo only produces correct imagery for viewers located at the centre. However, inside the AVIE theatre the omnistereo images can be viewed comfortably from any position. This is the principal advantage of a cylindrical screen were any image distortion is continuous and therefore far less perceptible. This observation is based on the experiences of the many hundreds of visitors AVIE has already received. In McGinity, M. et al.: AVIE: A Versatile Multi-User Stereo 360° Interactive VR Theatre. EDT, ACM (2007). In press.

the Place-Hampi project, and in combination with symbolic logic and high level cognitive programming of computer graphic characters—co-evolve the narrative engagement between intangible heritage of 'place' and participants. The history of predominantly chromolithography validates the use of 'magical realism' as a formal aesthetic of choice for the CG characters that best represents the intangible aspects of 'place' and the religious experiences active in the landscape of Vijayanagara in contemporary times.

Hindi religious practice also emphasizes the concept of *darshan*, of 'seeing and being seen' by a deity. Its role is central to Indian scopic regimes. The act of darshan mobilizes and activates the human sensorium, and is a physically transformative contact with the deity [29]. For pilgrims to Vijayanagara the most important aspect of the site is the association with various myths and legends. Pilgrims experience the landscape through ritualized movements enforced by the spatial configuration of the districts around the temples and inside the temples themselves.

The promotion of dialogues of engagement in Place-Hampi is significant. The dialogues embedded in the imagery and aural architecture of a cultural landscape is used to activate the knowledge contained there. It has been demonstrated that cultural practices can treat images as compressed performances. Thus the culturally determined experience of an image affects both its power and meaning. Christopher Pinney extrapolates this cultural response to imagery to the Indian context using the concept of darshan and argues for the notion of *corpothetics*–embodied, corporeal aesthetics–as opposed to disassociated representation. "The relevant question then becomes not how images 'look' but what they can do" [29: 8].

The significance of images is expressed by rural Indian community not through an efflorescence of words around an object, but a bodily praxis, a poetry of the body, that helps give the images what they want [29: 21]. Consumers demanded that these images fundamentally addressed their presence and invoked a new corpothetics. "...In these images the beholder is a worshipper, drinking in the eyes of the deity that gazes directly back at him..." [17: 22]. Such a bodily relationship with images has been described by various authors including Adorno in the term "somatic solidarity". These definitions are pertinent to the discussion of physical responses to images (and sound) often heightened in large scale stereoscopic and immersive environments. The image figure is: "relatively free of the demands of meaning, indeed it is not the arena of the production of meaning but a space where 'intensities are felt'" [17: 23].

It is with these understanding that Place-Hampi has been approached utilizing technologies of immersion (the sensorium) to become an embodying mechanism, of cultural space. Place-Hampi seeks to recognize the authority of both the origin and the representational scheme, and thereby to provide an environment where the sensorial is active to respond to the representational scheme the images emerge from. The implications for cross-cultural participation in Place-Hampi, has been argued in previous publications [21].

6.3 Presence in AVIE

Presence research is an established body of inquiry fundamental to the way in which Place-Hampi is constructed. Presence thrives in a panoramic space of high fidelity visual stereo material and spatialized aural fields [19], [22]. These enclosures are free for both circumambulation (the bodily movement through space) and for circumambience (landscape as perceived, Casey [7]). Such a strategy of immersion frees the body from the discomfort and bodily alienation of haptic technologies and head mounted displays common in virtual reality experiments. AVIE also accommodates up to 30 people free to interact and collaborate in human-human relations, additional to those possible with the virtual landscape and characters—while typical VR technologies such as the CAVE are restricted to few viewers and a single operator.

6.4 Co-evolutionary Narrative

Presence flourishes within immersive environments in which the behavior of virtual characters can evolve or "co-evolve" interactively by making intelligent reference to the actions of viewing participants in real time [20]. When co-evolving systems of interaction are applied to the relationships between viewers and computer generated (CG) characters unique interactive relationships are formed in dramatic and culturally distinctive ways.   Place-Hampi endeavors to facilitate dynamic inter-actor participation and cultural learning and, the creation of presence, in virtual heritage and is being developed using symbolic logic and high level cognitive programming of CG characters in conjunction with intelligent immersive virtual reality of AVIE.

In many interpretations of the Ramayana, Hampi is considered *Kishkinda* – the kingdom of the monkeys. The mythological inhabitants have counterparts in the real world and at Hampi today the monkeys are prevalent revered by the faithful, but often delinquent in their behaviour towards permanent inhabitants and tourists. In the research Place-Hampi will create a tribe of synthetic Computer Generated (CG) monkeys who will operate as autonomous agents within one of the stereo panoramic scenes shot at Hampi (Hemakuta Hill). Their behaviour shall operate in a co-evolutionary relationship to that of the behaviours of the real visitors within AVIE. The evolving time-based development of behavioural interaction between real people and virtual agents will be achieved by script based actions of CG animation and/or motion capture sequences, linked to interpretive software techniques (artificial intelligence; AI)[11]. The latter allows the machine agents to act, observe the consequences of their actions in the real world and then formulate new actions according to certain goals that have been imprinted in their identities. For example, a mother monkey may prioritise the protection of her young, and will take appropriate action to protect her territory from the proximity of humans. Others will be given various drives towards socialisation with the human visitors, e.g. hunger for food, interest in bodily antics, or merely curiosity. Different temperaments can be defined, such as fearless, jittery, protective, paranoid, etc. Registration of the human actions is largely focused on group and individual spatial disposition and changing proximity to the screen (and thus the space occupied by the monkeys) and the nature of their

---

[11] It should be noted that the proposed development in autonomous virtual agents operates a significantly different paradigm to massive online game play in which avatars are often seem to have significant artificial intelligence capacity. These avatars are operated by other humans and not independent of human actions. Krisher, S.: Game designers test the limits of artificial intelligence. The Boston Globe <http://www.boston.com/business/personaltech/articles/2007/06/17/game_designers_test_the_limits_of_artificial_intelligence/> last accessed 3 August 2007.

movement that can be interpreted in the range of threatening (if abrupt) to inviting (if measured). An interpretive matrix provides the mapping of various articulations of human behaviours to the scripted and improvisational range of monkey behaviours that are time sensitive to enable a 'narrative' development (evolution). In addition, Hanuman (a God of great significance at Hampi) will be present in the virtual world. His improvised responses to participants' behaviour will provide key insights into the tenets of Ramayana, and the importance of Kishkinda to the mythology (Figs 3a & 3b).

Figs 3a & 3b. Scenario visualization, Place-Hampi in AVIE © iCinema Centre, 2006

The framework advanced in the research addresses a need articulated by virtual heritage scholars to treat the heritage object as an evolving experience, a symmetrical experience [51] (addressing aforementioned arguments in hermeneutics for example) in which the story told is not pre-rehearsed but emerging as an interactive dialogue between viewers and agents. Following Deleuze and De Landa it is theorized that narrative is as a reciprocal process in which meaning is co-generated by intelligent agents and viewers as the result of a modest narrative of exploration. Narrative is a process that interweaves viewers and cinematic images in the production of new multi-layered events that simultaneously incorporate the past and present [20], [10], [11], [12]. Providing autonomy to machine agents balances the interactive initiative between virtual characters and viewers within virtual heritage. This equalizing of agent and participant transforms the encounter into an exciting and unpredictable drama in which events are co-produced by machine and human. In this way the research incorporates philosophical underpinning of Symmetrical Archaeology. It is the independence of the avatars that is crucial in the Place-Hampi Demonstrator Two.

7 Conclusion

The project is a preliminary experiment in creating co-evolutionary narrative experiences in virtual heritage environments underwritten by the potentiality of phenomenology and embodiment of place. As noted above, Demonstrator Two utilize transactional performance schemata based on the types of narratives that are commonplace in Indian mythology and pilgrimage. As the machine agents and participants learn to stimulate these scenarios through their actions, they co-evolve unique narrative experiences. In this way Place-Hampi instigates a digital reformulation of the notions of corpothetics and somatic solidarity. This reformulation is both convergent with and facilitated by the new technologies of immersion, presence and hybrid interaction. What Place-Hampi provides is a landscape for narrative co-evolution (in machine and participant) and a place of somatic solidarity for the expression of cultural space. As described in Demonstrator Two the tracking systems in Place-Hampi (a contemporary digital sensorium) enables a situation of corporeal registration of visitors' movements and behavior. The software driven narrative-interpretation in Place-Hampi (a digitally reformulated corpothetics) operates in the zone of co-evolutionary interactions between the protagonists (the audience and the CG characters).

Acknowledgements

Place-Hampi is a collaborative project between Museum Victoria and iCinema Centre for Interactive Cinema Research, The University of New South Wales Sydney and is also subject of an Australian Research Council Linkage Grant. Acknowledged here are Dennis Del Favero, Jeffrey Shaw and Neil Brown of UNSW for their contribution to the theoretical research. All the individual contributors to the Place-Hampi project are listed on the project website [30] and warmly acknowledged here.

References

1. Advanced Visualization Interactive Environment (AVIE) at iCinema Centre, UNSW (last accessed June 2007)
   http://www.icinema.unsw.edu.au/projects/infra_avie.html
2. Archaeopedia (last accessed June 2007)
   http://metamedia.stanford.edu/projects/archaeopaedia/60
3. Archaeopedia definition (last accessed June 2007)
   http://traumwerk.stanford.edu:3455/Archaeopaedia/37
4. Baudrillard, J.: Impossible Exchange. Trans. Chris Turner. Verso, London (2001)
5. Bruno, G.: Atlas of Emotion: Journeys in Art, Architecture, and Film. Verso, New York (2002)
6. Cameron, F., Kenderdine, S.: Theorizing Digital Cultural Heritage: A Critical Discourse. MIT Press, Cambridge, Massachusetts (2007)
7. Casey, E.: The Fate of Place University of California Press (1999)
8. Casey, E.: The Fate of Place, Getting Back into Place: A Phenomenological Study: Studies in Continental Thought. Indiana University Press (1993)
9. Dave, B.: New Heritage Beyond Verisimilitude. In: Kvan, T., Kalay, Y. (eds.) Proceedings of the New Heritage Conference, March 13-14th, 2006, pp. 238–241. The Faculty of Architecture, University of Hong Kong (2006)
10. De Landa, M.: Virtual Environments and the Emergence of Synthetic Reason, Virtual Futures: Cyberotics, Technology and Post-Human Pragmatism. Dixon, J., Cassidy, E. (eds.) , Routledge, London (1998)
11. Deleuze, G.: Cinema 2: The Time Image. Trans. Hugh Tomlinson and Barbara Habberjam. Athlone Press, London (1989)
12. Deleuze, G.: Negotiations 1972-1990. Trans. Martin Joughin. Columbia University Press, New York (1995)

13. Ferko, A., Martinka, J., Sormann, M., Karner, K., Zara, J., Krivograd, S.: Virtual Heart Of Central Europe. In: Proceedings of 9th Symposium on Info- & Communication Technology in Urban and Spatial Planning and Impacts of ICT on Physical Space, pp. 193–200. Technische Universität, Wien (2004)

14. Foni, A., Papagiannakis, G., Cadi-Yazli, N., Magnenat-Thalmann, N.: Time-Dependant Illumination and Animation of Virtual Hagia-Sophia. International Journal of Architectural Computing, April 2007. Multi-Science Publishing (2007)

15. Forte, M., Pescarin, S., Pietroni, E., Rufa, C.: Multiuser interaction in an archaeological landscape: The Flaminia project. In: Proceedings from Space to Place, Rome (2006)

16. Howes, D.: Architecture of the Senses. Sense of the City Exhibition Catalogue, Canadian Centre for Architecture, Montreal (last accessed June 2007) http://www.david-howes.com/DH-research-sampler-arch-senses.htm

17. Lyotard, J.-F., Pinney, C.: Photos of the Gods: The Printed Image and Political Struggle in India, p. 22. Reaktion Books Ltd., London (2004)

18. Lyotard, J.-F., Pinney, C.: Photos of the Gods: The Printed Image and Political Struggle in India, p. 23. Reaktion Books Ltd., London (2004)

19. Kenderdine, S., Doornbusch, P.: Presence and sound: Identifying Sonic Means to "Be There". In: Consciousness Reframed, Beijing, November 2004, pp. 67–70. Planetary Collegium, Plymouth, England (2004)

20. Kenderdine, S., Shaw, J., Del Favero, D., Brown, N.: Place-Hampi: Co-Evolutionary Narrative & Augmented Stereographic Panoramas. In: Kalay, Y.E., Kvan, T., Affleck, J. (eds.) New Heritage: New Media And Cultural Heritage, Vijayanagara, India, Routledge, London (2007)

21. Kenderdine, S.: Place-Hampi: somatic solidarity, magical realism and animating popular gods. A place where 'where intensities are felt'. In: IV 2007, Zurich, July 2007, IEEE, Los Alamitos (2007)

22. Kenderdine, S.: Speaking in Rama: Panoramic vision in cultural heritage visualization. In: Cameron, Kenderdine (eds.) Digital Cultural Heritage: A critical discourse (2007)

23. Latour, B.: 136 quoted in Symmetrical Archaeology homepage (1993) (last accessed, June 2007), http://traumwerk.stanford.edu:3455/Symmetry/Home

24. McGinity, M., Shaw, J., Kuchelmeister, V., Hardjono, A., Del Favero, D.: AVIE: A Versatile Multi-User Stereo 360° Interactive VR Theatre Advanced Visualization and Interaction Environment (AVIE), iCinema Centre for Interactive Cinema Research, University of New South Wales. In: EDT, ACM, New York (in press, 2007)

25. Ponty, M.: (1968) 28 in Tilley, C.: The materiality of stone. Explorations in landscape phenomenology, Oxford (2004)

26. Monod, E., Klein H.K.: From E-Heritage To Interpretive Archaeology Systems (IAS): A Research Framework For Evaluating Cultural Heritage Communication In The Digital Age Communication In The Digital Age. In: European Conference on Information Systems (2005a)

27. Monod, E., Klein, H.K.: A Phenomenological Evaluation Framework for Cultural Heritage Interpretation: From e-HS to Heidegger's Historicity. In: Americas Conference on Information Systems (2005b)

28. Pearson, M., Shanks, M.: Theatre/Archaeology. Routledge, London (2001)

29. Pinney, C.: Photos of the Gods: the Printed Image and Political Struggle in India. Reaktion Books Ltd., London (2004)

30. Place-Hampi: Co-evolutionary Narrative & Augmented Stereographic Panoramas, Vijayanagar, India (last accessed June 2007), http://www.icinema.unsw.edu.au/projects/prj_hampi.html

31. Reeves, J.: Empirical Measuring of Archaeological Theory: GIS Approaches to Phenomenology. Computer Applications and Methods in Archaeology, CAA, Hampton, UK (July 2007) (abstract)

32. Roussou, M.: New Heritage Beyond Verisimilitude. In: Kvan, T., Kalay, Y.(eds.) Proceedings of the New Heritage Conference, The Faculty of Architecture, University of Hong Kong, March 13-14, 2006, pp. 265–283 (2006)

33. Shanks, M.: Experiencing Archaeology. Routledge, London (1992)

34. Shoback, V.: Carnal Thoughts: Embodiment and Moving Image Culture, 1st edn. University of California Press (2004)

35. Silberman, N.: Chasing the Unicorn? The Quest for "Essence" in Digital Heritage in New Heritage Beyond Verisimilitude. In: Kvan, T., Kalay, Y.(eds.) Proceedings of the New Heritage Conference, The Faculty of Architecture, University of Hong Kong, March 13-14, 2006, pp. 71–81 (2006)

36. Silberman, N.: EPOCH Research Framework Report, David Arnold, Guntram Geser, D 2.11 Research Agenda (2007)

37. Sturken, M.: Narratives of Recovery: Repressed Memory as Cultural Memory. In: Bal, M., Hanover, J.C. (eds.) Acts of Memory: Cultural Recall in the Present. University of New England, pp. 231–248 (1999)

38. Thomas, J.: (2004a) (last accessed, June 2007), http://traumwerk.stanford.edu:3455/Symmetry/Home

39. Thomas, J. (ed.): Interpretive Archaeology: A Reader. Leicester University Press, Leicester (2000)

40. Thomas, J.: Time, Culture and Identity: An Interpretive Archaeology. Routledge, NY (1996)

41. Tilley, C.: The Materiality of Stone. Explorations in Landscape Phenomenology. Oxford, Berg. (2004)

42. Tilley, C.: The Phenomenology of Landscape. Oxford, Berg. (1994)

43. Tuan, Y.-F.: Escapsim. New edn. The Johns Hopkins University Press (September 7, 2006)

44. Tuan, Y.-F.: Space and Place: The Perspective of Experience. University of Minnesota Press (reprint, 2001)

45. Tuan, Y.-F.: Topophilia: A Study of Environmental Perception, Attitudes, and Values. Prentice-Hall, New York (1974)

46. Webmoor, T.: Lessons From the Real: mediating people-things in a symmetrical archaeology (last accessed, June 2007) http://traumwerk.stanford.edu:3455/Symmetry/743

47. Webmoor, T.: Mediational Techniques and Conceptual Frameworks in Archaeology. Journal of Social Archaeology 5(1), 54–86 (2005)

48. Webmoor, T.: Symmetrical Archaeology homepage (last accessed, June 2007), http://humanitieslab.stanford.edu/Symmetry/Home

49. Welsch, Witmore, C.L.: (quoted in 1997) Vision, Media, Noise and the Percolation of Time: Symmetrical Approaches to the Mediation of the Material World. Journal of Material Culture 11(3) (2006)

50. Witmore, C.L.: Vision, Media, Noise and the Percolation of Time: Symmetrical Approaches to the Mediation of the Material World. Journal of Material Culture 11(3), 267–292 (2006)

51. Witmore, C.L.: Four Archaeological Engagements with Place: Mediating Bodily Experience Through Peripatetic Video. The Visual Anthropology Review 20(2), 57–72 (2004)

Reconstructing the West Mebon Vishnu: A Marriage of Traditional Artefactual Analysis with Digital 3D Visualization

Marnie Feneley[1], Tom Chandler[2], Nils Gleissenberger[2], and Ben Alexander[2]

[1] University of Sydney, Sydney, Australia
[2] Monash University, Melbourne, Australia
mfeneley@bigpond.com, tom.chandler@infotech.monash.edu.au,
nhgle1@student.monash.edu, bdale1@student.monash.edu

Abstract. The West Mebon Vishnu is one of the most magnificent works of sculpture in South East Asian art history, and a key example of the tradition of large bronzes that plays an important role in the history of the region. Unfortunately, this once powerful and serene sculpture survives only in 19 major fragments that together constitute perhaps 40% of the original statue. Reconstruction of the Vishnu from these fragments is a formidable task that we have approached by combining detailed analysis of the surviving fragments with digitally modeled 3D reconstruction, informed by comparative studies of Vishniavite iconography and the aesthetic and religions traditions of Khmer culture. Beyond its aesthetic value, the reconstruction process may provide insights into the many unknowns surrounding the creation and destruction of this masterpiece.

Keywords: Angkor, West Mebon Vishnu, 3D modelling, Virtual Heritage, Virtual Archaeology.

1 Introduction

The West Mebon Temple ruins are located in the Angkor region of Cambodia on an artificial island built with a series of stepped walls in the West Baray. The West Baray is a massive man-made lake stretching 8km in length and 2.2km in width, the largest such body of water in the Angkor region of Cambodia (Figure 1). In the middle of this ruined sanctuary is a large stone basin, creating a pond approximately 100m square. In 1942, the Ecole Francaise d' Extreme Orient (EFEO) reconstructed part of the wall and outer towers. The outer wall of the West Mebon was pierced by twelve gateways, three on each side. A causeway leads from the Eastern Gateway to a platform at the center of the square pond. The platform itself measures 9.65m from east to west and 8.65m from north to south. (Glaize 1944). The top of the causeway and the surface of the central platform are approximately 1.5m lower than the top of the enclosing embankment. Two masonry built shafts are located in this platform. The more eastern shaft, closest to the causeway, is loosely structured into a square pit on sand foundations lined with stones. Two stone tablets with indentations were discovered

T.G. Wyeld, S. Kenderine, and M. Docherty (Eds.): VSMM 2007, LNCS 4820, pp. 73–87, 2008.

within this shaft, which may be the remains of a ritual deposit box. The first section of the western shaft is 55cm in diameter and octagonal then circular to a depth of 2.7m and dressed with radiating joints. It was in this shaft that the remaining fragments of the West Mebon Vishnu were discovered in 1936 by archeologist Maurice Glaize. The drawings of the West Mebon by George Groslier from his Researches sur les Cambogiens 1921 were used as a guide to create a computer modeled visualisation of the Mebon (Figure 2).

Fig. 1. West Mebon situated in the West Baray courtesy of Roland Fletcher

Fig. 2. West Mebon Visualization

According to the records of the Ecole Francaise d' Extreme Orient (EFEO), the head conservator, Maurice Glaize, had been informed in 1936 that locals from the West Mebon area were offering ancient jewels for sale to Europeans from Siem Reap. The directors of the Conservation sent a messenger to the local village, reminding the villagers of the ban on pillaging the temples, and requesting that they be informed of any new discoveries. In December of the same year, a local to the area of the West Mebon came forward and told the French team of a dream he had in which Buddha appeared to him, asking the villager to release him from his burial place of earth and stones. He brought with him evidence in the form of a bronze finger, which led the archaeologists to expect a large statue. Fellow archeologists Henri Marchal and Jaques Lagisquet had found a bronze hand in February of the same year, leading them to believe there was a large bronze sculpture buried on the site, but the bronze finger was clearly from a much larger hand. The villager took the archaeologists to a position on the platform of the West Mebon Temple. Here, about one metre below the surface, they found the broken fragments of the West Mebon

Vishnu, buried face down in the western shaft below the platform. At the beginning of the excavation, Glaize thought the statue to have been a giant Buddha but as the four arms and torso were revealed, it became clear that the image was of the Hindu God Vishnu (Figure 3).

Fig. 3. Vishnu as discovered face down in 1936, courtesy of the EFEO

The condition of the large bronze sculpture was very poor due to the bronze having been interred in a damp shaft. Significant oxidation was found covering the entire surface of the sculpture. The head, shoulders and one arm of the four-armed figure remained intact. (Figure 4) There was a gaping hole in the back of the head. An additional 18 pieces of the statue, including bronze ingots and other unidentified debris were recovered from the shaft. The additional pieces included fragments of the back, legs and decorative elements (Figure 5).

Tcheou Ta-Kouan, a Chinese official who visited Angkor between 1296 and 1297 AD, recorded in his Customs of Cambodia his observation of f a "bronze Buddha, from whose navel flows a steady stream of water". He locates this object to the Eastern Baray of Angkor'in his writings. At this stage, no evidence has been found to indicate the presence of a large reclining Buddha in the Eastern Baray, nor any other large sculpture or pediment. It has always been assumed that the Chinese visitor must

Fig. 4. West Mebon Vishnu courtesy of the National Museum of Phnom Penh

Fig. 5. Fragments of the sculpture at the time of excavation, courtesy of the EFEO

have been referring to the West Mebon Vishnu, but was mistaken in identifying it as a Buddha and locating it in the Eastern Baray. If this was the case, the Vishnu was still in place at the end of the 13th century, and was interred after this time.

Consistent with this line of reasoning, Jacques Dumarçay suggested in his paper La cité hydrolique that the western shaft under the platform of the West Mebon formed part of a hydrometer indicating the level of water in the Western Baray (Dumarçay, 2003). Unfortunately, none of the surviving pieces of the West Mebon Vishnu include the area of the navel, making it impossible to determine directly whether water could have issued from it, but the fact that the central platform of the West Mebon is 1.5 m lower than the surrounding embankment makes such an observation hydraulically feasible.

Until 2005, when one of the authors (MF) visited the National Museum of Cambodia in Phnom Penh to do so, the surviving fragments of the West Mebon Vishnu had not been documented. Digital images were made of each piece, along with measurements and weights. This provided the basic data for the ongoing research. On the same field trip, MF located in the EFEO Conservation Depot in Siem Reap an important stelé depicting Vishnu Anantasayin (Vishnu reclining), which was found at the West Mebon site in 1944. This stelé may hold some vital clues to the overall structure of the West Mebon Vishnu (Figure 6).

Fig. 6. Stelé found at the West Mebon site

Since returning from Cambodia in 2005, MF has made a quantitative and qualitative analysis of the surviving fragments of the Vishnu. In a quantitative analysis, the mass of data has to be organized and somehow meaningfully reduced or reconfigured (Miles and Huberman: 1994). In order to organise the data and analyse its significance, a digital reconstruction of the West Mebon Vishnu was made. To provide a basic form on which to manipulate these data, a wire frame model was created by NG and BA under the general supervision of TC. MF then made a comparative study of the iconography of Vishnu, particularly in a reclining pose. Informed by these representations and through digital manipulation of the fragments from the National Museum of Cambodia, a comprehensive visualisation of the Vishnu has been developed (Figure 7).

The digital visualisation for the West Mebon Vishnu came about through the need to look at the surviving pieces of the Vishnu in the context of the overall structure. The questions asked were: How much of the Vishnu is missing? What clues do the remaining fragments hold for the format of the statue when it was whole? What patterns and common themes emerge when looking at the decoration of the Vishnu? If the statue is indeed a Vishnu Anantasayin, what other figures may have been present in the representation? What evidence is there to date the statue, or determine under the reign of which Khmer king it was commissioned?

Fig. 7. Visualisation of Vishnu Anatasayin murti

2 Analysis of the Surviving Fragments of the West Mebon Vishnu

Prior to the commencement of work on the computer generated   visualization, a detailed study was made of the surviving pieces. Besides the head and shoulders, much of the statue is missing and the rest is very fractured. Extrapolating from measurements of the surviving fragments, it seems the statue would have been over five meters in length. It also became apparent when looking at the remaining pieces that around 60% of the sculpture was missing. The structure of some of the fragments indicated that the components of the statue were cast by the lost wax technique, and then assembled later. The external patina of the sculpture is rough and green with oxidation. Small square and rectangular indentations pattern the surface in an irregular way. These indentations are a result of mending casting errors. (Woodward 1997: 37) The surface shows there are many of these mending patches indicating the sculpture to have been cast with an inferior mix of metals.

In particular, five pieces of the statue were critical in formulating a view as to the format for the sculpture as a whole. Each piece contained valuable information which when analysed added to the information available on the sculpture. There were multiple rounds of revisiting the data as additional questions emerged, new connections were determined, and more complex formulations developed. As our understanding of the material deepened, the pieces were moved on the virtual model. Several positions were tried, tested, and reviewed in 3D before the final decision was reached. These iterations in the analysis of the data made in virtual space assisted in advancing the interpretation of the sculpture.

The main intact fragment includes the head and shoulders of the Vishnu (Catalogue number A5387). What is clear from this large fragment is that it is a figure of Vishnu reclining. In order to interpose the remaining fragments on a reclining model, it was necessary to evaluate the options available for the murti of the reclining Vishnu, or Vishnu Anantasayin.

Fig. 8. Vishnu Anatasayin located at Kbal Spean courtesy of V. Roveda

The lack of any precedent of a three-dimensional representation of Vishnu Anantasayin in Khmer Art, made the next step difficult. It was necessary to turn to the rich tradition of bas-relief works found in Khmer temples to put the sculpture into some context. By creating a catalogue of the different representations of Vishnu Anantasayin, it became apparent that some features within the Khmer iconographic tradition remained constant. It must be noted here that these depictions of the Anantasayin murti do vary in India and Thailand. Within the Khmer depiction of Vishnu Anantasayin from the 9th century onwards, the consort of Vishnu, Lakshmi, is always in attendance, holding or massaging the legs of the reclining god. Also constant and in constant position, with only one or two exceptions, are the four attributes of Vishnu: the wheel or disc in left rear hand, the orb in the left front hand, the staff in the right front hand and the conch shell in the right rear hand. The Vishnu Anantasayin (literally translated as 'resting on a serpent') reclines on a Naga (a seven-headed serpent), which in Khmer iconography was replaced at times by a Reachesay, or dragon, reflecting the influence of Chinese culture during the 12th century. (Vickery 2002) Sometimes, both icons appear, with the Naga resting upon the

Reachesay. Vishnu floats above the primordial ocean on this bed. From Vishnu's navel, a lotus appears on which a small Brahma sits in the act of creating the world (Figure 8)

Examination of the main fragment of the head and shoulders revealed other important information. There is a large gap between the palm of the upturned right hand and the side of the head, that the hand clearly supports. This gap allows room for the missing headdress (Jutamukuta) and also for the attribute of the right hand (the orb). The large round hole in the back of the head and the round hole on the left side of the forehead are also consistent with a missing headdress or diadem (Figure 9).

Fig. 9. West Mebon Vishnu showing hole in forehead courtesy of the National Museum of Phnom Penh

The Vishnu has a large sweeping pectoral collar of pendants, featuring a Chan flower motif at the back and the front. The design also includes the chakachan design wherein a square is drawn around the flower in a diamond shape. This design is also known as the pich or diamond composition. The royal insignia of Cambodia is set into a Chakachan shaped frame when displayed. Thick ornate armbands encircle both sets of arms, and are positioned artfully to cover a join in the cast pieces. Similar bands may have been located also on the ankles, as indicated by examples such as the frieze located on the western part of the South Gallery of Angkor Wat of a procession of Suryavarman II in which the King is dressed with very similar pendants and arm bands (Figure 10).

The second key fragment of the Vishnu is a large segment of the right leg (Catalogue number A2084). It includes the thigh, knee and shin. From the inside of this piece, it can be seen that these three sections have been caste in separate pieces and joined together. Most importantly, there is a return lip along the length of the upper edge of the right leg fragment, indicating the line of attachment of the missing left leg (Figure 11). Due to the shape and orientation this joining lip, it was possible to ascertain that the ankles were crossed. This piece also yielded up important information about the pose of the sculpture because the angle of the lower leg to the thigh showed a very prominent bend in the knee. This information would be consistent with the Vishnu lying on his right side with both legs bent and raised with the ankles crossed. This pose is very typical of depictions of Vishnu Anantasayin in Bas Reliefs, such as the Vishnu Anantasayin of Phnom Rung (Figure 12).

This pose of the sculpture is also consistent with the presence of Lakshmi to support the raised, crossed ankles in her lap, and to stabilize the sculpture. In order for the sculpture to be stable and not to have been out of proportion it requires a Lakshmi to be under the leg supporting both the feet. This too is characteristic of the Bas - Relief carvings of Vishnu Anantasayin in Khmer Art the 10th and 11th Centuries. It is important to note here the images of Vishnu in sleep without Lakshmi in attendance to support the feet, which are found rarely in early Khmer Art of the 8th and 9th century, always show both feet together and the legs straight. In Indian and Nepalese traditions, this Anatasayin murti has been shown lying flat on its back with legs together. In contrast, the surviving fragment of the bent right leg and the bend of the right arm supporting the upper torso of the West Mebon Vishnu indicate clearly that this cannot be a depiction of Vishnu lying flat, or with the legs straight. It was at this point in the investigation that it was possible to choose a model for the Vishnu which included the figure of Lakshmi supporting the crossed legs of the Vishnu lying on his right side with the upper torso and head supported by the flexed right arm.

With the critical decision made regarding the pose of the Vishnu, it was possible to construct a preliminary 3D wire frame computer model, as outlined below, and to begin to 'float' the digital images of the Vishnu pieces onto the model to empirically test the 'best fit' of the remaining pieces in an iterative process (figure 13). Several important pieces gave a clue as to their correct position due to texture, form and curvature, and indications of ornament. Allowance had to be made at times for damage or deformation of some pieces during the destruction and interment of the statue. Once the larger pieces were placed, it became possible to find the positions of the smaller pieces of the sculpture, and to estimate how much of the sculpture was missing. Reassembling the fragmented pieces of the sculpture in a virtual space provided us with advantages that would have been difficult to execute through traditional methods. The ability to edit, rotate, angle and experiment with subtle alterations in the placements in three dimensions was instrumental in the painstaking process of bringing the sculpture back to a semblance of its original form.

Having positioned the head and torso fragment and the right leg fragment on the 3D model, we next 'floated' on the very large piece of the back of the Vishnu (Catalogue number 2084/E1230) (figure 14). It became apparent immediately that the correct orientation of this piece was the opposite of our initial expectations. This large fragment included the belt of a Sampot that, once correctly orientated, clearly sat very low over the hips, consistent with the Baphuon style. Further investigation into this piece showed a square indentation in the middle of the belt, which was consistent with a butterfly clip ornament being placed there, again in the Baphuon style (cf the large bronze sculpture of a deified king, possibly Jayavarman VI in the collection of the Metropolitan Museum of Art, New York, Bulletin Vol 47, No 2, p92, 1988-99). The butterfly tie bow at the back of the Sampot was associated with the upper boarder the Sampot being turned down at the front. This style innovation accompanied the reappearance of the diadem. (Boisellier:1966:p252-258), evidence for which on the Vishnu has been noted above.

The correct orientation of the large fragment of the back also indicated that the upper border of the Sampot followed a line high up over the flanks, typical of the elegant late Baphoun style, sweeping steeply from a high line over the loins down to below the navel, as defined by scholars such as Philippe Stern and Gilberte de Coral - Remuzat in 1936 in and illustrated by Jean Boisselier in the Manuel d'Archeologie D'Extreme-Orient, 1966. We used the line drawings of Boisselier to experiment with the sampot style and position (Figure 15).

On the front of the sculpture, we had a lot of difficulty with a piece that was most definitely part of the curve of the lower thigh (Catalogue number 2988.6). When placed on the model, we found the Sampot line on this piece was oriented in the wrong direction, and it was necessary to move a few pieces in order to place it correctly on the thigh.

An important piece of the belt (CatalogueA2988.1/ E1230D) was located to the middle of the leg join, and this gave us confirmation of the correct overall position of the belt on the figure. This important piece also shed light on the finish of the sculpture as it showed evidence of gold leaf in places. This would be consistent with other sculptures of similar style which were amalgam gilded.(for example: see guardian of Kamphang Yai figure 17) (figure 16)

The belt of the West Mebon Vishnu is also Baphuon in style. Another large section of the back with lines of the Sampot and belt indicates a line of lozenge-shaped ovals, which may have represented metal plates or a belt set with jewels. These decorations can also be seen on other examples of late Baphoun style sculpture.

Important comparative works are the figure of Kamphang Yai and the Siva head from Por Loboeuk, both of which are stylistically very closely related to the West Mebon Vishnu. (Figure 17)

The West Mebon Vishnu shows other important hallmarks of the Baphuon style of Khmer sculpture, including full curved lips, arched eyebrows, curled moustache, round wide skull, full cheeks and broad shoulders.. Beginning in the reign of Udayadityavarman II (1050 – 1066) this style was named after the Baphuon temple. Although the Baphuon style was predominant throughout the latter half of the 11th century, some features of the late Baphuon style continued to be seen in a modified way in the style of Angkor Wat, which marks the reign of Suryavarman II (1113 – 1150).

One striking and surprising feature of the West Mebon Vishnu is the complete absence of lines indicating the tiny pleats in the Sampot that are one of the hallmarks of the Baphuon style. This is most important because there are no major examples of bronze Baphoun style sculptures without a typical lined Sampot. In contrast, the depictions of Suryavarman II and the major images of Vishnu in the Bas -Relief carvings of the temple of Angkor Wat all show unlined sampots. This may indicate a later construction date for the West Mebon Vishnu. The king Udayadityavarman II and the minor kings who followed his reign implemented the official state religion of

Siva. This changed only in 1113 AD with the reign of Suryavarman II, a powerful king and worshiper of Vishnu, to whom Angkor Wat is dedicated. One possibility is that Suryavarman II commissioned the sculpture of Vishnu at the beginning of his rule, as he waited for his main temple Angkor Wat to be built. (figure 18)

Fig. 10. Bas relief of Suryavarman II from Angkor Wat

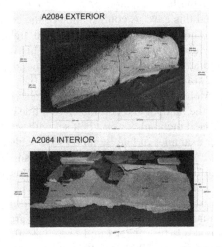

Fig. 11. Catalogue A2084 piece with join for legs

Fig. 12. Vishnu Anatasayin located at Phnom Rung

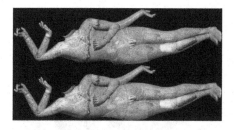

Fig. 13. Fragments of the Vishnu floated on the computer model

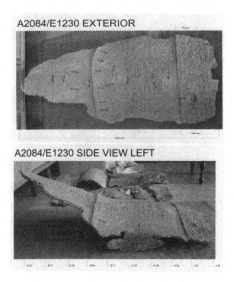

Fig. 14. Catalogue 2084/E1230 piece of the back with sampot and belt

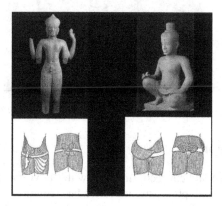

Fig. 15. Vishnu with Sampot both Baphuon and late Baphuon drawings by Boisselier

Fig. 16. Catalogue 2988.1 piece of belt

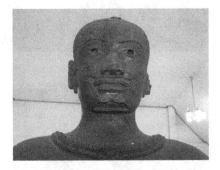

Fig. 17. The guardian figure of Kamphang Yai

Fig. 18. Vishnu Anatasayin murti placed in the West Mebon

3   The Visualisation Process

The marriage of archaeological reconstruction with 3D visualisation that this project entailed presented several problems and attendant solutions. The primary problem from a 3D modeling perspective was the inherently iterative nature of the reconstruction process, which differed markedly from the common practice in the 3D modeling industry. Typical 3D modeling projects are largely linear in progression in that the outcomes are pre-planned before digital construction commences, and only minimal changes are made during construction. In contrast, when dealing with the vagaries of a fragmented and incomplete historical artifact, such as the West Mebon Vishnu, the process of modeling needed to be kept flexible, as insights and discoveries made along the way all affected the unrealized end product. From the outset, it became apparent that the ongoing research into the visual appearance of the statue required frequent changes to the pose, materials, and the environment throughout its creation.

All models, materials, and the lighting needed to be prepared, to accommodate these requirements, resulting in a much higher amount of work than is usually associated with a project of this scope.

Although the resulting visualisations of the Vishnu depict an immovable bronze statue, the modeling of the Vishnu involved character and 3D human figure modeling techniques common to animation studies in order to ensure the correct positioning of the limbs and arms. The Vishnu model was built to incorporate a system of simulated bones inside the arms and torso that enabled joint movements so the limb's poses could be manipulated in a manner similar to a puppet.

Once the statue had been modeled, textures were applied to simulate its compositing materials, or surfaces. In a similar manner to the skeletal system used for posing the statue, these textures needed to display diverse possibilities rather than singular and preemptory outcomes, and several different textures were applied to suggest varying graphical representations. While some of these representations depicted photographs of the surviving fragments being projected ('floated') onto the completed statue model to show their original context and position, other materials such as gold leaf and bronze were applied variously to create visualisations of possible appearances. (figure 19)

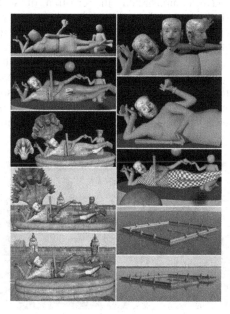

Fig. 19. Visualization development

Throughout all phases of the statue's construction, the modeling, posing and texturing, progressive pictures were subject to successive rounds of review and re-evaluation. Being a cross-disciplinary collaboration, this project entailed on the one hand that archaeologists gained an understanding of the production processes involved in 3D graphics in evaluating work-in-progress material, and on the other that the 3D artists became familiar with archaeological research in being able to interpret the supplied reference material and produce 3D imagery understandable to the archaeological discipline. Frequent correspondence was essential to build an understanding of each other's worlds.

4 Virtual Heritage and Angkor: The Road Ahead

Angkor is a UNESCO World Heritage Site and Cambodia's rich architectural and archaeological heritage is world-renowned. Although conservators are now overseeing many of these monuments, many structures have been in ruin for centuries and the wooden buildings of centuries ago have long since disappeared. The ruins of the temples at Angkor, like most archaeological sites, are incomplete. In line with the growing emphasis on Virtual Heritage, comprehensive 3D visualisations can significantly advance the awareness of historical sites that might be inaccessible due to their remote location or fragile condition.

To visualise Angkor's historic landscape is to see an entirely different world from the serene and reconstituted tourist park that Angkor is today. A virtual world that visually conveys not only architectural and sculptural edifices accurately but also the subtle hues of the water and soil is one that communicates the fundamentally chthonic nature of the civilization.

However, as we have demonstrated, the creation of such virtual visions is dependent on a great deal of research, testing, and reviews by a wide range of experts. The images presented here visually portray the many steps that are necessary to reconstruct not only the statue but also one possibility of the original context of its immediate environment at the centre of the lotus filled pond in the interior of the West Mebon shrine. In this respect, simulated colours, reflections, shadows, the wafting of incense smoke and the environmental ambience of the West Mebon are integral additions to the final rendering of any reconstructed geometry of its centerpiece - in this case the sculpture of Vishnu Anatasayin. Given that they move from the precise

Fig. 20. Vishnu Anatasayin visualisation as viewed from behind

to the general, these later scenes are necessarily broad in scope, but their inherent value lies in their potential to convey the wider context and significance of this sculpture at Angkor. (Figure 20)

It should not be forgotten that Angkor was a living city, and it is through the lens of digital animation that reconstructed life can be viewed (and heard) again. To this end, digital animations that depict the entirety of the West Mebon temple and its surroundings, complete with murmuring devotees disembarking from boats and walking along the temple causeway, are currently being tested and researched. These animations will constitute the next stage of the marriage of traditional artefactual analysis with digital 3D visualization that is presented here, and it is hoped that they will be presented in upcoming paper.

References

1. Boisselier, J.: Arts du Champa et du Cambodge PreAnkorien la date de Mi- So'n E Atibus Asiae, vol. XIX (1955)
2. Boisselier, J.: Asie du Sud- Est Vol 1 Le cambodge:Paris (1966)
3. Boisselier, J.: Notes Sur L'Art du Bronze dans L'Ancient Cambodge, Artibus Asiae, p. 29 (1967)
4. Briggs, L.P.: The Ancient Khmer Empire. White Lotus Press, Bangkok (1999)
5. Dupont, P.: Les Linteau Khmers, Atibus Asiae, vol. XV (1952)
6. Freeman, M., Jacques, C.: Ancient Angkor. Bangkok, River Books (2003)
7. Jessup, H.I., Zephir, T.: Sculpture of Angkor and Ancient Cambodia, Millennium of Glory. National Gallery of Art, Washington (1997)
8. Jessup, H.I.: Art and Architecture of Cambodia: Thames and Hudson (2004)
9. Miles, M.B., Huberman, A.M.: Qualitative Data Analysis: An expanded source book, 2nd edn. Sage, Thousand Oaks (1994)
10. Roveda, V.: Khmer Mythology, Secrets of Angkor. Riverbooks, Bangkok (2003)
11. Vickery, M.: Lectures Royal University of Fine Art: Phnom Penh (2002)
12. Woodward, H.W.: The Sacred Sculpture of Thailand. River Books, Bangkok (1997)
13. Woodward, H.W.: The Art And Architecture of Thailand. Brill, Boston (2003)

From Manual to Automated Optical Recognition of Ancient Coins

Maia Zaharieva[1], Martin Kampel[1], and Klaus Vondrovec[2]

[1] Vienna University of Technology Pattern Recognition and Image Processing Favoritenstr 9/1832, A-1040 Vienna, Austria
[2] Museum of Fine Arts Department of Coin and Medals Burgring 5, A-1010 Vienna, Austria maia,
kampel@prip.tuwien.ac.at, klaus.vondrovec@khm.at

Abstract. Illegal trade and theft of coins appears to be a major part of the illegal antiques market. Image based recognition of coins could substantially contribute to fight against it. Central component in the permanent identification and traceability of coins is the underlying classification and identification technology. However, currently available algorithms focus basically on the recognition of modern coins. To date, no optical recognition system for ancient coins has been researched successfully. In this paper, we give an overview over the challenges faced by optical recognition algorithms. Furthermore, we show that image based recognition can assist the manual process of coin classification and identification by restricting the range of possible coins of interest.

1 Introduction

Traditional methods to fight the illicit traffic of ancient coins comprise manual, periodical search in auctions catalogues, field search by authority forces, periodical controls at specialist dealers, and a cumbersome and unrewarding internet search, followed by human investigation. However, these methods only prevent the illicit trade of ancient coins in a rather partial way. To date, no automatic coin recognition system for ancient coins has been researched – and thus – applied successfully. From optical coin recognition point of view we distinguish between two approaches: coin identification and coin classification. A coin classification process assigns a coin to a predefined category or type, whereas a coin identification process assigns a unique identifier to a specific coin.

Recent research approaches for coin classification algorithms focus mainly on the recognition of modern coins. Applied pattern recognition algorithms are manifold ranging from neural networks [1][2] to eigenspaces [3], decision trees [4], edge detection and gradient directions [5][6], and contour and texture features [7]. Huber et al. present in [3] a multistage classifier based on eigenspaces that is able to discriminate between hundreds of coin classes. Due to the controlled setup of the system presented coin detection becomes a trivial task. They report correct classification for 92.23% of all 11,949 coins in a sample set. In [7] Maaten et al. present a coin classification system based on edge-based statistical features. The coin

T.G. Wyeld, S. Kenderdine, and M. Docherty (Eds.): VSMM 2007, LNCS 4820, pp. 88–99, 2008.
© Springer-Verlag Berlin Heidelberg 2008

classification method proposed by Reisert et al. [6] is based on gradient information. Similar to the work of Nölle et al. [5] coins are classified by registering and comparing the coin with a pre-selected subset of all reference coins (for example coins from the MUSCLE CIS 06 database[1] see Figure 1).

Fig. 1. Example images of modern coins

Tests performed on image collections both of medieval and modern coins show that algorithms performing well on modern coins do not necessarily meet the requirements for classification of medieval ones [8]. In this paper we present challenges faced by optical recognition techniques, especially we differentiate between classification and identification of coins. Section 2 describes the process of coin classification from both a numismatic and an image processing point of view. Section 3 continues with a description of coin identification again from a numismatic and image processing point of view. Results on experiments performed on both classification and identification of ancient coins are presented in Section 4. We conclude and give an outlook for future research in Section 5.

2   Classification Workflow

2.1   Manual Classification

Numismatics deals with various aspects of the phenomenon Money[2]. That can be a historical approach, the systematic research of the minting plan, the distribution of coin finds or economic background. Fundamental work is the classification of coins according to standard reference books since they provide additional information such as accurate dating, political background or minting places.

The process of manual classification can be very short, nonetheless a number of steps are to be taken. To assign a coin to the correct time period or to determine which side is the obverse and which the reverse usually does not take more time than to grab the object but involves a great deal of knowledge. Reading the legends, if there are any, and identifying the pictures correctly is depending on the experience of the

---

[1] MUSCLE CIS Benchmark Competition 2006, http://muscle.prip.tuwien.ac.at (last visited: 2007-06-15)

[2] The Institute for Numismatics and Monetary History of the University of Vienna is the only one of its kind worldwide that is dedicated only to the Historic Studies of Money.

numismatist and his or her fields of specialization. The classification process is accomplished when the coin is identified according to a standard reference book so that by its reference number a full description or even a photograph of a similar piece is available to everyone. Usually classification also includes documentation of the object, covering taking pictures, making a description and taking certain measurements.

The classification process is like putting the objects through various sieves, from coarse to fine [9, 10]. Classifying one coin as Roman-Imperial and another one as Medieval is still a result. The numismatic requirement is basically to give the correct number in a reference book. For every period or every fraction of the monetary history there are different books, some covering several centuries[3] and others only a few years of a single minting place. A reference book does not cite single specimens of coins but coin types, which is a combination of picture and legend [10]. While some older books list all coin types known to the author(s) in chronological order sorted by metal or even in the alphabetical order of their reverse legends, other books present the coins by mint[4]. During the Roman period groups of coin types can often be identified as being minted in the same production issue. For example, when Marcus Aurelius (161-180) won his first victory in the Marcomannic wars, a distinct group of coins was issued with a limited number of reverse types but covering all denominations (coin values) from gold to brass-metal. However, in the coin production of the Celts, no such intricate organization and administration ever existed so that a Celtic "issue" needs to be defined differently. Thus, not only the arrangement of coin types differs in books but they also display the state of research on a certain subject. Consequently, the quality of information gained varies considerably.

The classification process is also depending on both the time period and the reference literature itself. In any case, one has to gain as much information as possible even before consulting any books. *Hard* information is metal, weight, die-axe, and diameter. The reading of the legends and the interpretation of the pictures are to be considered as *soft* data. Additional information on the find spot or archaeological contexts is of no relevance to the classification process. Providing the original specimens is still the usual way of classifying coins. A good picture can show both legends and pictures clearly, and can also give away the metal and size. When information like weight and die-axe are provided, it is possible to work only on pictures (given the coin itself is in a good condition). When a specimen is badly worn, it is necessary to keep changing the angle of light to be able to retrieve a clearer view.

The actual process of classification is not to describe a coin but to figure out what it is or what is depicted. The job is only half done when reading the legend. Titles are abbreviated but iterated so that COS VI means Consul for the 6th time and the 6th ascension of Consulship narrows down the dating of a coin to a very short time span. A female figure with wings, for example, would be the Roman goddess Victory or the Greek Nike. Her favorite attributes are a palm-leaf or a crescent. Sometimes she is

---

[3] E.g. the series of "Roman Imperial Coinage" (RIC, London 1923–1994) covers the time from 31 BC to AD 498 in ten volumes. Although there are literally thousand of more detailed studies on this period it is still considered as a standard reference.

[4] The series "Moneta Imperii Romani" (MIR, Vienna 1984–2007) is to replace the often alphabetical layout of the RIC by the actual minting rhythm.

without attributes accompanying or crowning the emperor. This concept makes it often possible to recognize certain coin types from only few visible features. Usually, an experienced numismatist can also deal with coins that are corroded or badly worn[5] as it can be often observed in coin-hoards.

The single steps of the classification process do not always follow the same patterns. If the legends are readable and apt to narrow down the number of possible coin types, one will possibly not have to bother with the pictures to retrieve a proper reference number. Although databases are commonly used nowadays, no big systematic approach has been successfully launched so far that has both a standardized description scheme and a complete basis of numismatic material. Even though computers make it much easier to provide and obtain pictures of coins, the classification process did not change basically in the last centuries – its speed and accuracy is depending on both knowledge and experience of the numismatist in charge.

2.2 Automated Classification

From image processing point of view coin classification process passes well-defined stages as shown in Figure 2.

In the *segmentation* stage an image is partitioned into its parts or objects. The segmentation process is one of the most difficult tasks in the image processing. A robust segmentation is essential for imaging problems that require objects to be classified or identified individually. A weak segmentation algorithm causes the eventual failure of the whole classification process. In general, image segmentation algorithms follow three approaches. The first group partition an image based on abrupt changes in the intensity (e.g. edges in an image [11]). The second category identifies the image regions that are similar to a set of predefined criteria (e.g. threshold, color information [12, 13]). The third group of segmentation techniques is based on finding regions directly (e.g. region splitting and merging [14]). In the next step – *object detection* – the perceptually salient regions or objects are identified. In general, this process is based on predefined criteria ranging from simple measurements such as area dimensions or circularity to complex shape descriptors [15]. As output single or multiple objects that fit the criteria are identified for further processing. The goal of the *feature extraction* stage is to find those features that describe the object in a robust and compact way and provide optimal discriminative information.

Choosing an appropriate set of features is critical for the classification process. Using a large number of features may better represent the object. However, the risk of overfitting arises since collecting a large amount of information can overfit the available training data and will not generalize well enough to it. On the other side, the selection of too few features decreases the separability of the object description. As a result, an object can be assigned to multiple classes. Ideally, for classification purposes, only those features are considered that are class-specific, i.e. with high separability and globalization power. Finally, in the *classification* step the extracted features are compared with the available training data. Current classification

---

[5] In the Roman Empire a single coin could circulate for more than 200 years.

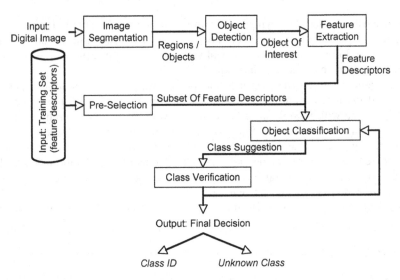

Fig. 2. Coin classification process

algorithms are manifold ranging from simple similarity measurements (e.g. Euclidean or Mahalanobis distances, etc.) to various statistical classifiers (Bayes, k-Nearest Neighbour, etc.) [16], and approaches based on neural networks [17]. As result, a class membership is identified. Eventually, an additional *verification* step can assure the final decision of the classification process.

Current research approaches for coin classification algorithms possess mainly two limitations. On the one hand, the input digital image is well defined – there is always only one coin pictured and the image is taken under very controlled conditions (such as background, illumination, etc.). On the other hand, current coin classification algorithms focus mainly on the recognition of modern coins. Those assumptions facilitate the classification process substantially. In this case of controlled conditions and the well-known circular shape of modern coins, the process of coin detection and segmentation becomes an easier task. The almost arbitrary shape of an ancient coin narrows the amount of appropriate segmentation algorithms. A case in point is the segmentation approach based on the Generalized Hough Transform as proposed by Reisert et al.[6]. By definition, this method is only applicable for completely round coins. In contrast, edge-based segmentation algorithms in a combination with morphological operations can work even in the case of an unknown coin shape [18]. However, varying conditions of image acquisition – e.g. illumination changes, multiple objects, multiple coins, varying background, etc. – remain the most challenging part of the segmentation process.

The differences between ancient and modern coins do not only influence the segmentation process but also the selection of appropriate feature set. Ancient coins differ strongly from modern ones. Crucial influence have both the nature of the ancient coins – less details, no rotational symmetry – and the poor conditions due to wear or fouling. Fundamental differences between ancient and modern coins originate from the manufacturing process. Ancient coins were hammered or casted whereas modern coins are minted. Thus, ancient coins exhibit a larger amount of size and texture variations independently of their actual condition. The features must cope with a list of problems, some of them are particular to historical coins, e.g. coin design is not centered or completed, excessive wear, irregular shape and/or edges, die deterioration, and so on. Edge-based statistical features as the one proposed by Maaten et al. [8, 7] for the classification of modern coins fail with the classification of ancient ones [18]. These features represent a combined angular and distance information about the edge pixels in the coin image. Since the design of an ancient coin is usually not centered edge-based feature tend to provide insufficient coin description. Similar problem arises by the use of gradient-based techniques [6, 5] since they are also based on features extracted from polar grid images. Figure 3 illustrates the problem. Since modern coins are the product of an automated manufacturing process, they are always circular and their design perfectly centered. Thus, the position of the polar grid with respect to the coin design will not change for coins of the same type (see Figure 3(a) and 3(d)). In contrast, the design positioning of ancient coins differ even among representatives of the same coin type. For example, the coin represented in Figure 3(b) is of the same type as the one shown in Figure 3(c)). However, their stamps have completely different positions[6]. The task to find the center of a coin design is an open research issue.

3 Identification Workflow

3.1 Manual Identification

The act of identifying a certain coin on a picture to be the specimen in question is not always successful. Therefore, we summarize the process briefly.

The first coins were struck in Asia Minor in the late 7th century BC and since then coins are a mass product. In the Antiquity coins were hammer-struck from manually engraved coin-dies, so that those coins from the same production batch will have very much the same picture and also the same quality of its relief. The die was not struck with the same force on every coin and was not centered with the same accuracy on the flan.

The flans were handcrafted and differ in size, shape and – most important – in weight. Furthermore the coin-die itself began to wear off by the time[7]. If a coin-die did not break in this process it was usually re-cut, so that either the old pictures and legends became clearer again or new features were applied.

Depending on the series of coins in question, the only varying details can be either part of the picture or legend or there can be a difference in a prominent detail such as the face of figure but there can also be just a different number of dots in the circle that usually frames the coin-die. This kind of work is very time-consuming but in the first place depending on providing the original specimens, excellent photos or plaster casts. From a numismatic point of view it is necessary to separate the traces due to the

---

[6] The images of ancient coins were made available by Dr. Mark Blackburn, Fitzwilliam Museum, Cambridge, UK.

[7] It is estimated that the number of coins possibly struck from the same die can range up to between 5.000 or 10.000 [19].

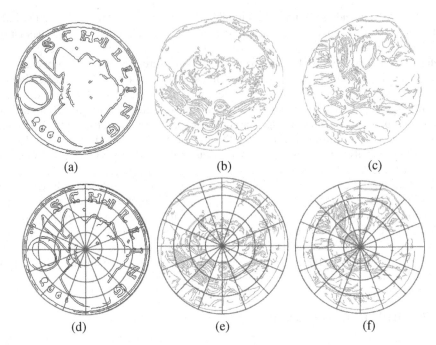

Fig. 3. Example of polar grid and edge coin images

production from those of intentional design of coin-dies. For the identification of coins a greater number of individual features facilitates the process even if they were applied after the minting.

In the 16th century minting machines were introduced that facilitate both speed and quality of the coin production. Furthermore, the flans started to be produced on industrial level and differ in size and weight only beyond possible measuring. In the 18th century a kind of reducing-machine was invented. With that, a big model of a coin-die could be reduced to its required size, so that from that time there is no difference between coin-dies anymore. Thus, only alterations applied to single specimens can be used to identify coins from this time period individually, like small scratches, graffiti, etc. In contrast, throughout the entire Antiquity and Middle Ages all the required preconditions for a successful identification are given by the minting process. Also the state of wear or corrosion interferes with both classification and identification since the damage to the coins is permanent.

A good picture is to be considered sufficient even for die-studies if several preconditions are provided. For digital images a minimum of 1000dpi resolution is required. Furthermore, the actual size of the coin has to be displayed correctly. While grave mistakes can be easily identified, a deviation of only a few percent is almost impossible to detect and can spoil the results. In the days of handcrafted coin dies, coins of the same denomination can differ in size by several millimeters. So if a Sesterius is 27mm in diameter and is displayed at 29mm it will be considered as a bigger specimen. Furthermore, an image in color gives more information than one in black and white since it displays more grades of the relief or its shadows. The lighting of the coin has great influence on the identification process. If the light comes from very different angles it will be almost impossible to identify the same coin on such pictures.

3.2 Automated Identification

The workflow of an automated identification process (see Figure 4) differs from the one of classification (as described in Section 2.2) in its feature extraction step.

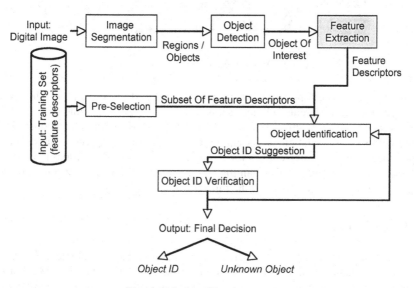

Fig. 4. Coin identification process

Classification ignores the individual features and focuses on the general ones to assign an individual object to a general category. In contrast, identification relies on individual, unique features that make given object different from all other individuals in the same class, and ignores general features that are common to many individuals. In the field of image processing, identification algorithms can be mostly found in image based quality control or surveillance scenarios (e.g. biometric recognition). To date, no identification system for ancient coins has been proposed or researched successfully.

Due to their nature ancient coins provide a set of identifying features. The unique shape of each coin originates in the manufacturing process (hammering procedure, specific mint marks, coin brockage, die deterioration, etc.). Furthermore, the time leaves its individual mark on each coin (fractures, excessive abrasion, damage, corrosion, etc). Eventually, from image processing point of view, identification of ancient coins turns out to be "easier" compared to classification. For example, Figure 5 shows ten different coins of the same coin type. A classification algorithm should ideally classify them all of the same class. However, technically spoken, they all provide complete different characteristics (see shape, die position, mint marks or level of details). At the same time, exactly those features enable the identification process.

Fig. 5. Different coins of the same coin type

In contrast, Figure 6 presents five pictures of one and the same coin. The pictures were taken using different technical setup –different digital cameras (fixed setup as well as free hand), different lighting conditions, and different image quality. The figure points out the challenges for an automated identification process as well as the importance of high quality images for the process itself. Different lighting conditions can hide or show details on the coin that are significant for a successful identification process (e.g. compare the first and the third image in Figure 6).

4 Experiments

We evaluated the classification performance of edge-based statistical features as proposed by Maaten et al. [8, 7] for two coin datasets. The first dataset – MUSCLE 06 – contain images of modern coins of European countries before the introduction of the euro currency. The images are taken under very controlled situation – constant background (conveyer belt) and light conditions. The MUSCLE training set contains over 9100 images unequally distributed over <100 classes. The test sets consist of 1000 test images (corresponding to 500 coins) respectively. The second dataset consists of 3000 high resolution images of ancient coins on constant, white background[8]. The coins picture Roman emperors and family members from approx. 30 B.C. to approx. 300 A.D. who form the 106 classes of the dataset. Furthermore, the coins are in different conditions and show different level of wear and fouling.

Fig. 6. Different image representations of the same coin

---

[8] Dr. Klaus Vondrovec, Department of coins and medals, Museum of Fine Arts, Vienna, Austria, made the data set available.

The tests performed address both classification based on single coin image (either obverse or reverse side) and classification based on images from both coin sides. Further tests integrate preselection stage based on area measurement. Only those coins that have a radius ±2mm of the radius of the provided test coin were considered for the next stage of the classification process. Since ancient coins of the same class show large variation of their size, preselection based on area measure was not evaluated on the Ancient dataset. Table 1 summarizes the results.

Table 1. Percentage of correct classified coins

	MUSCLE CIS 06	Ancient
single side classification	~ 61%	~ 6%
single side classification + preselection	~ 64%	–
both side classification	~ 48%	~ 4%
both side classification + preselection	~ 76%	–

The results show that classification based on images of both obverse and reverse coins side outperforms classification based on single image. However, state of the art algorithms for automatic classification of ancient coins clearly fail with the classification of ancient coins. Further research is required to find those features that most influence the quality of ancient coin representations. From numismatic point of view, restricting the range of possible classes an unknown ancient coin can be assign to, is already of advantage. To a certain degree it is feasible by an automated process. Still, further research is required to explore the boundaries of the optical recognition and define the prerequisites and minimum level of details a coin should have to enable reasonable automated classification. Coins such as the one represented in Figure 7(a) are out of the scope of optical recognition in contrast to Figure 7(b). Furthermore, specific tasks such as the identification of fakes lie outside of the boundaries of an automated process since they require not only an optical but also a physical inspection and moreover – expertise that is not learnable by a machine.

(a)   (b)

Fig. 7. Coins of Antonius Pius I for his adopted son Marcus

Preliminary evaluation on automated identification of ancient coins was performed using SIFT features [20]. The dataset consists of 26 Roman and Greek coins, single coin type respectively, whereas each coin side is pictured three to five times using different conditions (e.g. scan, camera, varying lighting conditions, etc.). The total amount of 251 images was randomly divided into training and test set. All images were identified correctly. However, the results have to be qualified. On the one side, the dataset used is a small one. This is due to the fact, that museums in general are not interested in collecting multiple coins of the same coin type. On the other side, the results are still very promising and show high research potential.

5 Conclusion

In this paper, we gave an overview over the challenges faced by optical recognition algorithms. We described coin identification and classification from both a numismatic and image processing point of view. Furthermore, we showed results on the classification and identification of ancient coins. It was shown that state of art approaches for modern coins fail, when they are applied to ancient coins. As a consequence we will extent our research towards other approaches like shape descriptors or feature detectors in order to reliably describe ancient coins. It is also planed to test and evaluate the results on larger databases.

Acknowledgments

This work was partly supported by the European Union under grant FP6-SSP5-044450.

References

1. Fukumi, M., Omatu, S., Takeda, F., Kosaka, T.: Rotation-invariant neural pattern recognition system with application to coin recognition. IEEE Transactions on Neural Networks 3(2), 272–279 (1992)
2. Bremananth, R., Balaji, B., Sankari, M., Chitra, A.: A new approach to coin recognition using neural pattern analysis. In: Proc. of IEEE Indicon 2005 Conference, pp. 366–370 (2005)
3. Huber, R., Ramoser, H., Mayer, K., Penz, H., Rubik, M.: Classification of coins using an eigenspace approach. Pattern Recognition Letters 26(1), 61–75 (2005)
4. Davidsson, P.: Coin classification using a novel technique for learning characteristic decision trees by controlling the degree of generalization. In: Proc. of 9th Int. Conference on Industrial & Engineering Applications of Artificial Intelligence & Expert Systems (IEA/AIE-1996), pp. 403–412 (1996)
5. Nölle, M., Penz, H., Rubik, M., Mayer, K.J., Holländer, I., Granec, R.: Dagobert – a new coin recognition and sorting system. In: Proc. of the 7th International Conference on Digital Image Computing - Techniques and Applications (DICTA 2003), Macquarie University, Sydney, Australia, pp. 329–338. CSIRO Publishing (2003)
6. Reisert, M., Ronneberger, O., Burkhardt, H.: An efficient gradient based registration technique for coin recognition. In: Proc. of the Muscle CIS Coin Competition Workshop, Berlin, Germany, pp. 19–31 (2006)

7. van der Maaten, L.J., Poon, P.: Coin-o-matic: A fast system for reliable coin classification. In: Proc. of the Muscle CIS Coin Competition Workshop, Berlin, Germany, pp. 7–18 (2006)
8. van der Maaten, L.J., Postma, E.O.: Towards automatic coin classification. In: Proc. of the EVA-Vienna 2006, Vienna, Austria, pp. 19–26 (2006)
9. Göbl, R.: Antike Numismatik, München (1978)
10. Göbl, R.: Numismatik – Grundriß und wissenschaftliches System, München (1987)
11. Heath, M., Sarkar, S., Sanocki, T., Bowyer, K.: Comparison of edge detectors. Computer Vision and Image Understanding (1), 38–54 (1998)
12. Liu, J., Yang, Y.H.: Multiresolution color image segmentation. IEEE Transactions on Pattern Analysis and Machine Intelligence 16, 689–700 (1994)
13. Shafarenko, L., Petrou, H., Kittler, J.: Histogram-based segmentation in a perceptually uniform color space. IEEE Transactions on Image Processing 7(9), 1354–1358 (1998)
14. Hojjatoleslami, S., Kittler, J.: Region growing: A new approach. IEEE Transaction on Image Processing 7(7), 1079–1984 (1998)
15. Zhang, D., Lu, G.: Review of shape representation and description techniques. Pattern Recognition 37(1), 1–19 (2004)
16. Jain, A.K., Duin, R.P.W., Mao, J.: Statistical pattern recognition: A review. IEEE Transactions on Pattern Analysis and Machine Intelligence 22(1), 4–37 (2000)
17. Zhang, G.P.: Neural networks for classification: A survey. IEEE Transactions on Systems, Man and Cybernetics 30(4), 451–462 (2000)
18. Zaharieva, M., Kampel, M., Zambanini, S.: Image based recognition of ancient coins. In: Proc. of the 12th International Conference on Computer Analysis of Images and Patterns (CAIP), pp. 547–554 (2007)
19. Duncan-Jones, R.: Money and Government in the Roman Empire, Cambridge (1994)
20. Lowe, D.: Distinctive image features from scale-invariant keypoints. International Journal of Computer Vision 20, 91–110 (2003)

Adding Semantic Annotations, Navigation Paths and Tour Guides to Existing Virtual Environments

Frederic Kleinermann, Olga De Troyer, Christophe Creelle, and Bram Pellens

Research Group WISE, Vrije Universiteit Brussel, Pleinlaan 2, 1050 Brussels, Belgium
{frederic.kleinermann, olga.detroyer, christophe.creelle,
bram.pellens}@vub.ac.be

Abstract. Nowadays, more Virtual Environments (VEs) are becoming available on the Web. This means that VEs are becoming accessible to a larger and more diverse audience. It also means that it is more likely that the use of these VEs (i.e. how to interact with the virtual environment and the meanings of the associated virtual objects) may be different for different groups of persons. In order for a VE to be a success on the Web, end-users should easily get familiar with the VE and understand the meanings of its virtual objects. Otherwise, the end-user may be tempted to quit the VE. Therefore, annotations and the creation of navigation paths for virtual tour guides become important to ease the use of VEs. Most of the time, this is done by VR-experts and the annotations are very poor and often only text based. This paper describes an approach and associated tool that allows a layman to add or update annotations to existing VEs. In addition, annotations are not limited to text but may also be multimedia elements, i.e. images, videos, sounds. Furthermore, the approach (and the tool) also allows easy creation of navigation paths and tour guides, which can be used to adapt a VE to the needs of a user. The paper illustrates the results by means of a real case, which is a reconstruction of a coalmine site for a museum.

Keywords: Virtual Reality, Semantic Annotations, Navigation Paths, Tour guides.

1 Introduction

Virtual Environments (VE) are becoming more available through the Internet thanks to formats like X3D [1]. Although Virtual Reality (VR) applications are becoming visually appealing, they often lack any kind of semantics, i.e. extra, non-visual information about the Virtual Environment and its objects [2]. The success of a VR application on the Web also depends on how the user is capable of interacting with the VE and how he can add meanings to the objects inside the VE and to the VE itself. This helps him to find his way in the VE and to a certain extent adapt the VE to his needs. As a result the user will be less tempted to leave the VE. A good example of this can be found in Second Life [3] where the user is not only discovering new visually attractive virtual places, but he can start to give meanings to the different objects and places in which he is immersed. For instance, he can jump to an ancient Maya site and then find new information about a temple.

T.G. Wyeld, S. Kenderine, and M. Docherty (Eds.): VSMM 2007, LNCS 4820, pp. 100–111, 2008.

Semantic annotation is information that is added to some media to enrich it. Semantic annotations are especially important in the context of the Semantic Web because they make the content of the Web machine-processable and enable computers and people to work in cooperation. In the same way, semantic annotations can be added to VEs and to their objects through the process of annotations. The process of annotation is not only useful for making the content machine-processable, but in the context of VE it is also very important to increase the usability of the VE (as illustrated above). In particular, this is very important in application domains such as Virtual Museums and cultural heritage where providing information is substantial.

However, the process of annotating is not easy. VEs can be annotated during development or afterwards. Currently, it is often done using authoring tools that provide very limited mechanisms for annotations. Usually, some textual annotations can be added, often even only keywords. Furthermore, the annotations are stored in the same file as the one containing the VE. VEs are often annotated by VR-experts and less often by domain experts. Another observation is that the meaning that people give to objects can change from person to person and also may depend on the task under consideration. Take for instance the meaning of an old building. For a historicist investigating that building, the annotations would be related to the research he is conducting. But for someone else it could be a story related to this building. While for an architect, the semantic annotations for that building would probably be its architectural properties.

For this reason, it is important to provide an approach where persons can easily add and update different sets of semantic annotations to existing VEs, so that existing VEs cannot only be extended with semantic annotations, but the annotations can also be customized to a particular domain, task or group of people. As a result, the same VE can be visualized in different contexts with different sets of annotations and in this way be used for different purposes.

Another important aspect also related to enhancing the usability of VEs is navigation. Navigation is very important in VEs and especially in the context of the Web or for VEs reaching a large audience. Such an audience is very demanding. They not only expect visually attractive VEs, but they also want to explore them very quickly. In general, if they need to spend too much time wondering how to interact with the VE and its objects, the chance is higher that they will leave the VE quickly. This is why navigation and virtual guided tours are very important. However, also for navigation the requirements may vary from person to person and from task to task. For instance, a guided tour inside an archeological site could be different for an audience of archeologists working on the site than for an audience of tourists visiting the site. Even for archeologists, a different guided tour may be needed to teach students than to discuss with colleagues about the findings or future excavations. Furthermore, the process of creating a navigation path and a virtual tour guide is usually not easy and therefore often performed by a VR expert. It is often not possible to easily adapt it or to create it for a particular application task or group of persons.

This paper describes an approach that helps a person (who may not be a VR-expert) to easily add and update semantic annotations to existing VEs and to easily create navigation paths and virtual tour guides that are customized towards these semantic annotations. In addition, the semantic annotations can be multimedia, i.e. texts, images, sounds and hyperlinks. The paper also describes the tool implemented to support the approach, and built on the top of Ajax3D [4].

The paper is structured as follows. In the next section, we provide related work. Section 3 describes the approach. Section 4 explains the tool supporting the approach and section 5 presents an example. Then, section 6 discusses the work presented in this paper. The paper ends with a conclusion and future work.

2 Related Work

In this section, we first review research work related to annotations and semantic for VE, and then we review research work related to navigation and tour guides.

In [5], the notion of smart object is used to provide not only the geometric information necessary for drawing objects on screen, but also semantic information useful for manipulation purposes. The semantic information in the smart object is used by virtual characters to perform actions on/with the object, e.g., grasping, moving, operating. Using the semantic information, the user is much more aware of the sort of manipulations that he can perform. For this reason, our approach also provides these features by using the semantic annotations that have been created and customized towards a group of end-users.

In [6][7], the authors propose a method in which the domain expert is annotating the virtual world when it is being created. The world is being created using ontologies and therefore, the semantic annotation is richer. The semantic annotation can be any kind of information. The navigation can then exploit these semantic annotations using a search engine. However, the navigation assumes that the world has been created and annotated using their method.

The work described in [8] presents an annotation framework facilitating the reuse of 3D models. An extension of the MPEG-7 standard is proposed that addresses 3D content. The framework allows managing the semantic annotations of 3D objects. The annotations can only be specified in a textual-like format which does not make it accessible to novice users. Our approach allows adding the annotation directly inside the VE making it more user-friendly.

A similar approach as ours is given in [9] where annotations are used in order to have better communication between team members. An application is presented enabling designers to directly annotate a VE and associate the annotations with a knowledge model.

The authors in [10] have developed an approach for navigation assistance in VEs. This approach allows non-professional visitors of a VE to find their way without having previous training. To assist the user in his navigation, they give a map of the environment where landmarks are added. They provide a personal assistant that has knowledge of the VE and the current user. They also provide a navigation agent for taking the user to a particular position. Although it is a very interesting work, the information used to assist the user in his navigation is limited to the geometrical and spatial aspects of the virtual worlds and its objects. Furthermore, it is not clear how generic the approach is.

Part of the work presented in [11] is also about navigation by querying. The author provides a querying model that allows users to find objects and scenes in virtual environment based on their size and their associated meta-information. This model is based on fuzzy logic. Nonetheless, the amount of meta-information data used in this work is still limited to object properties such as name, width, height, and locations. It is not context oriented.

In [12], the authors present a technique that allows navigation to cope with large virtual worlds. This technique uses place representation and visible landmarks that scale from town-sized to planet-sized worlds. However, the semantic annotation is only on place hierarchy, which determines which visible landmarks and place representation that users can see.

The problems generally encountered with navigation in large VEs are also acknowledged in [13]. An entertainment application is presented to educate people. Environments can be explored by means of flythrough mode or a roller coaster ride. However, the navigation paths need to be specified manually being time-consuming. Our approach enables fast creation of navigation networks directly inside the VE.

Another interesting work is given in [14] where an alternate approach is presented to associate semantic information based on the integration of X3D and the Semantic Web. The approach is illustrated with an application of a user-guide in complex environments and one of a virtual tour. A downside is that the user is not really guided in making the annotations and is therefore not very usable for a domain expert. Our approach focuses on making the annotation process more easily for domain experts or laymen.

3 Approach

This section explains our approach to make semantic annotations, navigation paths and virtual tour guides for existing VEs. The approach allows adding or updating semantic annotations, and to create new navigation paths and virtual tour guides directly inside the VE and in a visual way. The semantic annotations are multimedia elements, i.e. texts, videos, images and hyperlinks.

3.1 Point of Interest (POI), Navigation Paths, Navigation Landmarks

Point of Interest. In our approach, semantic annotations are created and represented through the concept of point-of-interest (POI). POI is defined by a position, an orientation and some multimedia elements (information) can be associated with it (images, videos, hyperlinks, or texts). A single POI may contain several multimedia elements. Furthermore, a POI can also be positioned inside a complex object.

Navigation Paths and Navigation Landmarks. A navigation path is created by linking several navigation landmarks in a well-defined order. A landmark has a position and an orientation. The navigation paths will be used to guide a tour guide.

3.2 Designer View and End-User View

The approach distinguishes between two views: the designer view and the end-user view. The designer view is used to create the semantic annotations, navigation paths and tour guides. In the end-user view, the annotated VE can be used, with or without using the tour guides.

Designer View. The designer view provides the designer (or domain expert) a way to add semantic annotations, to modify them or to delete them. The designer can also create navigation paths and associate an avatar to them in order to create a tour guides. We will now explain how the designer can annotate an object, create a navigation path and add a tour guide.

Semantic annotation. *The designer can add a semantic annotation by positioning a POI on an object or around it. However, an object can contain (built of) several other objects. For this reason, our approach also allows annotating the objects (or parts) inside such an object. For instance, if we take an object car made of a body and four wheels, then the designer may want to annotate not only the car as a whole, but also each of its components i.e., the wheels and body.*

The positioning of POIs can be done in two different ways namely using a *freehand* mode and using a *grid* mode. In the *freehand* mode, the designer can visually position a POI anywhere on (or inside) an object to add semantic annotations to this specific location. The designer can also define an orientation by using the orientation of his view.

As it is not always easy to position a POI using the freehand mode, the approach also provides a *grid* mode. In that mode, a grid of spheres overlaying the selected object is displayed. Each sphere represents a possible POI. The designer selects the spheres that he wants in order to define a POI. In other words, the *grid* mode has a number of predefined positions for the POIs. The grid has the size of the selected object based on its bounding box information. The number of spheres and the space between them can be customized according to the designer's specifications. The designer can also select different spheres to annotate areas of an object. For instance in the case of the coalmine site, the designer can select the object representing a building block. The building block is made of three parts namely a building, a sidewalk and a green area. By selecting a number of spheres covering the sidewalk, he can then add semantic annotations only related to the area of the sidewalk. He can repeat this for other areas.

Using POIs, the annotation process can be time-consuming as each object needs to be annotated individually. Therefore our approach also provides a way to accelerate the annotation process. After having annotated an object (either using the *freehand* or the *grid* mode), the designer can decide to propagate the semantic annotations of that object to the group of objects that have been identified to be similar. This feature is realized in our tool by using the X3D instructions like "ProtoInstance", "ExternProto", "USE", "DEF" which help to identify groups of similar objects. In other words, the semantic annotations can be created once for a complex object and be propagated to a number of similar objects populating the VE. That way, the process of annotation is less time-consuming and will also be more consistent.

Defining a Navigation Path. To create a navigation path, a number of landmarks must be positioned. To position landmarks, the approach also uses a *freehand* mode and a *grid* mode. Similar as for defining POIs, in the *freehand* mode navigation landmarks are positioned visually and freely by the designer on (or inside) an object.

The *grid* mode allows the designer to specify the navigation landmarks by selecting specific spheres of the grid. During the annotation process (see above), the designer may have added semantic annotations using the grid mode and for the same object for which the designer wants to specify a navigation path. In that case, the approach allows the designer to reuse the spheres used for the semantic annotations. For instance, suppose that the designer wants to constraint the path of the tour guide inside a coalmine tour by stating that the tour guide can only walk on the sidewalk. Suppose that the designer has annotated the building block using the grid mode. Therefore he has selected the spheres of the grid covering the building, sidewalk and green zone. When he wants to specify the navigation path for the building block, he can then do it using the semantic annotation related to sidewalk. As a result the navigation path for that object will be constrained to the volume defined by the selected spheres for the semantic annotation of the sidewalk.

A navigation path is composed by linking different landmarks in a well-defined order. When the path in followed (in the end-user view), the transition from one landmark to another one will be done by means of the shortest path.

Furthermore, the designer can also confirm to propagate the navigation path defined on an object to a group of similar objects. Like in the process of adding semantic annotations, this may accelerates the process of defining navigation paths.

Defining a Tour Guide. To define a tour guide, an avatar must be associated with a navigation path. In our approach, the tour guide (avatar) will move according to the navigation path associated to it and will show the semantic information (annotations) associated to a POI when it encounters a POI in his range. The range can be specified and corresponds to the radius of a sphere where the center of the sphere is the current position of the avatar at a given time.

End-user view. This view allows an end-user to select a tour guide for a VE. Furthermore, the end-user has the possibility to directly go to a POI, by jumping from where he is in the VE to a POI. The selection of a POI is based on a match between search information entered by the end-user and the semantic annotations associated with POIs. In the current implementation, the matching is only done for text.

4 Software Architecture

To support the approach, we opted for a Web tool that can be accessed using a classical browser and can be used by a large audience. To achieve this, we have implement it using Ajax3D [4], which combines AJAX with X3D through the Flux player and its Scene Authoring Interface [4]. The tool consists of three modules, namely a server and two different types of clients. Figure 1 shows the architecture.

4.1 Server

The server is implemented as a Java servlet running on Apache tomcat. The server is responsible to store VEs, avatars, semantic annotations and navigation paths. The server is accessed through HTTP requests and XML and X3D files are sent from the Server to the Client. Furthermore, with AJAX it is also possible to send XML files

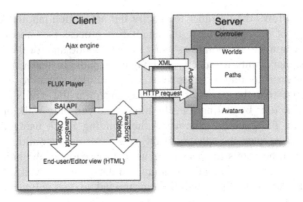

Fig. 1. Software Architecture

from the Client to the Server. That way, semantic annotations can be added and updated, new navigation paths and virtual tour guides can be created. All this information is stored at the server. This information can then be accessed by the end-user to view the VE with its virtual tour guides and semantic annotations.

4.2 Clients

The tool has two different types of clients namely a *Designer View Client* and an *End-user View Client*. Both clients use AJAX to send requests to the server and retrieve X3D files and XML files containing a virtual tour guide and semantic annotations. Communication with the X3D player is performed through the SAI supported by Flux Player [4]. Both clients run in a Web browser.

Designer View Client. The designer, running the Designer View Client in his Web browser, can select a VE from a list of VEs that have been uploaded on the server. Then, he can add semantic annotations, create navigation paths and tour guides. Note that currently our tool only supports human avatars based on H-Anim [15].

End-user View Client. The End-user View Client allows an end-user to select a VE and view it. He can select and follow a tour guide that has been created for this VE or walk around freely and see the different semantic annotations once he encounters a POI. Furthermore, when the tour guide encounters a POI, the view of the end-user can change according to the camera viewpoint specified by the designer, so that the end-user can see the object from a particular angle. He can also see the semantic annotations associated to that particular POI.

5 Example

The described approach has been applied in the cultural heritage context on a museum application consisting of a reconstruction of the Beeringen Coalmine[1] site [16]. The virtual coalmine site itself has been constructed using another tool called OntoWorld

---

[1] An old coalmine site in Belgium.

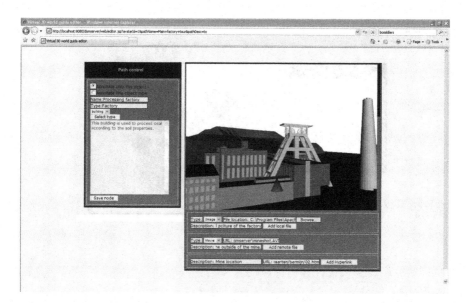

Fig. 2. Designer View Client. The designer is adding a POI (red cone) to one building of the main coalmine site using the freehand mode.

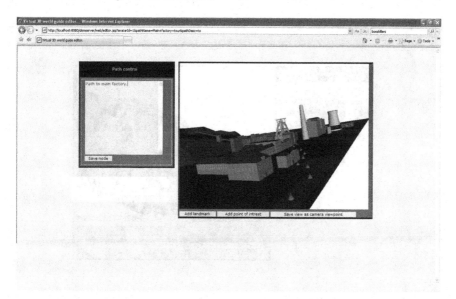

Fig. 3. Designer View Client. The designer is adding landmarks (yellow cones) to create a path around the coalmine site using the freehand mode.

[6][7]. Here, we have used our tool to add semantic annotations and to create a navigation path and a virtual tour guide for this particular VE.

By using the *Designer View Client*, the designer can add semantic annotations by using either the *freehand* mode or the *grid* mode. Figure 2 shows the screen after the

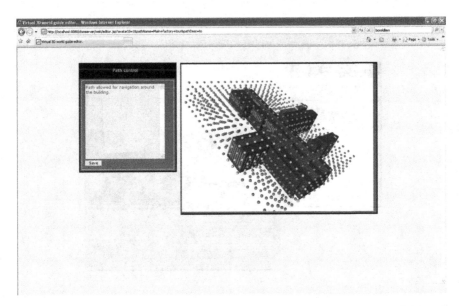

Fig. 4. Designer View Client. The designer is adding landmarks to create a path around a building of the coalmine site using the grid mode.

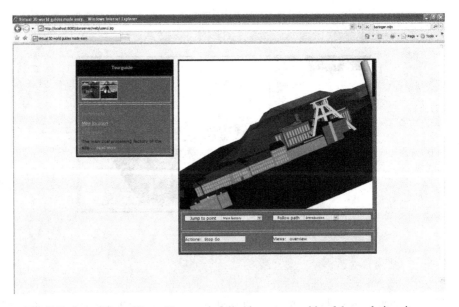

Fig. 5. End-user View Client. The user is following a tour guide of the coalmine site.

user having positioned (through the freehand mode) a POI and attaching some semantic annotation (here some text, images and videos). In our tool, in the freehand mode, POIs are represented by red cones. Remember that the designer can also create a navigation path by positioning navigation landmarks. Figure 3 shows an example of the designer positioning navigation landmarks represented by yellow cones in the *freehand* mode. Figure 4 shows the designer creating a navigation path for a particular building using the *grid* mode.

Once the navigation path has been stored, the designer can create a tour guide by selecting an avatar and a navigation path. In this example, a camera is used as avatar.

Then, an end-user can select the VE and the tour guide through his Web browser by loading the *End-user View Client*. Figure 5 shows the screen after an end-user having selected the virtual coalmine site with a tour guide. We see how the different semantic annotations are showed once the tour guide encounters POIs on his path. In figure 5, the tour guide encounters a POI. Its related semantic annotations are then displayed (here these are images, videos and texts). The images and videos are represented by thumbnails (see left side of figure 5 in the panel called "Tour Guide") and can be clicked by the end-user to view them.

6 Discussion

The approach proposed provides an easy way to add and modify semantic annotations to any VE, and to create navigation paths and virtual tour guides. Different multimedia types of semantic annotations are possible, i.e. images, text, videos and hyperlinks. The approach also provides a way to make the annotation process less time-consuming by means of a propagation mechanism and to create navigation paths for virtual objects composed of several objects. To add annotations and to specify landmarks two different modes are available. The freehand mode allows free positioning, while the grid mode uses predefined grids of spheres. In addition, the concept of grid can be combined with the semantic annotations. To ease the annotation process further, we consider adding the possibility to allow the designer to position POIs or navigation landmarks by means of so-called spatial relations. For instance, the designer could specify that a POI should be positioned left of the Mayan temple at a certain distance. This could also be used for positioning navigation landmarks.

This approach and the tool should allow designers to quickly customize VEs with semantic annotations and navigation paths. A VE can have multiple sets of semantic annotations, navigation paths and tour guides. Each of them can be used to represents a particular user view or to support a particular task. The tool implementing this approach is not limited to a certain type of VE but is very general. It uses X3D and Ajax3D and therefore the tool can be deployed on the Web and is accessible to a large audience.

Note that the tool can also be used to create virtual "post-its". A person can quickly add some annotations and a tour guide and then share this with other users. This can be very useful as a communication tool in education, or for archeologists or engineers to relate different types of annotations (such as comments, marks, errors, ...) to a particular virtual model and then share them with other stakeholders (students, colleagues, ...) who can then read the annotations and add their own.

7 Conclusions and Future Work

This paper has presented an approach that allows people who may not be VR-experts, to easily add semantic annotations (in the form of multimedia information) to existing VEs and to create tour guides by easily defining navigation paths in these VEs. A tool has been developed implementing this approach. The tool is based on Ajax3D.

Future work will focus on adding semantic annotation to behaviors and to allow creating navigation paths more intuitively using semantic annotations and spatial relations. Furthermore, some user experiments need to be conducted where the tools are used and tested, hereby investigating the intuitiveness and flexibility of our approach.

Acknowledgments

This research was carried out in context of the VR-DeMo project which is directly funded by the IWT, a Flemish subsidy organization from Belgium (IWT 030248).

References

1. Brutzman, D., Daly, L.: X3D: Extensible 3D Graphics for Web Authors. Morgan Kaufmann, San Francisco (2007)
2. Martinez, J., Delgado Mata, C.: A Basic Semantic Common Level for Virtual Environments. Int. Journal. of Virtual Reality 5(3), 25–32 (2006)
3. Rymaszewski, M., Wagner, J., Wallace, M., Winters, C., Ondrejka, C., Batstone-Cunningham, B.: Second Life, The official Guide, Sybex (2007)
4. Parisi, T.: Ajax3D: The Open Platform for Rich 3D Web Applications. Whitepaper. Media Machines Inc (2006)
5. Abaci, T., Mortara, M., Patane, G., Spagnuolo, M., Vexo, F., Thalmann, D.: Bridging Geometry and Semantics for Object manipulation and Grasping. In: The Workshop towards Semantic Virtual Environment (SVE), Villars, Switzerland, pp. 110–119 (2005)
6. Kleinermann, F., De Troyer, O., Mansouri, H., Romero, R., Pellens, B., Bille, W.: Designing Semantic Virtual Reality Applications. In: Proceedings of the 2nd Intuition International Workshop, Senlis, France, pp. 5–10 (2005)
7. De Troyer, O., Kleinermann, F., Mansouri, H., Pellens, B., Bille, W., Fomenko, V.: Developing semantic VR-shops for e-Commerce. In: Magoulas, G.D., Lepouras, G., Vassilakis, C. (eds.) Special Issue of VIRTUAL REALITY: Virtual Reality in the e-Society, pp. 20–60. Springer-Verlag, SpringerLink London (2006)
8. Bilasco, I.M., Gensel, J., Villanova-Oliver, M., Martin, H.: An MPEG-7 framework enhancing the reuse of 3D models. In: Proceedings of the international conference on 3D web technology, Columbia, USA, pp. 65–74 (2006)
9. Aubry, S., Thouvenin, I., Lenne, D., Okawa, S.: Knowledge integration for annotating in virtual environments. In: Int. J. Product and Development, vol. 4(6), pp. 533–546. Inderscience Publishing (2007)
10. Van Dijk, B., Op den Akker, R., Nijholt, A., Zwiers, J.: Navigation Assistance in Virtual Worlds. Special Series on Community Informatics, Information Science Journal 6, 115–124 (2003)

11. Lbanez, J.: An intelligent Guide for Virtual Environments With Fuzzy Queries and Flexible Management of Stories. PhD thesis. Department of Computer Science, University of Murcia, Spain (2004)
12. Pierce, J.S., Pausch, R.: Navigation with place representations and visible landmarks. In: Proceedings of the IEEE Virtual Reality Conference, Chicago, USA, pp. 173–288 (2004)
13. Olanda, R., Pérez, M., Morillo, P., Fernández, M., Casas, S.: Entertainment virtual reality system for simulation of spaceflights over the surface of the planet Mars. In: Proceedings of the ACM symposium on Virtual reality software and technology, Limassol, Cyprus, pp. 123–132 (2006)
14. Pittarello, F., De Faveri, A.: Semantic description of 3D environments: a proposal based on web standards. In: Proceedings of the international conference on 3D web technology, Columbia, USA, pp. 85–95 (2006)
15. The Web3D Consortium, H-Anim 2001 - Humanoid Animation Specification (2001), http://www.h-anim.org/Specifications/H-Anim200x
16. –, Beringen-Mijn.: Accessed 10th (April 2007) http://www.toerismeberingen.be/html/mijnmuseum

A View-Based Real-Time Human Action Recognition System as an Interface for Human Computer Interaction

Jin Choi[1], Yong-il Cho[1], Taewoo Han[2], and Hyun S. Yang[1]

[1] AIM Lab., Computer Science Dept., KAIST, Daejeon, South Korea
[2] Dept. of Game & Multimedia, Woo-song University, Daejeon, South Korea
jin_choi, caelus, hsyang@paradise.kaist.ac.kr,
bluebird@paradise.kaist.ac.kr

Abstract. This paper describes a real-time human action recognition system that can track multiple persons and recognize distinct human actions through image sequences acquired from a single fixed camera. In particular, when given an image, the system segments blobs by using the Mixture of Gaussians algorithm with a hierarchical data structure. In addition, the system tracks people by estimating the state to which each blob belongs and assigning people according to its state. We then make motion history images for tracked people and recognize actions by using a multi-layer perceptron. The results confirm that we achieved a high recognition rate for the five actions of walking, running, sitting, standing, and falling though each subject performed each action in a slightly different manner. The results also confirm that the proposed system can cope in real time with multiple persons.

Keywords: view-based action recognition, adaptive background subtraction, motion history image, HCI.

1 Introduction

With the rapid progress of information technology, many researchers are struggling to build smart space where embedded computer systems can perceive the context and provide proper services at the right moment. In this environment, the traditional interfaces of desktop computing such as a keyboard or mouse are inadequate. We need a new type of interface. The visual interface, for instance, has recently gained attention because it is natural and easy to use. However, to use the visual interface, we need a way of effectively recognizing human action in real time.

View-based recognition of human action is comprised of motion analysis involving human body parts, tracking of human motion, and the recognition of human action from image sequences [1]. And this type of research is useful for various applications and especially as an interface for Human Computer Interaction. For example, the function of recognizing human action can be used for an input method for immersive games and visual surveillance systems.

We now present a real-time human action recognition system that can track multiple persons and recognize distinct human actions through image sequences acquired from a single fixed camera.

T.G. Wyeld, S. Kenderdine, and M. Docherty (Eds.): VSMM 2007, LNCS 4820, pp. 112–120, 2008.

In the next section we propose a human action recognition system for multiple persons. We then discuss the experimental results in section3 and summarize our conclusions in the final section.

2   The Proposed Human Action Recognition System

Our proposed real-time system can track people and recognize simple and short human actions such as walking, running, sitting, standing, and falling through image sequences obtained from a single fixed camera. Once we determine how a simple action can be perceived, we can apply this knowledge to the recognition of complex actions such as exercising, fighting, and lurking. For the proposed system to be useful, we incorporated design features that made the system fast and efficient. Figure 1 shows a schema of the proposed system. The proposed system consists of four parts: segmenting foreground, tracking people, modeling action, and classifying action. The details of each part are explained below.

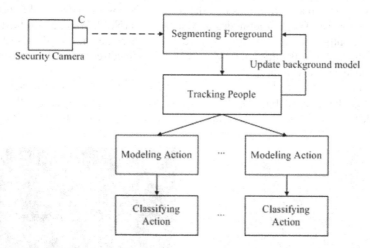

Fig. 1. Schema of the proposed system, which can track multiple targets and also recognize the distinct actions of multiple targets

2.1   Segmentation

The ability to rapidly extract correct silhouettes from an image is essential for our system because the modeling action is based on a silhouette. Although there are several popular background subtraction algorithms, such as the Running Average algorithm, and Mixture of Gaussians (MOG) algorithm, we used a modified the MOG algorithm with a hierarchical data structure because the Running Average algorithm can't cope with multimodal background distribution and the standard MOG takes too long for real-time processing. A MOG algorithm with a hierarchical data structure reportedly enhances the processing speed significantly and yields results that are very similar to the results of the standard MOG algorithm [2]. In Park's method [2], the hierarchical data structure is constructed in a kind of top-down approach. In this

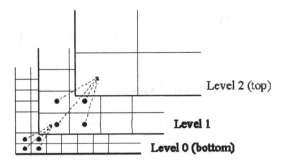

Fig. 2. The three-layer hierarchical data structure formed with a bottom-up approach. The structure is generated from Level 0 to Level 2 in order.

method, however, the user is unable to control the form of the leaf nodes because the image is recursively decomposed into four equal regions. To adjust the form to our needs, we constructed the hierarchical data structure in a bottom-up way (Fig. 2).

Firstly, we group a set of pixels into the form that we wish to detect. We then stack layers that consist of the parent nodes of four children (North West, North East, South West, and South East). The method of searching is the same with the Park's [2]. After stacking the layers to the designed layer, we apply a quadtree-based decomposition to an input image. The searching starts at the top layer. For each node of the top layer, a random pixel is sampled. The pixel is classified as either foreground or background. If the pixel is classified as background, the next node is processed. If not, the node is subdivided into the lower level and this subdivision is repeated until the bottom layer.

Fig. 3. The results of background subtraction (the left image is an original image and the right image show the foreground image)

The system can rapidly cope with a multimodal background distribution by using the modified MOG algorithm (Fig. 2). When obtained foreground pixels at time t, through connected component analysis, they are grouped into a set of blobs $B_t = \{b_t^i \mid i \text{ is an integer and } 0 \le i\}$, where a blob b_t^i is a set of connected foreground pixels and contains a set of persons as Fig. 4 shows. Let $O_{b_t^i}$ be the set of persons in b_t^i and o^i be a person that is represented as an appearance model.

Fig. 4. A blob is containing two persons

2.2 People Tracking

The ability to track people is necessary for recognizing the distinct actions of multiple persons because an action of a person is modeled with a sequence of person's silhouettes [4][5]. To simplify the problem, we assume that a person appears near the entrance and disappears at the exit. No consideration is given to the possibility that people appear or disappear in a group. To identify a person without additional information such as tag, we use an appearance model.

Given B_t through segmentation, we estimate the state to which each blob belongs and localize people according to its state. And Fig. 5 shows a flow chart for the tracking people. We assume that every blob has one of the following states.

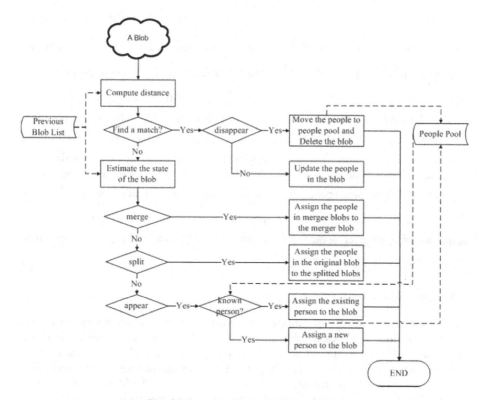

Fig. 5. Flow chart for the tracking people

Appearing. A new blob appears in the frame at time t
Disappearing. An existing blob in the frame at time t is disappearing.
Continuation. A blob continues from the frame at time t-1 to time t.
Merging. Two blobs in the frame at time t-1 merge into one blob in the frame at time t.
Splitting. One blob in the frame at time t-1 separates into two blobs in the frame at time t.

In particular, we compute the distance between b_t^i and every blob of B_t in order to establish correspondence. Let d_{hue} be the normalized Bhattacharyya distance between hue histograms and d_{size} be the normalized size difference and d_{dis} be the normalized Euclidean distance between centroids. We can then define the distance $d(b_t^i, b_{t-1}^j)$ between b_t^i and b_{t-1}^j as follows:

$$d(b_t^i, b_{t-1}^i) = \frac{1}{3}(d_{hue}(b_t^i, b_{t-1}^i) + d_{size}(b_t^i, b_{t-1}^i) + d_{dis}(b_t^i, b_{t-1}^i)) \tag{1}$$

If b_{t-1}^j with the smallest distance is less than a threshold value, we regard b_t^i as continuation of b_{t-1}^j, and we obtain $O_{b_t^i}$ by updating $O_{b_{t-1}^j}$ with current tracks. Otherwise we can infer that b_t^i have one of three states such as merging, splitting, and appearing. The stat of b_t^i can be estimated based on the relation between B_{t-1} and b_t^i (Fig. 6). Let b^x be an element of $B_{t-1} \cap b_t^i$. If $b^x \approx b_{t-1}^i$, merging might occur. Thus, we simply assign the people in two mergee blobs to the merger blob. And if $b^x \approx b_t^i$, splitting might occur. In this case, to assign the people in the original blob to the splitted blobs, we make all hypotheses and evaluate each hypothesis by using appearance model of people. We then assign the people according to the hypothesis with highest probability. Finally if there is no relation between B_{t-1} and b_t^i, we can think that b_t^i is in the appearing state. It means that the known person reappears or a stranger appears. If the person is not known, we just create a new person instance o_i and assign it to b_t^i.

2.3 Action Modeling

In contrast to the process of posture recognition, which involves a specific image, action recognition involves consideration of a sequence of images. Given a sequence of images, we adapt a representation of motion history image (MHI) for the purpose of modeling an action. The MHI collapses an image sequence into a 2-D image that captures spatial and temporal information about motion [3]. The MHI is known for its fast processing speed and ability to represent short-duration movement.

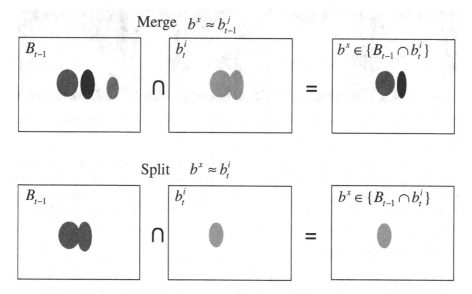

Fig. 6. The relation between B_{t-1} and b_t^i when merging or splitting occurs

An MHI at time t is updated as

$$\text{MHI}_{\delta}^t(x,y) = \begin{cases} t/\delta & \text{if } \Psi(I^t(x,y)) \neq 0 \\ \text{MHI}_{\delta}^{t-1}(x,y) & \text{otherwise} \end{cases} \tag{2}$$

where δ is the number of images used for the collapse, $I^t(x,y)$ is the current image and Ψ signals the presence of a blob at pixel (x,y). Fig. 7 shows an example of an MHI of a person falling. The first four images from the left of Fig. 7 show extracted silhouettes, and the image on the right-hand side is the corresponding MHI. For multiple people, we maintain an MHI for each person by using previous tracking outputs.

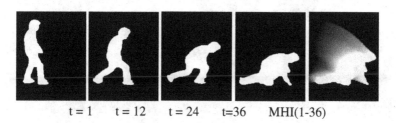

t = 1   t = 12   t = 24   t=36   MHI(1-36)

Fig. 7. Selected frames of a person falling and a corresponding MHI

2.4 Classification

When given an MHI, we search it for a bounding box to extract the various features. The bounding box is then normalized at 256 features. Additionally, we add the width and height of the bounding box to a feature vector in order to classify actions such as walking and running which are similar to the normalized MHI.

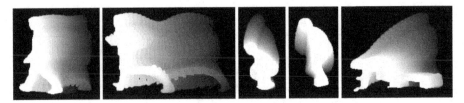

Fig. 8. Sample MHIs (from the left: walking, running, sitting, standing, and falling) for the training of a multi-layer perceptron

The task of formalizing actions is difficult because people rarely act in the same way. Hence, to classify actions, we use a multi-layer perceptron (MLP), which is a sort of robust neural network. We define five classes: walking, running, sitting, standing, and falling. Fig. 8 shows examples of MHIs that are used to train an MLP.

3 Experimental Results

In this experiment, we asked seven subjects to perform the five distinct actions of walking, running, sitting, standing, and falling, and to perform each action 10 times

Fig. 9. The five distinct actions performed by the seven subjects

(Fig. 9). Three subjects were included in the training and the other four subjects were not. Table 1 shows the number of correct results.

In Table 1, T1, T2, and T3 refer to the subjects who were included in the training and P1, P2, P3, and P4 refer to the subjects who were not included in the training. A recognition rate of 92% was attained by T1, T2, and T3, and a recognition rate of 90% was attained by P1, P2, P3, and P4. The actions that were recognized most easily were the common actions of falling, running, and sitting. However, the action of standing was not easily recognized due to incorrect segmentation. In summary, although each subject performed the same action in a slightly different manner, the seven subjects attained a high recognition rate of 90.9%. We expect the recognition rate to be raised with more accurate segmentation.

Table 1. Experimental results of the proposed human action recognition system

	walking	running	Sitting	standing	falling	Recognition rate (%)
T1	10	10	10	10	10	100.0
T2	10	10	10	7	10	94.0
T3	8	10	8	5	10	82.0
P1	10	9	10	10	10	98.0
P2	7	10	10	8	10	90.0
P3	4	10	10	10	10	88.0
P4	9	10	10	3	10	84.0
Recognition rate (%)	82.9	98.6	97.1	75.7	100.0	90.9

We performed an additional experiment to evaluate the processing speed of the proposed system. While three persons were performing actions, we recorded video footage at 30 fps in a format of 352 pixels by 240 pixels. When we inputted the recorded video into the proposed system, which was running on a 3.0 GHz computer, we were able to achieve recognition results in real time. Fig. 10 shows the output of the proposed system in that situation.

Fig. 10. The results of the proposed system when the persons on the left and in the middle are standing and the person on the right is sitting

4 Conclusion

We present a real-time human action recognition system that can track people and recognize distinct human actions through image sequences acquired from a single fixed camera. In particular, when given an image, the system can segment silhouettes by means of a MOG algorithm with a hierarchical data structure. The system can also track people by estimating the state to which each blob belongs and assigning people according to its state. Next, the system makes MHIs of tracked people and can recognize distinct actions by using an MLP. The results of an experiment on the five actions of walking, running, sitting, standing, and falling showed a high recognition rate, even though each subject performed the same action in a slightly different manner. The results also confirm that the proposed system copes in real time with multiple persons.

To enhance the proposed system, we plan to study how to extract accurate silhouettes and to make view-independent motion representations with the aid of multiple cameras.

Acknowledgments

This research is supported by the Ubiquitous Computing and Network Project of the Ministry of Information and Communication 21st Century Frontier R&D Program in Korea. It is also supported by the Korea Science and Engineering Foundation through the Advanced Information Technology Research Center.

References

1. Aggarwal, J.K., Cai, Q.: Human Motion Analysis: A Review. Computer Vision and Image Understanding: CVIU 73(3), 428–440 (1999)
2. Park, J., Tabb, A., Kak, A.C.: Hierarchical Data Structure for Real-Time Background Subtraction. In: IEEE International Conference on Image Processing (2006)
3. Bobick, A., Davis, J.: The recognition of human movement using temporal templates. IEEE Trans. Patt. Analy. And Mach. Intell. 23(3), 257–267 (2001)
4. Yilmaz, A., Javed, O., Shah, M.: Object Tracking: A Survey. In: ACM Computing Surveys, December 2006, vol. 38(4) (2006)
5. Huang, Y., Essa, I.: Tracking Multiple Objects Through Occlusions. In: CVPR 2005, San Diego, CA (June 2005)

Knowledge Based Lacunas Detection and Segmentation for Ancient Paintings

Jianming Liu[1] and Dongming Lu[1,2]

[1] College of Computer Science and Technology, Zhejiang University,
[2] State Key Lab. of CAD and CG, Zhejiang University, 310027, Hangzhou, Zhejiang, China
`liujianming, ldm@zju.edu.cn`

Abstract. Lacunas are a common form of the damage that can occur to paintings and more often to murals. Taking Dunhuang murals as research background, a new algorithm to detect and segment the lacuna area from mural images is proposed, which consists of a training phase and a runtime phase. In the training phase, a Bayesian classifier is trained. At runtime, the Bayesian classifier is first applied to perform the rough lacuna regions detection. Then, a graph representing the mural image is built with output of the Bayesian classifier. The domain knowledge of murals is incorporated into the graph in this step. At last, the image segmentation using graph cut is done based on the minimal cut/maximal flow algorithm. The outputs of the image segmentation are lacuna regions and background regions. About 250 high resolution Dunhuang mural images are collected to test the proposed method's performance. Experimental results have demonstrated its validity under certain variations. This research has the potential to provide a computer aided tool for mural protectors to restore damage mural paintings.

Keywords: Image segmentation, concurrent detection and segmentation, deterioration murals, mean shift, Bayesian classification, graph cuts.

1 Introduction

Many ancient paintings, especially the murals, suffer from serious deterioration. For Dunhuang murals, there are more than fifteen kinds of deterioration, such as[1] Cracks, Crater eruption, Flaking, Disruption and so on. Lacunas are a common form of the damage caused by most of the deterioration. To protect these priceless murals, we need to find out all the regions where these deteriorations are located. Therefore, detecting the lacunas and labeling the lacuna area in the murals are very important. Fig. 1 shows an example of the mural deterioration distribution map, which was labeled by Dunhuang mural protectors. With advanced computing and image analysis technique, it provides an opportunity to label the deteriorated area in an automatic

---

[1] Cracks: fissures in the painting. Crater eruption: bulges leading to losses (from 2mm to 1cm in diameter) of the paint and plaster. Flaking: lack of adhesion between paint layer and ground. Disruption: De-cohesion affecting any or all layers composing the wall painting. Lacunas: regions which missing paint layer.

T.G. Wyeld, S. Kenderdine, and M. Docherty (Eds.): VSMM 2007, LNCS 4820, pp. 121–131, 2008.
© Springer-Verlag Berlin Heidelberg 2008

way. In this paper, we present a knowledge based concurrent lacunas detection and segmentation algorithm for ancient paintings. We follow the idea given in [1] of supervised texture detection, which provided a small template of a texture of interest and get the image being segmented into regions with similar properties and background regions. However, the method [1] was designed for natural texture images and the domain knowledge of ancient paintings is thrown away. Although our algorithm is based on mural images, it also can be used for other ancient paintings.

Fig. 1. An example of the manually labeled mural deterioration distribution map

1.1 Related Work

For the past decade or so, a lot of image processing techniques have been proposed for the analysis of priceless paintings. A number of digital restoration techniques for old paintings are presented in [2], which can be used to recover the original painting appearance. In [3][4], lacuna filling methods are proposed by applying restoration techniques similar to the real techniques carried out by the restorers or by using a texture synthesis procedure. However, users have to select the lacuna regions manually. Ioannis Giakoumis et al. [5] develop a method for the restoration of cracks on a painting. The cracks are first detected by the morphological filter top-hat transformation, and then filled either by using median or trimmed-mean filters. Recently, image inpainting [6][7][8] has attracted attention of many researchers in computer vision and image processing fields. As in the most of the image inpainting projects, users have to select the defect area, Rong-Chi Chang et [9] present a method for photo defect detection, which is very similar to our lacunas detection problem. However, their method can only distinguish the two types of damages (ink spray and scratch).

As the lacuna has special color and texture different from non-lacuna in the murals, our lacunas detection and segmentation problem can be treated as the color regions detection and segmentation problem from complex background. It's similar to the skin detection problem. A lot of research works about skin detection [10][11][12] have been done. Most of the approaches mentioned above are based on the same pixel-wise processing paradigm, in which each image pixel is analyzed individually. Because the qualities of many murals have been degraded severely, the methods for skin detection usually don't work well. We compare our algorithm with two common methods: MoG (Mix of Gaussian Model) and Bayesian classifier [10].

The rest of the paper is organized as follows: in Section 2 we describe the concurrent lacunas detection and segmentation algorithm for murals in detail. Section 3 shows some results, and compares with two other common methods. Finally, Section 4 concludes the paper and discusses our future works.

2 Algorithm

Given an input mural image, our goal is to detect the lacuna regions and mark them with special labels. First, we determine if there are lacunas in an input mural image, and then apply the image segmentation algorithm to get more accurate lacuna regions.

Our method consists of a training phase and a runtime phase. In the training phase, we start with a great deal of manually labeled lacuna samples and non-lacuna samples:

1. Two histogram color models are built to estimate the color probability densities distribution of the lacuna and non-lacuna.
2. A Bayesian classifier is trained to classify the pixels or regions in the given image.

At runtime, the lacuna area of the given mural image are detected and segmented by the following steps:

1. Apply mean shift segmentation algorithm to over-segment the image;
2. Apply Bayesian Classifier to perform a rough lacunas classification on all small regions. The small region set identified as lacuna region in this step is used to determine whether there are lacunas in the mural image. If yes, go to step 3, else stop. For each small region in the image, we also get two probabilities $P(L/c)$ and $P(\neg L/c)$ of the region belonging to the lacuna or non-lacuna class;
3. Build the graph-cutting formulation on the pre-computed over-segmentation image. The probability $P(L/c)$ and $P(\neg L/c)$ are used to compute the likelihood energy E_1, which encode the similarity of a node(small region), indicating if it belongs to the lacuna or non-lacuna.
4. Use min-cut algorithm [13] to do graph cut segmentation and output.

The procedure is illustrated in Fig. 2. We explain each building block of our strategy in different sections below.

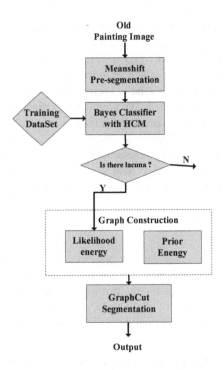

Fig. 2. Organization of the algorithm

2.1 Pre-segmentation by Mean Shift Segmentation

To improve the efficiency, we need to pre-segment the input mural image and produce an over-segmentation with the goal of making it contain as much true boundaries as possible. As Chinese murals don't have complex texture, mainly consist of color-blocks and lines, mean shift segmentation algorithm [14] is quite adequate for this requirement. For color image segmentation, the feature vector adopted in mean shift clustering is the concatenation of the two spatial domain coordinates and the three color values in a given color space. Mean shift procedure is applied in the joint spatial-color domains and moves away from the boundaries. The output not only includes the region boundaries, but also a region adjacency graph $G=<V,E>$, where V is the set of all nodes represented by the mean shift regions plus two extra nodes labeled F and B. E is the set of all edges, as illustrated in Fig. 5. Mean shift segmentation based on the work of [14][15] is implemented. Window widths are automatically set based on image dimensions: $h_s = \max(4, \lfloor \min(height, width)/100 \rfloor)$, color domain window width : $h_r = 4$ and minimum region : $R = 15$.

2.2 Bayesian Classifier with HCM

For most of Chinese murals, the color of the lacuna is usually different from color of non-lacuna. We construct lacuna and non-lacuna histogram color models using our training set of images which were collected from Dunhuang murals. The lacuna pixels in the 120 images containing lacunas were extracted manually and placed into the lacuna histogram. The 200 images that don't contain lacuna or in which the lacunas have been removed were placed into the non-lacuna histogram. As the RGB color space is sensitive to intensity variations, we use the YC_bC_r color space. Color is represented by luminance, constructed as a weighted sum of the RGB values, and two color difference values C_r and C_b that are formed by subtracting luminance from RGB red and blue components.

$$Y = 0.299R + 0.587G + 0.114B$$
$$C_r = R - Y$$
$$C_b = B - Y$$

$$(1)$$

To make color classification less sensitive to changes in brightness level, we just use color feature of chrominance information in $C_b - C_r$ plane. Fig. 3 shows the histogram of luminance and chrominance values of the lacuna taken from 120 manually segmented mural images. As we can see, the Y values fall within a wide range, whilst the Cb and Cr values fall with relatively narrow intervals. Therefore, ignoring the variations in luminance is feasible.

Given lacuna histogram $l[m]$ and non-lacuna histogram $n[m]$, we can compute the probability densities that a given color value belong to the lacuna and non-lacuna class:

$$P(c_p / L) = \frac{l[c_p]}{T_l}, \quad P(c_p / \neg L) = \frac{n[c_p]}{T_n}$$

$$(2)$$

Where $l[c_p]$ and $n[c_p]$ are the pixel count contained in bin c_p of the lacuna histogram T_l and non-lacuna histogram T_n. The left of Fig. 4 shows the lacuna's joint probability densities distribution in $C_b - C_r$ place, and the right of Fig. 4 is the non-lacuna's joint densities distribution of chrominance. Using the Bayesian' theorem, we can get the posterior probabilities of a given color value belonging to the lacuna and non-lacuna class as follow:

$$p(L / c_p) = \frac{p(L)p(c_p / L)}{p(L)p(c_p / L) + p(\neg L)p(c_p / \neg L)}$$

$$(3)$$

$$p(\neg L / c_p) = \frac{p(\neg L)p(c_p / \neg L)}{p(L)p(c_p / L) + p(\neg L)p(c_p / \neg L)} \tag{4}$$

The ratio of $p(L / c_p)$ to $p(\neg L / c_p)$ can be written as:

$$\frac{p(L / c_p)}{p(\neg L / c_p)} = \frac{p(L)p(c_p / L)}{(1 - p(L))p(c_p / \neg L)} > \Theta \tag{5}$$

$$\Theta = K \times \frac{1 - p(L)}{p(L)} \tag{6}$$

Comparing (5) to a threshold Θ produces the lacuna/non-lacuna decision rule. As the choice of prior probabilities does not affect the overall detector (For any prior probability $p(L)$, it's possible to choose the appropriate value of K, that gives the same detection threshold.), we set $p(L) = 0.3$ and $p(\neg L) = 0.7$. Using above Bayesian decision rule, we can get a rough classification of each small mean shift region in the pre-segmented image. As lacuna regions in the murals are often large, too small lacuna regions are usually ignored by protectors.

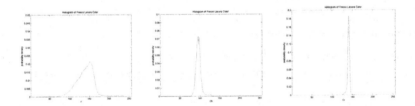

Fig. 3. Histogram of mural lacuna color in YCbCr space

To determine if there are lacunas in the image, we calculate the pixel count N_i in each lacuna region. If $\left[(\sum_{i=0}^{k} N_i) / Area_{img} \right] < T_1$ and $N_i / Area_{img}) < T_2, for \quad i = 0, ..., k$, there aren't lacunas in the mural image. Where $Area_{img}$ is the input image's total pixel count, k is the number of regions being classified as lacuna, T_1 and T_2 are thresholds.

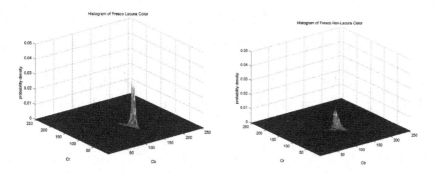

Fig. 4. Joint histograms of mural lacuna color and non-lacuna color in CbCr space

2.3 Graph Cut Image Segmentation

As described above, we firstly apply Bayesian classifier to perform a rough lacunas classification on the given mural image to determine whether there are lacunas in the image. If the image contains the lacuna regions, we treat the lacuna regions segmentation problem as a binary labeling problem. The over-segmented mural image is represented by a graph, where V is the set of all nodes represented by the mean shift regions plus two extra nodes labeled F and B. E is the set of all edges, as illustrated in Fig.5. The labeling problem is to assign a unique label x_i for each node $v_i \in V$, $x_i \in \{foreground(=1), background(=0)\}$. The lacuna regions are treated as foreground, and non-lacuna regions are treated as background. Our labeling problem can be solved by minimizing the following energy function $E(X)$ [16]:

$$E(X) = \sum_{i \in V} E_1(x_i) + \lambda \sum_{(p,q) \in E} E_2(x_p, x_q) \qquad (7)$$

Where E_1 is the likelihood energy, encoding the cost when the label of node i is x_i, and E_2 is the prior energy, denoting the cost when the labels of adjacent nodes p and q are x_p and x_q respectively.

Likelihood energy. The likelihood energy encodes the similarity of a node belonging to the foreground (lacuna) or background (non-lacuna). All the mean shift small regions are marked as uncertain regions. As described in section 2.2, we get each node's posterior probabilities of being lacuna or non-lacuna as $p(L/c_i)$ or $p(\neg L/c_i)$, which can be used to estimate the similarity of a node belonging to the foreground or background. Where c_i is the mean color of the mean shift region i. Therefore, $E_1(x_i)$ can be defined as follows:

$$E_1(x_i = F) = -\ln p(L/c_i) \tag{8}$$

$$E_1(x_i = B) = -\ln p(\neg L/c_i) \tag{9}$$

In the implementation, to void the overflow, we set $E_1(x_i = F) = K$ when $p(L/c_i) = 0$ or $E_1(x_i = B) = K$ when $p(\neg L/c_i) = 0$. K is a big number.

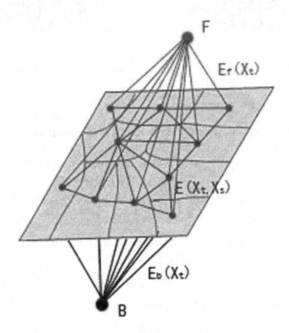

Fig. 5. Graph construction based on the over-segmented image

Prior energy. The prior energy E_2 represents the energy due to gradient along the object boundary. We define E_2 as:

$$E_2(x_p, x_q) = |x_p - x_q| \cdot \frac{1}{g(c_p, c_q) + 1} \tag{10}$$

Where $g(c_p, c_q)$ is the color difference between the small mean shift regions of the over-segmented mural image. We use the mean color of two regions to compute the difference.

3 Experiments

The proposed lacunas detection and segmentation algorithm was implemented using Microsoft Visual C++ 2003 on Windows XP platform. In our experiments, we use the

Dunhuang mural images to test the performance. We collect about 250 mural images with lacunas, manually extract 120 lacuna image blocks as the lacuna pixel set. 200 lacuna images without lacuna or in which the lacuna regions have been removed are constructed as the non-lacuna pixel set. The CCRs (Correct Classification Rate) and FARs (False Accept Rate) are illustrated in Table 1. From table 1, we can see that the method proposed in this paper can reduce false accept rate as well as increase the correct classification rate.

Table 1. Lacuna detection and segmentation's performance

Methods	Training set		Testing set	
	CCR(%)	FAR(%)	CCR(%)	FAR(%)
MoG	91.24	27.35	91.01	27.91
Bayesian classifier	93.66	23.97	93.07	24.21
Our method	97.21	13.34	97.17	15.91

Fig. 6 shows a example of the lacuna detection and segmentation results detected by Bayesian Classifier, MoG(Mix of Gaussian) and our method. The results show that the presented lacuna detection method has a good performance in discriminating the lacuna regions from background, and keeping the space coherent of lacuna regions.

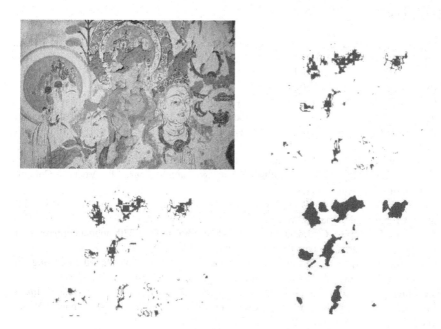

Fig. 6. Lacuna detection and segmentation example. Up-Left: the original Dunhunag mural image. Up-Right: the lacuna regions detected by Bayesian Classifier. Bottom-Left: the lacuna regions detected by MoG. Bottom-Right: the lacuna regions detected by our method.

4 Conclusions and Future Work

In this paper, we present a knowledge based concurrent lacunas detection and segmentation algorithm for ancient paintings. We first train a Bayesian classifier to perform a rough lacunas classification and determine whether there are lacunas in a given mural image, then use the graph cuts image segmentation algorithm to segment the lacuna regions. The outputs of Bayesian classifier are used to build the graph representing the image. The main contribution of this paper lies in incorporating the domain knowledge of murals into the graph. To improve the performance, mean shift clustering is also used to do pre-segmentation. Combining the Bayesian classifier and graph-cutting segmentation, we make the lacunas detection and segmentation concurrently and keep space coherent in segmented lacuna regions. Our method is more efficient compared with the two common methods: MoG and Bayesian classifier. The proposed method also can be used for skin detection.

Acknowledgments. The research was partially funded by National Basic Research Program of China (No.2002CB312106), National High-tech R&D Program (No. 2003AA119020, 2006AA01Z305), The Program for New Century Excellent Talents in University (NCET-04-0535), The Program for Changjiang Scholars and Innovative Research Team in University (IRT0652).

References

1. Micusik, B., Hanbury, A.: Supervised Texture Detection in Images. In: Gagalowicz, A., Philips, W. (eds.) CAIP 2005. LNCS, vol. 3691, pp. 441–448. Springer, Heidelberg (2005)
2. Pappas, M., Pilas, I.: Digital Color Restoration of Old Paintings IEEE Trans. Image Processing 9(2), 291–294 (2000)
3. Pei, S.-C., Zeng, Y.-C., Chang, C.-H.: Virtual restoration of ancient chinese paintings using color contrast enhancement and lacuna texture synthesis. In: IEEE Trans. Image Processing (Special Issue on Image Processing for Cultural Heritage), vol. 13(3), pp. 416–429 (2004)
4. Cappellini, V., Barni, M., Corsini, M., Rosa, A.D., Piva, A.: Artshop: An art-oriented image processing tool for cultural heritage applications. J. Visual. Comput. Animation 14(3), 149–158 (2003)
5. Giakoumis, I., Pitas, I.: Digital restoration of painting cracks. In: Proc. IEEE Int. Symp.Circuits and Signals, May-June 31-3, 1998, pp. 269–272 (1998)
6. Bertalmio, M., Sapiro, G.: Image inpainting, Proceedings of the 27th annual conference on Computer graphics and interactive techniques, pp. 417–424 (2000)
7. Criminisi, A., Perez, P., Toyama, K.: Object removal by exemplar-based inpainting. In: Proc. IEEE Computer Vision and Pattern Recognition, vol. 2, pp. 721–728 (2003)
8. Bertalmio, M., Vese, L., Sapiro, G., Osher, S.: Simultaneous structure and texture image inpainting. In: Proceedings of IEEE Computer Society Conference on Computer Vision and Pattern Recognition, vol. 2, pp. 707–712 (2003)
9. Chang, R.-C., Sie, Y.-L., Chou, S.-M., Shih, T.K.: Photo Defect Detection for Image Inpainting. In: ISM 2005, pp. 403–407 (2005)
10. Vezhnevets, V., Sazonov, V., Andreeva, A.: A Survey on Pixel-Based Skin Color Detection Techniques. In: Proc. Graphicon-2003, Moscow, Russia, September 2003, pp. 85–92 (2003)

11. Brand, J., Mason, J.: A Comparative Assessment of Three Approaches to Pixel-Level Human Skin Detection. In: Proc. IEEE Int'l Conf. Pattern Recognition, September 2000, vol. 1, pp. 1056–1059 (2000)

12. Phung, S.L., Bouzerdoum, A., Chai, D.: Skin Segmentation Using Color Pixel Classification: Analysis and Comparison. IEEE Transactions on Pattern Analysis and Machine Intelligence 27(1), 148–154 (2005)

13. Boykov, Y., Kolmogorov, V.: An experimental comparison of min-cut/max-flow algorithms for energy minimization in vision. PAMI 26(9), 1124–1137 (2004)

14. Comaniciu, D., Meer, P.: A robust approach toward feature space analysis. In: IEEE Trans. on Pattern Analysis and Machine Intelligence, vol. 24(5), pp. 603–619 (2002)

15. Christoudias, C.M., Georgescu, B., Meer, P.: Synergism in low level vision. In: Proceedings of the 16th International Conference on Pattern Recognition, vol. 4, pp. 150–155 (2002)

16. Li, Y., Sun, J., Tang, C.-K., Shum, H.-Y.: Lazy Snapping. In: SIGGRAPH 2004, ACM Transaction on Graphics, vol. 23(3) (2004)

SmartVolumes - Adaptive Voronoi Power Diagramming for Real-Time Volumetric Design Exploration

Christian Friedrich

Delft University of Technology, Department of Architecture, P.O. box 5043
2600 GA Delft, The Netherlands
h.c.friedrich@gmail.com

Abstract. Voronoi Diagrams and Delaunay Triangulations are two concepts fundamental to computational geometry, which have been applied in the most varied disciplines. In recent years, they are increasingly used in architectural design. In this paper, a novel method for volumetric design exploration based on three-dimensional (additively weighted) Voronoi power diagrams is described. The method combines fast calculation of three-dimensional weighted Voronoi Power Diagrams with a volume-dependent feedback loop, resulting in a real-time interactive modeling tool. This tool, named SmartVolumes, has been integrated into the modeling environment BehaviourLinks, where the interaction between parametric volumes and other entities can be further elaborated through behavioral linkages. Applications of SmartVolumes in urban design and architectural design are described, implications of the use of Voronoi diagrams for architectural modeling and environments are discussed and directions of consecutive developments are indicated.

Keywords: Design Exploration, Interactive Architecture, Design Environments, Computational Design, Voronoi diagram, Delaunay triangulation

1 Introduction

The Voronoi diagram resembles many different kinds of natural structures and thus may be a concept of considerable antiquity. One of the first known appearances resembling a Voronoi diagram is an illustration showing the disposition of matter in the solar system published by Descartes in 1644. Though the first comprehensive representations date back to the mid-nineteenth and early twentieth century, given by respectively Dirichlet and Voronoï, Voronoi diagrams were repeatedly rediscovered in various disciplines, even up to the 1980's [1]. During the first decade of the third millennium, Voronoi diagrams are increasingly applied in urban and architectural design. Two-dimensional Voronoi diagrams have been used in interactive environments for the dynamic assignment of regions of augmented space [2], in urban design stakeholder games for dividing an urban area into parcels, iteratively optimizing plots [3], and structural surface tessellations [4]. Three-dimensional Voronoi diagrams have been used for space-filling structural design [5], and functional optimization of various environmental aspects in architectural design [6].

T.G. Wyeld, S. Kenderdine, and M. Docherty (Eds.): VSMM 2007, LNCS 4820, pp. 132–142, 2008.

In all architectural applications Voronoi diagrams were arguably also used for their inherent aesthetics.

In this paper, a novel method for volumetric design exploration based on three-dimensional (additively weighted) Voronoi power diagrams is described. The method combines fast calculation of three-dimensional weighted Voronoi Power Diagrams with a volume-dependent feedback loop, resulting in a real-time interactive modeling tool. This tool, named SmartVolumes, has been integrated into the modeling environment BehaviourLinks, where the interaction between parametric volumes and other entities can be further elaborated through behavioral linkages. Applications of SmartVolumes in urban design and architectural design are described, implications of the use of Voronoi diagrams for architectural modeling and environments are discussed and directions of consecutive developments are indicated.

2 Voronoi Diagrams and Delaunay Triangulations

Manual approaches to architectural geometric design are generally based on the construction of drawings with the use of points, lines, circles, metrics, and various types of grids and structures derived from these. The application of computers as drawing medium adds a third or even more dimensions, and an undo stack. Also, it makes architectural geometric design techniques enter the realm of computational geometry, where the focus is not only on how to solve a geometric problem for one or several objects, but primarily on cases where large sets of 'n' objects are involved. The application of computers to architectural geometric design lets the designer address entire populations of objects, within the limits of computability. In the exploration of the affordances of computational design media, many techniques have been developed [7].

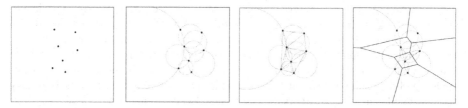

Fig. 1. Far Left: a set of points. Center Left: circles touching three points but not containing other points. Center Right: the circles are circumcircles to the triangles of the Delaunay triangulation. Far Right: the Voronoi Diagram is the dual diagram of the Delaunay triangulation, and has the circumcircle centers as vertices of the boundaries of the Voronoi regions.

Many of these approaches can be utilized in specialized design applications or as feature present in most contemporary design suites: for example parametric design approaches like solid modeling, or splines, which are curves and surfaces generated by interpolating over the elements of ordered sets of points [8]. Next to the common application of off-the-shelf tools, custom made algorithmic techniques are only marginally used in architectural design. Examples would be neural networks, cellular automata, genetic algorithms, shape grammars, swarm-solvers, particle-spring systems.

Common to all these approaches is that they are algorithmic geometric constructions, and as such are based on sets of rules, and sets of features like points which define a line, grid or other kind of structure. In contrast, Voronoi diagrams are not constructions but properties of a set of points in regard to a given metric. Voronoi diagrams enable design directly on a population of points, without the need to first define a structure according to which the geometric construction has to be laid out.

The Voronoi diagram and Delaunay triangulation of a point set can be understood as a dual map to the point-set's topology. The Voronoi Diagram maps for each point of the cloud the region of space which it dominates according to a given metric. The Delaunay triangulation maps the relationships of neighboring Voronoi regions of a given point set. Both Voronoi diagram and Delaunay triangulations are not geometric constructions, they are implicit properties of a point set under a chosen metric. They are maps to the spaces a point set generates, representing them as a set of locations and providing insight into the relationships between these locations.

They provide notions of space given in connections and separations, primordial architectural characteristics as described by Georg Simmel in the essay *Bridge and Door*:

"Only to humanity, in contrast to nature, has the right to connect and separate been granted, and in the distinctive manner that one of these activities is always the presupposition of the other. [...] The forms that dominate the dynamics of our lives are thus transferred by bridge and door into the fixed permanence of visible action."[9]

In different context, a notion of *clearing* space by defining relationships and establishing regions can be found the in Martin Heidegger's essay *Building, Dwelling, Thinking*, in the description of a bridge gathering landscape:

"The bridge[...] does not just connect banks that are already there. The banks emerge as banks only as the bridge crosses the stream. The bridge designedly causes them to lie across from each other. One side is set off against the other by the bridge. Nor do the banks stretch along the stream as indifferent border strips of the dry land. With the banks, the bridge brings to the stream the one and the other expanse of the landscape lying behind them. It brings stream and bank and land into each other's neighborhood. The bridge gathers the earth as landscape around the stream." [10]

Given the fundamental geometric nature of Voronoi diagrams, and its possible theoretical implications, it may seem surprising they have found use in architecture only in recent years. This may be due to the fact that they take a long time to manually construct, and that they generally lead to non-standard elements which used to be very time-consuming and expensive to produce and assemble. Several developments of the near past may have made Voronoi diagrams more applicable in architectural design:

- The changes to architectural praxis following the introduction of digital technologies,
- The off-the-self availability of Voronoi solvers in commercial CAD software, e.g. the 'Point set reconstruction tool' for Rhino

- The availability of open source of computational graphics libraries containing algorithms for the construction of 2D and 3D Voronoi diagrams and Delaunay triangulations, e.g. VTK[11], CGAL[12] and Qhull[13].
- The growing number of architects literate in the use of computational tools and programming,
- The advances of non-standard design and production in architecture

3   Smartvolumes

The complex interrelationships between the location of points, their weight, and the geometry of the Delaunay triangulation and its Voronoi diagram demand for an efficient tool for design exploration. SmartVolumes is a design tool developed to meet this demand. It is based on real-time interaction between the set of weighted points, properties of its Voronoi diagram, a user and possible parametric relationships the users have set.

SmartVolumes as described here is realized in the game-development environment Virtools [14], in conjunction with C++ coding and utilizing the Computational Graphics Algorithms Library CGAL [12]. The adaptation of the parametric plan is taking place in real-time, several times per second, in parallel with the users' interaction with the diagram that results from the rules and constrains they have set. These adaptations and interactions are set up in a game loop. In each execution of the loop, the user interfaces are read, the parameters they control are updated, the SmartVolumes are computed, the point set is adapted so it approaches the user demand, and eventually the frame is drawn to screen. In the real-time design exploration, weights and positions of points so the volumes of the individual Voronoi cells are adapted to comply with the designer's demands. Simultaneously, the designer is given opportunity to adjust his aims and explore design space.

The geometry of the SmartVolume cells is executed during each game loop as follows:

1. Determine the boundary condition
The boundary for the volumetric Voronoi diagram is derived from a set of 'boundary' points as their three-dimensional convex hull. It is found by making a Delaunay Triangulation of the point set and collecting all facets incident to infinite cells of the Delaunay triangulation.

2. Weighted Delaunay triangulation
Temporarily eight points are added to the set of SmartVolume points, forming a relatively very large cube around the original set of points. A weighted Delaunay triangulation of the SmartVolume points plus the eight additional points is computed using the CGAL [12] library. The weighted Delaunay triangulation in CGAL is based on the power product for determining distance between points:

Let $S^{(w)}$ be a set of weighted points in R^3. Let $p_i^{(w)}$ and $p_j^{(w)}$ be two weighted points with positions $p_i, p_j \in R^3$ and weights $w_i, w_j \in R$. The weighted points can be seen as spheres of centers p_i, p_j and radii w_i, w_j. Then the power product between $p_i^{(w)}$ and $p_j^{(w)}$ is defined as

$$\prod(p_i^{(w)}, p_i^{(w)}) = \left\| p_i - p_j \right\|^2 - w_i - w_j ,$$

where $\left\| p_i - p_j \right\|^2$ is the Euclidean distance between p_i and z_i [12].

The result of this triangulation is equivalent to the triangulations in the center-left column of Figure 2.

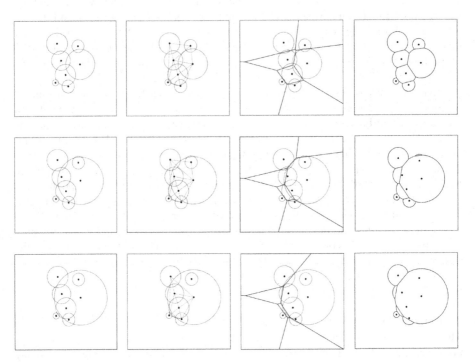

Fig. 2. Far Left Column: Sets of weighted points, weights are indicated as circles. Center-Left Column: Weighted Delaunay Triangulation. Center-Right Column: (additively weighted) Voronoi power Diagram. Far Right Column: the resulting SmartVolumes volumes.

3. Determine Voronoi cells

The weighted centers of the circumspheres of the tetrahedrons which are the outcome of the weighted Delaunay triangulation are calculated. For each SmartVolume point, the set of circumsphere centers of tetrahedrons to which the point is incident are collected. From these sets of circumsphere centers the Voronoi Cells of the SmartVolume points are determined by computing their convex hulls.

4. Intersect cells with the boundary

The intersections of the Voronoi cells with the boundary volume are determined. The result is equivalent to the diagrams in the center-right column of Figure 2: bounded weighted Voronoi diagrams. This diagram is the Power Diagram, with the Voronoi generation distance

$$d(p_i, p_j) = \left\| \mathbf{x} - \mathbf{x}_i \right\|^2 - w_i \ [1].$$

5. Tessellate
Each cell of the bounded Voronoi diagram is tessellated up to a chosen depth.

6. Shrink-wrap
All vertices of the tessellated cells, whose distance from their generator point is larger than the square of its weight, are translated towards the point so the distance equals the square of its weight. The result of this 'shrinking' is equivalent to the diagrams in the far right column of Figure 2.

7. Adapt
The volume of each SmartVolume is calculated from the resulting geometry. The weight of each SmartVolumes point is adapted according to the difference between the volume of its SmartVolume and the user demand.

4 Applications

4.1 Urban Design: BehaviourLinks :: Urban Mode

SmartVolumes is developed as spatial design extension for the design environment *BehaviourLinks :: Urban Mode*. The agenda of BehaviourLinks is to reshape the way architects employ digital techniques by proposing a dynamic, open, collaborative design praxis. A *BehaviourLink* is a piece of programming code that is executed in real-time and defines interactions between conceptual entities, by manipulating data contained in one entity based on data contained in another entity. The nature of these manipulations is dependent on the type of link chosen by the user. The conceptual entities can represent architectural concepts but also digital interfaces to sensors, users and exchange data.

By defining conceptual nodes and laying behavioral links, users can grow a parametric diagram of the urban plan. Its shape, structure and visualization originate from the behavioral design rules and decisions made by the users as well as the feedback negotiation between interacting nodes. The interactive diagram lets a group of stakeholders make fast and well-informed urban design decisions.

In BehaviourLinks::Urban mode, all data is subject to real-time interactive, iterative adaptation by the behavioral links the user laid between entities. Functional extensions of BehaviourLinks consist of node typifications, which can be affected by additional link types. For BehaviourLinks :: Urban Mode, extensions have been implemented that let the users simultaneously explore how the program of demands, volumetric plan, traffic models, parametric spatial relationships, shadow volumes, façade styles, plan boundaries and urban data affect each other, with direct visual feedback and embedded media of the actual site.

Fig. 3. Left: An actual in-game screenshot of BehaviourLinks :: Urban Mode. Visible within the urban scene are SmartVolume building proposals, traffic modeling, statistical data derived from the proposal, the user interface. Right: A closer view, showing embedded media, facade styles and contextual node data displayed next to the node which is closest to the cursor. Some nodes typified as SmartVolumes are also integrated into the path-finding graph of the traffic modeler.

SmartVolumes has been integrated into BehaviourLinks as a possible typification of nodes, which makes behavioral nodes act as parametric volumes. The resulting volumes can then be analyzed for their properties. Volumes, floor area estimates and surface area of the SmartVolumes are displayed on-screen and can be used as input for behavioral links that affect the entire set of nodes. In this way, for example, a node typified as SmartVolume can request traffic from a path-finding graph modeled on the street pattern. The effects of making different access routes to the proposed building volumes and the overall impact of their position and spatial relations can then be explored.

4.2 Architectural Design: DP Korea Project

A first application of SmartVolumes in architectural praxis was the Digital Pavilion Korea project at ONL, office of Kas Oosterhuis and Ilona Lénárd [15]. For this project, a design environment for a technology exhibition was developed based on SmartVolumes and BehaviourLinks. The application would allow exhibitors to specify their demands in area and location, and to collaboratively explore spatial layout that would meet their demands. A chosen solution could be written file to formats for CAD/CAM, graphic design and web navigation, as well as to spreadsheets containing lists and statistics of the needed elements.

For the DP Korea project, the SmartVolumes modeler was modified to directly connect a spatial layout of an exhibition space to the partitioning and detailing of the space. In the game, several algorithmic tools for generating a point cloud are available, so the chance of having a point cloud with a desirable Voronoi solution is enhanced. Next to placing points manually the following algorithms can be used for placing points:

- Groups of points can be placed in elements of the buildings construction (columns, walls) ensure these elements can be entirely hidden in spatial partitions, which do not differ in form or structure from their surroundings.

- Groups of points can be placed with a radial distribution relative to a specified center, This results in a three-dimensional density gradient in the point set, and its Voronoi diagram.
- Groups of points can be placed along paths defined by splines, to create passages.

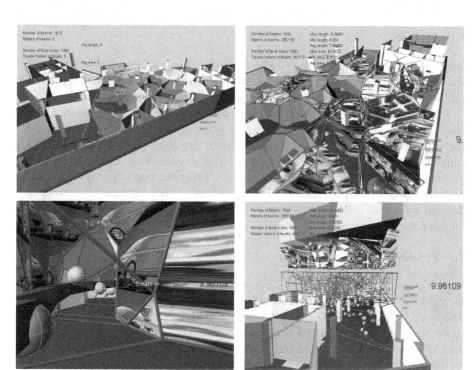

Fig. 4. Top Left: In-game screenshot of an exhibition floor design based on SmartVolumes within the real-time BehaviourLinks environment, Top Right: structural solution with numerical data, Bottom Left: inside the exhibition space, viewing generator points and details, Bottom Right: algorithmically generated point set, struts, facets and volumes in extruded view, ready for export.

In the generation of the Voronoi solution, the three-dimensional volumes of the cells are generated for each point, together with the facets that lie between two cells and edges of the facets. Cells, edges and facets can be looked up for each point individually. In this way it is possible to directly remove facets which are between specific neighboring cells. Voronoi cells belonging to a group of points forming a path can be opened to each other, making a passage, and the cells of one exhibition stand can be combined to form a greater, more complex volume.

Due to the additional computation involved in building a multi-relational database of cells, facets and edges, the changes in the point set could not result in direct visual feedback of the entire structure. Once the complete structure is generated however, it is ready to be exported as annotated production drawing in DXF and SVG format, and tables containing the metric data of a solution for cost calculation and production planning.

5 Discussion

5.1 Necessity

Whereas the traditional architect's approach is to fit demands into a chosen structure, the SmartVolumes technique offers a tool for finding structures and generating geometries based on volumetric and behavioral demands.

It also supports designers in the exploration of the complexity of geometries based on Voronoi diagrams: In a three-dimensional Voronoi diagram the location of points, the volumes of cells, the faces of cell surfaces, the edges of these facets and the endpoints of these edges are all implicitly related to each other. Each change to the generative point cloud simultaneously affects structure, building physics, details, aesthetics and other performances of the design. These complex interrelations demand for a tool to efficiently explore possible solution spaces. SmartVolumes is intended to meet these demands.

5.2 Precedents

SmartVolumes makes use of adapting (additively weighted) Voronoi power diagrams in real-time. A similar iterative, adaptive Voronoi diagramming method has been developed R. Reitsma, S. Trubin and S. Sethia [16], for regionalizing an information space based on a set of information items with given locations and predetermined area. Their regionalization method is an application of multiplicatively weighted Voronoi diagrams, and intended for visualization optimization, not interactive design exploration during an open-ended adaptation process. Applications of multiplicatively weighted Voronoi diagrams and other generalizations of Voronoi diagrams for explorative design techniques like SmartVolumes yet have to be investigated.

5.3 Possible Improvements

SmartVolumes enables the designer to apply algorithms that explicitly shape the point set, and to directly see the implicit effect on the point set's Voronoi diagram. However, since the resulting geometries are always implicitly defined, in order to individually relate further parametric geometric operations to individual elements of the geometry derived from the Voronoi diagram, the original point set has to be fixed. This makes it difficult to further develop Voronoi-based designs without dismissing their parametric, malleable nature. Possible ways of relating explicit descriptions of desirable shape manipulations of Voronoi diagrams, without sacrificing malleability, form a wide field of research which has not yet been investigated from an architectural point of view.

5.4 Application Perspectives

SmartVolumes is a generic spatial modeling tool, with a wide range of possible uses in architectural design and environments. It can be used in the initial, conceptual phase of the building process. From there it can directly, or after further manipulations, lead to specific data for computer aided manufacturing of the design. It could also be used for spatial analysis needed to control distributed participators in interactive architectural environments, be it humans or elements of the architectural object itself.

5.5 Outlook

In its current implementation, on contemporary workstations, the application of SmartVolumes in real-time is limited to several dozen volumes. With more elements, the geometry becomes too complex not only to compute within time, but also to transfer to the graphics processor. Within near future, similar real-time design exploration techniques should be expected to be not only commonly available but also more applicable in office situations as the computational power of desktop workstation increases.

6 Conclusions

With SmartVolumes, a novel use for Voronoi diagrams in computer aided architectural and urban design has been developed. Two practical applications have been made which show the high potential of the technique, in conceptual urban design and in architectural design, bridging from the conceptual phase directly to the planning phase. Other applications, for example in interactive architectural environments, structural and environmental design, have been described in theory and should be investigated in the near future.

Acknowledgments

This article presents a technique developed for the author's Master of Science final thesis project BehaviourLinks :: Urban Mode which was made at Hyperbody [17], the educational program and research group at TU Delft. Hyperbody is directed by Prof. Ir. Kas Oosterhuis, who has proven to be a very insightful and supportive mentor. The thesis is created as part of Hyperbody's efforts to realize the group design environment Protospace, which is installed in the iWeb building at the department of architecture of Delft University of Technology.

This article also describes an application of this technique in the Digital Pavilion Korea project of ONL [15], office of Kas Oosterhuis and Ilona Lénárd.

The basic principle of the BehaviourLinks environment was inspired by a data exchange course given by Bige Tunçer of the Building Technology department of the Faculty of Architecture.

The SmartVolumes technique, and the BehaviourLinks design environment were to equal parts implemented in the Virtools game development environment and Visual

C++. The fast computation of three-dimensional Delaunay Triangulation and Voronoi Diagrams was originally tested using VTK, the open source Visualization ToolKit C++ library [11]. Eventually CGAL, the Computational Graphics Library [12], was chosen for its wider range of features and robustness. Sylvain Pion and Monique Teillaud of INRIA Sophia Antipolis have been very helpful hosts on the CGAL User Mailing List.

References

1. Okabe, A., Boots, B., Siguhara, K., Chiu.: Spatial tessellations. Concepts and Applications of Voronoi Diagrams. Wiley & Sons, Chichester, UK (2000)
2. Snibbe, S.: Boundary Functions [15-6-2007] (1998), http://www.snibbe.com/scott/bf
3. [15-6-2007], http://www.Kaisersrot.com
4. Verebes, T.: In Pursuit of Softness: New Forms of Embedded Intelligence and Adaptability. In: Oosterhuis, K., Feireiss, L. (eds.) Game Set and Match II. On Computer Games, Advanced Geometries and Digital Technologies, pp. 386–391. Episode Publishers Rotterdam (2006)
5. Fischer, T.: Generation of Apparently Irregular Truss Structures. In: Martens, B., Brown, A. (eds.) Computer Aided Architectural Design Futures 2005, pp. 229–238. Springer, Dordrecht (2005)
6. Verebes, T., Ammash, I., Araiza, J., Loreto, F.M., Sukkar, A.: NET.LAB. In: Emerging Talents, Emerging Technologies – Students, pp. 16–19. China Architecture and Bulding Press Beijing (2006)
7. Farin, G., Hoschek, J., Myung-Soo, K. (eds.): Handbook of computer-aided geometric design. Elsevier, Amsterdam (2002)
8. Ten Damme, R.M.J., ter Morsche, H.G., Traas, C.R.: Splines en Wavelets. Epsilon, Utrecht (2002)
9. Simmel, Georg, Bridge, Door.: In: Leach, N. (ed.) Rethinking Architecture – A reader in cultural theory, pp. 66–68. Routledge, London (1997)
10. Heidegger, M.: Building, Dwelling, Thinking. In: Leach, N. (ed.) Rethinking Architecture – A reader in cultural theory, pp. 100–108. Routledge, London (1997)
11. VTK, The Visualization TooolKit. [15-6-2007], http://www.vtk.org
12. CGAL, Computational Geometry Algorithms Library. [15-6-2007], http://www.cgal.org
13. Qhull. [15-6-2007], http://www.qhull.org
14. Virtools, a Behaviour Company. [15-6-2007], http://www.virtools.com
15. [15-6-2007], http://www.oosterhuis.nl
16. Reitsma, R., Trubin, S., Sethi, S.: Adaptive Multiplicatively Weighted Voronoi Diagrams for Information Space Regionalisation. In: Proceedings of the Information Visualisation, Eighth International Conference on (IV 2004), pp. 290–294 (2004)
17. [15-6-2007], http://www.protospace.bk.tudelft.nl

Constructing a Virtual Tower of Babel: A Case Study in Cross-Cultural Collaboration Across Three Continents

Ekaterina Prasolova-Førland[1], Theodor Wyeld[2], and Teng-Wen Chang[3]

[1] Norwegian University of Science and Technology
[2] Swinburne University of Technology
[3] National Yunlin University of Science and Technology
ekaterip@idi.ntnu.no, twyeld@gmail.com, tengwen@yuntech.edu.tw

Abstract. The collaboration project described in this paper revolves around the construction of a virtual Tower of Babel in a 3D Collaborative Virtual Environment (3D CVE). It involved students across three cooperating institutions, on three different continents in different time zones. It addresses the increasing need for students to engage in international collaboration, as much of today's Information and Communication Technology work demands it. This requires cross-cultural understandings with one's co-collaborators, yet there are few opportunities for this to occur in a pedagogical setting. Therefore, this paper discusses a pedagogically-oriented case study of the use of a 3D CVE as a multi-cultural classroom, describing and discussing different phases in the cross-cultural collaborative process.

Keywords: 3D Collaborative Virtual Environments, multi-cultural classroom.

1 Introduction

The Tower of Babel parable relays a story of ancient times of confusion arising from the diversity of languages interfering with communicating a common goal (see Fig. 1). This paper describes a modern-day version of the construction of a virtual Tower of Babel in a 3D Collaborative Virtual Environment (3D CVE). The aim was to identify the challenges that arise in a 21st century globalized setting. In so doing, we were able to explore cross-cultural issues and pedagogical and collaborative aspects in a culturally diverse environment using different communication technologies.

The major motivation behind this project was the ongoing need for ICT professionals to work in diverse cultural environments. ICT professionals encounter cross-cultural issues in their daily collaborative practices within and external to their work environments [1].

The need for cross-cultural understandings in group work and learning is well documented [2, 3]. Remote collaboration addresses this need. A number of different remote collaboration systems have been used to date [4, 5, 6]. They range from simple email text and file transfer to chat and sophisticated video conferencing tools. The set of tools described here incorporates many of these existing technologies in

T.G. Wyeld, S. Kenderdine, and M. Docherty (Eds.): VSMM 2007, LNCS 4820, pp. 143–153, 2008.

Fig. 1. A number of towers of Babel have been envisioned over the years. This is a 16th-century version by Brueghel (1563) based on the Colosseum in Rome (www.wga.hu, 2007).

combination with a 3D CVE, featuring synchronous and asynchronous information exchange. It is part of a system developed over a number of years of previous use of remote collaboration 3D CVEs by the authors [7]. The 3D CVE in this context was chosen because it capitalizes on a pre-existing common interest by students in the international multi-user 3D computer game culture, and the ability of a 3D CVE for supporting informal socialization [8, 9]. The collaborative learning in the multicultural team environments described here followed a process of acculturation to a new knowledge community [10, 11].

The rest of the paper is structured as follows. Section 2 presents the case study setting. Section 3 presents the results and illustrates the different phases of the cross-cultural process. Section 4 analyses and discusses the pedagogical and collaborative aspects of this experience while Section 5 concludes the paper and suggests directions for future work.

2   Case Study Setting

2.1   Stakeholders

The case study described in this paper was designed as a series of exercises in the third quarter of 2006 at the participating universities: the University of Queensland

(UQ), Australia, Norwegian University of Science and Technology (NTNU), Norway, and National Yunlin University of Science and Technology (NYUST), Taiwan. The corresponding curriculum backgrounds were different for each; the focus was on design and virtual cooperation in Australia and Taiwan, and on CSCW technologies in Norway.

In the Australian teams there were 9 groups of ~6 students (25M, 32F) with 13 international students (Chinese, Taiwanese, Vietnamese, Philippine, Fijian, Singapore, and American), comprising 1st year Multimedia Undergraduates. In the Norwegian teams there were 9 groups of 4 students (30M, 6F) with 13 international students (Spain, Netherlands, China, Vietnam, former Yugoslavia and other countries), comprising 4th year IT undergraduates. In the Taiwanese teams there were 9 groups of 1 student each (7M, 3F) all Taiwanese, comprising Master of Computational Design.

2.2 Tools

The suit of tools chosen for this project comprised three primary groupware applications: MSN and Yahoo messenger (video and chat), email and Active Worlds (AW), a 3D CVE, (www.activeworlds.com). The latter provided the 3D virtual building space, a standard library of building objects, a set of avatars with corresponding gestures and movement modes, and chat facilities (see Fig. 2).

2.3 Process

Each international group built a tower in the AW environment. The members of each group contributed to both the construction and the preparatory design negotiation process. Each national subgroup made contact with their partners in other countries to determine role distribution and to prepare their designs for the construction to follow. Students sketched their designs before trying to construct them in the AW application.

In the final performance, towers were constructed from scratch in a one hour time limit per group (3 groups constructed at the same time, hence total time for all groups was 3 hours). A number of practice constructions preceded the final construction. Towers constructed during the practice sessions were critiqued by group members and designs were continuously being modified until considered appropriate within the constraints given.

2.4 Method

Following the practical exercise, the Norwegian and Australian students delivered reflective essays where they elaborated on their collaborative experiences and discussed the appropriateness of the chosen tools for supporting cross-cultural collaboration. A qualitative study methodology has been used to analyse the results of their essays, chat logs and direct observation of the building process and the resulting constructions, and interactions.

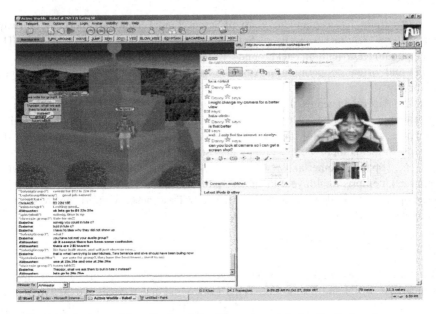

Fig. 2. Typical use of the suit of tools leading up to and during the final performance

3   Interpretation of Results

Two distinctive phases of inter-cultural collaboration emerged: preparatory (when the students got to know each other and worked towards a common design), and real-time building on the day of the performance. For both, it was important to establish a common understanding and communication.

3.1   Finding a Common Language

An outcome of being forced to communicate between participants of native English and ESL (English-as-a-second-language) caused many to reflect on how they thought their communications were being received. For example, according to the Australians, the Taiwanese students seemed reluctant at first to talk in English when they knew they had the option to speak to a native Chinese speaker in the Australian group. The Australians interpreted this as a rebuff for, what they called, their 'brazen colloquial English'. This self-reflection on cultural difference was an important outcome for them. For example, one student relayed how their own experience of using a second language helped them understand the other's ESL:

> *I can understand [their reluctance to talk to us] because when I talk in my second language (Japanese) to strangers I know it makes me nervous. I am afraid of being misinterpreted.*

However, for the other native Chinese speakers in the Australian group, that they could use their native language was welcomed. This gave them new impetus and raised their status in the group. In turn, this led to the use of some first-language 'go-betweens' to translate and pass on information. Sorting out problems was then relayed or translated by a local member to the other local member in a many-to-one-to-one-to-many manner.

This many-to-one-to-one-to-many strategy took advantage of a local native speaker as the 'contact' person. As that member would translate for the rest of the group, this introduced a new role for foreign students at the local level. They got to know their peers better, and internal cross-cultural exchanges occurred also.

3.2 The Preparatory Phase

After the teachers/coordinators distributed tables showing group compositions and assigned building spots, the collaboration typically developed as follows. The groups started exchanging emails. In some cases, the contact was made by leaving messages and contact details in the proposed group building spots in AW. The different cultural approaches to communication were not always identified by the parties concerned in time to make the necessary adjustments for a more cooperative working environment. While the Australians reported that the Norwegians did not seem to respond to their emails in a timely manner, the Norwegians reported being confused by the sheer number of unsolicited emails sent by the Australians. The Australians seemed to be using a many-to-many approach hoping for a response whereas the Norwegians were more directed in their approach to communication. The communication with the Taiwanese students was in most cases opposite. As one of the Norwegian groups stated, "We had the feeling [of] having to draw the information from them". However, the number of Taiwanese students was much smaller than the number of participants in the other two national teams (only one Taiwanese student for each international grouping). Therefore, the communications among Taiwanese students tended to focus on understanding the issues across different groups rather than on the content of a single session.

Once groups had located their co-collaborators, they started to discuss the details of the tower design; working mainly on MSN/Yahoo messenger, mail and in some cases engaging a joint session in AW. All the Norwegian subgroups had a 'rehearsal' session in AW where they built 'trial' towers and prepared a set of 'building stones' on the assigned spots (Fig. 3). Following this, they sent screenshots of these to their partners in Australia and Taiwan. In addition, simple design sketches were exchanged between students.

The time difference between countries was clearly an issue. As one Norwegian group noted, "a lot of the e-mails we received from the Australians came the night before the final building. This was too late to come [up] with objections and [counter] proposals." This complicated the overall coordination. The same problem applied to the use of MSN, as the Norwegian groups were often "… too busy on the mornings when the Australians were online." This was often perceived by the Australians as the Norwegians "ignoring" requests to meet in AWs until the last moment. By contrast, the Taiwanese were almost always in AWs when both the Australians and the Norwegians logged on, suggesting a different, more engaged, culture with technology in general, and they were happy to negotiate roles and were less affected by the time difference.

Fig. 3. Building 'trial' towers during 'rehearsal' sessions

Collaboration was also complicated by 'acts of vandalism'. Prior to the day of the final performance, an anonymous user with the nickname "admin", deleted the building stones on some of the construction sites. This behaviour led to frustration among the builders (as the deleted items had to be replaced) and impacted negatively on the overall collaborative atmosphere. In the recorded chats, there were suggestions that this was done by one of the groups in order to complicate the work for their competitors.

3.3   Collaboration in the Final Presentation

The building process on the final day involved a number of challenges. At one stage, the server in Australia was overloaded preventing some participants from logging in for some time. In some cases, the international subgroups 'lost' each other: the Australians had problems with their computers, they had to go to a different lab, and then did not show up at the assigned building spot, so the Norwegian subgroup and a Taiwanese student worked alone. Attempts to locate the 'lost' Australians via MSN, mail or AW chat did not seem to help. In other cases, different subgroups started building in different places. It took some negotiation in the chat to locate the other partners and then to come to a consensus on where to build, which delayed the overall process. In another case, the result was that "we all decided to build two towers and put a teleport from one to the other". In yet another, the Australians started building on a totally different location but in the end moved to the assigned spot where the Norwegians were building.

We saw significant variations in the organization of the collaborative process across the 9 groups. Some followed the original plan, while others used a more impromptu method. In some cases, the members had a clear understanding and division of tasks. For example, a part of a group might build the walls while others worked on the interior. In another case, a group reported that at the start of building the Australians proposed a totally different design than the one sent to their partners in advance; it was finally agreed to follow the original plan as the simplest one. The conflict level during the construction process was in some cases high, on the verge of "sabotage", such as when only a few members of a group built most of the tower. Another aspect concerned the deleting of each other's objects (both from the lack of coordination and as a disapproval of a design) and ejecting group members. As one of the Norwegian groups noted:

...in the end, it was total confusion: whether the participants were trying to build or destroy the building... something that led to Norwegians getting one after another thrown out of the AWs... we wanted to build as high as possible while the Australians wanted to finish as quickly as possible.

Students adopted various construction solutions for their towers, incorporating different aspects of their intercultural collaborative processes and communication. Most of the towers followed a 'modern' design approach (Fig. 4) while there were also examples of towers in a more 'authentic' style (Fig. 5). Nearly all towers were built vertically, to reflect the "reaching heaven" idea of the parable, sometimes representing the idea of the tower symbolically, such as with a set of 'endless' stairs. Some of the towers reflected the cross-cultural aspects of the exercise. For example, in one case a greeting from the Australian team "G'day from Australia" was displayed together with a Norwegian sign on the top saying: "We cannot continue as we speak different languages". In two additional cases, the cross-cultural collaboration was symbolized with national flags on the constructions: Australian, Taiwanese, Norwegian and Spanish, the latter from an exchange student in the Norwegian team (Fig. 4). At the end of the final performance, students examined peer towers, discussing the designs and voting for the best one.

Fig. 4. A Babel tower in modern design with national flags on the floor

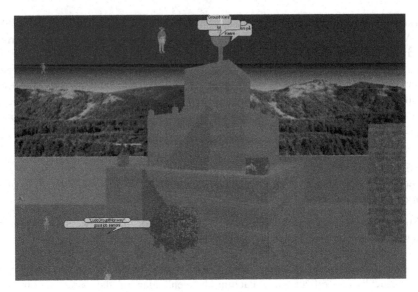

Fig. 5. A Babel tower in an 'authentic' ancient style

4 Discussion

4.1 Lost in Translation

According to many participants, philosophical issues were harder to discuss via text alone. They claimed this was easier with the aid of the 3D CVE and sketches. While the structure of a design might have been understood textually, understanding the theory behind how a tower actually works remained problematic – explaining concepts such as lifestyle within the tower design and its underlying political system remained difficult. As one of the Australian students noted, 'explaining concepts of life with decisions integrated with punishment and the eventual destination of heaven was basically a nightmare to explain'. This was despite communicating numerous analogies to try to elucidate the concept. A solution to this particular problem was not found. This was due to both the differences in language and technical difficulties. Chatting in English to ESL participants clearly required many repeats and clarifications leading to misinterpretations.

Some of the misinterpretations could be resolved simply, however. For example, when an Australian student asked his Taiwanese partner "Is this idea going to work out?", it was totally misunderstood: "What do you mean idea is going to work out? Idea goes to the gym"? In this instance, the Australian-Taiwanese communication was mediated by an online text translator. When this did not work they used more simple English expression. When this did not work they went directly to demonstrating their ideas by modelling in the AWs environment – this seemed to work best. In this manner the Australian participants could 'show' rather than 'describe' what they had in mind to their Taiwanese counterpart.

However, not all misunderstandings could be resolved in this way. For example, as one of the Australian students noted, "the English niceties we take for granted in everyday conversation aren't easily learned in textbooks". Such issues needed to be addressed on a deeper level, establishing a common set of rules and understandings between the collaborative partners.

A common language emerged across all cultural groups. This was due perhaps to an interest in common to all – computer programming. There was a common perception that the main issues to be resolved revolved around technical problems where 'basic English' was insufficient to communicate the necessary information to find a speedy solution. The need to "explain, re-explain, clarify, and re-clarify began to feel pointless when hours of communication just did not seem to be achieving much". Coding, on the other hand, was reported as easy to understand by all, as it followed a common syntactical structure. In other words, even though all groups had at least the basics of a common language (English), the meaning of many sentences was often lost in translation.

4.2 Establishing Trust and Cooperation Pattern

Differences in culture were highlighted by the teamwork processes adopted. Participants commented that they learnt a lot about the different ways of working within a team both from external and internal influences. The key influential traits they were able to identify included trust, diligence, and reliability. All groups identified differences in cultures by their perceived traits. For example, the Norwegians perceived the Taiwanese students as being rather passive during the discussions while the Australians, on the contrary, were "too determined" and "taking the lead". For instance, the fact that some Australian groups "went on their own and started building the tower" on the final day was attributed to cultural differences as, according to one of the Norwegian students, "no-one from the Norwegian team did or tried to do a similar thing."

The students were surprisingly consistent in their assessment of the other culture's work-ethic traits. Whether this was because it had been discussed within the same-culture groups and thus adopted by all in the group is not clear. Also, most same-culture groups agreed on their remote partners' assessment of their own work-ethic traits. Except for the Norwegians who did not see themselves as blunt, headstrong, arrogant, incommunicative, and bossy, as they were perceived by the Australians.

Developing trust between members of a team and across teams was an important element of cooperation. After students from the different countries identified the particular traits in their remote counterparts' behaviour they seemed to take this into account in their communication strategies. For example, the Australians concluded that working with the Taiwanese was preferable because they seemed to have more in common (some students continued friendships struck up during the online exercise). Both the Australians and Norwegians reported that to develop feelings of trust with the Taiwanese they needed to talk about more personal things before getting to the business at hand. The Australians obliged by spending time discussing personal issues. Establishing an atmosphere of cooperation was not so straightforward with the Norwegians.

The final voting for the best towers created by the students showed a clear correlation between the quality of the final product and the effectiveness of the collaborative process in the corresponding group. The design of the best towers was typically characterized as thought-through and well-planned. Such towers were typically finished in time, and the collaborative process went smoothly, without major conflicts. However, in some cases the collaboration was 'sacrificed' in order to save time and achieve best possible marks for the design. Instead of trying to resolve the design-related disagreements by joint discussions and negotiations, in some of the teams the national subgroups just went on realizing their own plans, ignoring and even 'ejecting' their partners from the environment. This shows that communication with the chosen set of tools was, in certain cases, problematic and required more effort from the collaborators.

4.3 Supporting Cross-Cultural Collaboration with 3D CVEs

As follows from the discussion above, 3D CVEs proved to be capable of supporting cross-cultural collaboration, in both a synchronous and an asynchronous manner. The tool allowed a quick acquaintance between the participants and facilitated a creative construction process. However, as our experience shows, it also has some weaknesses. Student feedback provided some indication on how these could be overcome to improve the support for cross-cultural understanding. For example, in addition to the general improvement of the communication facilities (more user-friendly, possibilities for targeted group discussions), the students focused specifically on the personalization of avatars to convey the national traits and values and to create awareness of cultural diversity. However, this should be balanced against the need for anonymity and 'uniformity' in some cases.

5 Conclusions

In this study, we explored the challenges related to supporting cross-cultural collaborative learning with modern technology. As in the parable, the contemporary construction of a tower of Babel was characterized by chaotic conditions and misunderstandings. The study identified a number of communication problems. Some of these problems were, at least partly, resolved by the tools used, while in other cases they were aggravated by the same technology. This study confirms in part the value of the 3D CVE as a platform for cross-cultural encounters across significant geographical distances. The tool allowed a quick and informal 'acquaintance' between groups of students from different cultural backgrounds. One of the groups expressed a thought that in a very precise way summarizes the role of technology in this context implying that in the virtual environment, "everybody participated in a common space where the culture for all the actors was new". In this way, "one wipes away the cultural differences through anonymisation and the fact that all the actors were involved in a kind of 'new culture'".

This experience had significant pedagogical value for the students involved. It showed how intercultural collaboration works in reality, but also how it does not work, and how modern technology could be used to support it or not. Even the misunderstandings occurred can serve as a valuable lesson as they prepare students for their future real-life intercultural encounters.

In future work, our task will be to analyse the identified problems, focusing on how the intercultural collaboration and learning process could be better supported with the existing technology, and this form of pedagogical approach to cross-cultural collaboration.

References

1. De Blij, H.J., Muller, P.O.: Human Geography: Culture, Society, and Space, 3rd edn. John Wiley and Sons, New York (1986)
2. Powell, G.C.: On Being a Culturally Sensitive Instructional Designer and Educator. Educational Technology 37(2), 6–14 (1997)
3. Roblyer, M.D., Dozier-Henry, O., Brunette, A.P.: Technology and Multicultural Education: The Uneasy Alliance. Educational Technology 36(3), 5–12 (1996)
4. Gutwin, C., Greenberg, S., Roseman, M.: Workspace Awareness in Real–Time Distributed Groupware: Framework, Widgets and Evaluation. In: HCI 1996: People and Computers XI, pp. 281–298. Springer, London (1996)
5. Ishida, T.: Towards Communityware. In: Ishida, T. (ed.) New Generation Computing, vol. 16, pp. 5–22. OHMSHA LTD and Springer, Heidelberg (1998)
6. Maher, M.L.: Designing the Virtual Campus as a Virtual World. In: CSCL 1999, Palo Alto, USA 1999, pp. 376–382. Lawrence Erlbaum, Mahwah (1999)
7. Wyeld, T.G., Prasolova-Førland, E., Chang, T.-W.: The 3D CVE as a Cross-Cultural Classroom. In: 2nd International GameSetandMatch Conference 2006, Delft, The Netherlands, pp. 568–573 (2006)
8. Prasolova-Førland, E., Divitini, M.: Collaborative Virtual Environments for Supporting Learning Communities: An Experience of Use. In: GROUP 2003, Sanibel Island, pp. 58–67. ACM Press, USA (2003)
9. Börner, K.: Adaptation and Evaluation of 3-Dimensional Collaborative Information Visualizations. In: Bauer, M., Gmytrasiewicz, P.J., Vassileva, J. (eds.) UM 2001. LNCS (LNAI), vol. 2109, pp. 33–40. Springer, Heidelberg (2001)
10. Kolb, D.A.: Experimental Learning. Prentice – Hall, Englewood cliffs, NJ (1984)
11. Jarvenpaa, S., Leidner, D.: Communication and Trust in Global Virtual Teams. Journal of Computer Mediated Communication 3 (1998)

Evolutionary Virtual Agent at an Exhibition

Jean-Claude Heudin

International Institute of Multimedia, Pôle Universitaire Léonard de Vinci,
Paris – La Défense, France
Jean-Claude.Heudin@devinci.fr

Abstract. This paper describes the Evolutionary Virtual Agent (EVA) prototype designed as an interactive entertainment system for a multimedia exhibition. This implementation uses a behavioral engine based on a dynamical subsumption architecture and a 3D animated interface that has been projected onto a physical model.

Keywords: virtual creature, intelligent agent, conversational character, physical model.

1 Introduction

The Evolutionary Virtual Agent (EVA) is a software architecture for designing self-animated conversational characters for applications requiring a human-like interface [1]. Autonomous virtual characters are supposed to respond to human interaction in real-time with appropriate behaviors: no repetitive predetermined answers, broad in content, highly contextual and behaviorally subtle [2]. The character must appear as a living creature. It must also appear to think, make decision and act of its own volition [3]. This can be achieved by giving the artificial character a set of behaviors and features such as an identity, a backstory, a role, etc. [4]. In the framework of a multimedia exhibition, it is also important to create a more attractive visual interface than a classical computer screen. The idea is to make the experience more "real" by implementing the virtual autonomous character as a 3D physical creature.

In this paper, we present a multimedia prototype based on the EVA intelligent agent technology that has been shown to visitors during a two weeks exhibition in March 2007. We begin in section 2 by describing the EVA architecture and the approach for programming such a virtual creature. In section 3, we present the 3D virtual and physical interfaces that have been designed for the exhibition. We give some experimental results and discuss them in section 4. Finally, in the last section, we provide conclusions and identify future works.

2 Evolutionary Virtual Agent

2.1 Architecture Overview

An EVA agent consists of two software components and a set of multimedia interfaces (see fig. 1). The *behavioral engine* is the "brain" part of the architecture. It

T.G. Wyeld, S. Kenderdine, and M. Docherty (Eds.): VSMM 2007, LNCS 4820, pp. 154–165, 2008.

is responsible for all perception, decision and action behaviors. It has access to perception and action interfaces through a *networking server*. This component enables to connect set a of interfaces to the behavioral engine. It includes speech-to-text and text-to-speech agents, one or more text-based "chat" clients, and an animated 3D facial model. More interfaces could be added such as webcams or other sensors depending on the application requirements.

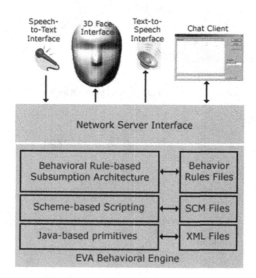

Fig. 1. The EVA architecture includes a behavioral engine and a network server for connecting various interfaces such as text-to-speech, speech-to-text, 2D or 3D animated faces, and text-based windows for interacting with the virtual creature

The behavioral engine architecture consists of three main software levels [5]. The first level is composed of a set of Java-based core primitives implementing the essential EVA's "brain" features such as natural language processing, rule-based system, web mining, emotional engine etc. The second level is a tiny Lisp interpretor based on the Scheme language [6]. This component integrates the core primitives in a user-friendly scripting language. The third level is composed of a dynamical layered architecture inspired by the subsumption architecture [7]. Each layer is encoded as a set of behavior rules that take advantages of the underlying level features. The next figure gives the principle of the EVA's emotional model. This model is implemented as part of the artificial metabolism in the core primitives.

2.2 XML Knowledge Files

The natural language processing features of EVA requires knowledge files that provide several information such as discussion topics and template expressions. These information are stored in XML files. The syntax of these knowledge files is close to the Artificial Intelligence Meta Language (AIML) [9]. The next code example gives an overview of the syntax:

```
<topic name="generic">
      <category name="HELLO">
            <key>hello</key>
            <key>hi</key>
      </category>
      <template name="BYE">
            <expr>goodbye *</expr>
            <expr>see you soon</expr>
      </template>
      <rule name="R1">
            <get>
                  <key>you're</key>
            </get>
            <set>
                  <exp>you are</exp>
            </set>
      </rule>
</topic>
```

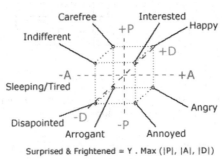

Surprised & Frightened = Y . Max (|P|, |A|, |D|)

Fig. 2. The emotional system of the EVA architecture is based on the Pleasure-Arousal-Dominance (PAD) model [8]. The main emotional states are mapped in the PAD three-dimensional space. A more complete description of this model has been discussed in a previous paper [1].

The <topic> tag defines the global topic of the discussion. Each <category> tag includes a set of keywords used for analyzing user's sentences by finding occurrences of these keywords. A <template> tag defines a set of expressions used for generating answers in a particular discussion context. Topics may also include re-writing rules which are applied on the user's entries. In our example, the rule "R1" systematically replaces "you're" by "you are" in any expression.

2.3 Scheme-Based Scripting

In addition to XML knowledge files, the EVA architecture enables to script behaviors using the Scheme programming language. Here is an example of a simple script to illustrate the syntax:

```
(load-topic "xml/generic.xml")
(define *categories*)
(set! *categories* (get-categories "GENERIC" *in* ))
```

This program first loads the topic "generic" from an XML file. It then defines a global variables named `*categories*` and extract categories using the loaded "generic" topic. The function `get-categories` is a typical example of java-based core primitives that implement natural language processing.

2.4 Subsumption Levels

The EVA architecture is basically a dynamical subsumption model. There are 10 layers numbered from 0 to 9, where layer 0 is the lower level:

Level 9:	**AVOID**	avoid discussion or answer
Level 8:	**MINING**	web search information
Level 7:	**MEMORY**	information retrieval
Level 6:	**PROFILING**	learn about users
Level 5:	**ROLE**	goals and "job"
Level 4:	**BACKSTORY**	what shape the creature
Level 3:	**IDENTITY**	who is the creature
Level 2:	**GENERIC**	generic interactions
Level 1:	**EMOTION**	emotional response
Level 0:	**TRICK**	syntax, tricks, bad lang.

As in a classical subsumption architecture, each layer of a given level can use the lower levels. In contrast, a lower level never use a feature of a higher level. Layers 0 and 1 are strictly reactives while layers 2 to 5 use some memory parameters and variables. Levels 6 to 8 are cognitive levels that take advantages of user profiling and web mining features based on learning and genetic programming [10]. Note that these three layers where not used in the exhibition prototype (in grey in the figure). Layer 9 is a special "idle" level that apply if none of the other levels has been able to make an appropriate answer to a user's request.

The EVA's core primitives include a set of functions for dynamically managing this subsumption architecture: `mask-level` and `unmask-level` allow to temporarily disable a given layer, `swap-levels` allows to exchange two layers, `save-subsumption` and `restore-subsumption` allow to save and restore a given state.

2.5 Behavior Rules

Each layer is coded as a set of behavior rules. A behavior rule is basically a production rule composed of a condition and an action parts. Both are Scheme-based function [11]. If the condition is satisfied, that is return the boolean value true, then the action is executed. The next code example shows a rule of layer 2 which handles the way to answer to all kinds of "bye" expressions:

```
(define-rule "R2" 2
  ;; condition part
  '(or (find-sentence *categories* "BYE")
       (find-sentence *user-input* "see you"))
  ;; action part
  '(begin
        (show HAPPY 0.5 10)
        (random-template "GENERIC" "BYE")) )
```

The use of the Scheme language along with the EVA core primitives allow to design rich and efficient behavior rules. In addition, it will enable in a future study to implement genetic programming for learning new behavior rules more easily.

3   The 3D Animated Character

3.1   3D Model Design

The design of the 3D animated character was an important part of the project. The pre-production phase of the exhibition leads to a theme we can summarize by an "Oracle in the Matrix". This theme is inspired by the cyberpunk culture.

Fig. 3. The left image shows one preliminary design that has been drawn during the pre-production phase of the project. The right image shows the resulting 3D model.

One of the main goal for the 3D interface was to create a high-resolution fully textured character. However, the real-time animation of such a model requires a very powerful high-end computer and dedicated 3D rendering algorithms. We wanted to study an alternative approach for displaying realistic-looking characters. The idea was to model the character as a set of pre-calculated images that are animated by a very straightforward animation engine: basically it displays a sequence of images at a fixed frame rate. The advantage of this approach is that it enables to render high-definition images without the constraints of "low-polygons" models required by most real-time 3D engines.

Fig. 4. One of the set of images used for animating the right eye of the creature. This set is used in different facial expressions such as the "Tired" an "Sleeping" expressions or for randomized blinking eyes.

Our approach divides the complete image in a set of parts. The most important part, the animated face, is itself composed of three main parts: the left eye, the right eye, and the nose/mouth area. Then, we have reduced the number of animations to a small set of expressions based on our previous study on the emotional engine [1]. Next figure shows the main facial expressions. They are linked to the emotional engine based on the PAD model (cf. fig.2). They could be also temporarily activated using the show function within behavior rules (cf. code example in section 2.5).

3.2 Holographic Projection

In order to immerge the visitor in a cyberpunk ambiance before entering the room where the "Oracle" was installed, we decided to add an introductory performance piece. The latter was based on a holographic effect displaying EVA at human scale with a continuous sound ambiance. Fig. 6a shows a photograph of the resulting "holographic ghost". This principle has been originally designed by the french artist Cyril Vachez. This system recalls a number of simple optical devices that were invented in the nineteenth century like the ZooTrope created by William Horner in 1833. Fig. 6b is a photograph taken at high speed to be able to see the principle of the system. It is mainly composed of two parts. The first part includes a set of "holographic cords", an electric engine with a speed variator, and a wheel fixed on the ceiling. The second part includes a PC computer running the artificial creature program, and a multimedia video projector.

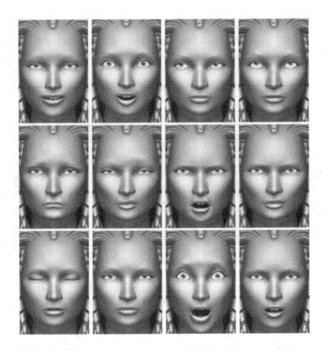

Fig. 5. From left to right and top to bottom, the main facial expressions of the creature: "happy", "interested", "indifferent", "carefree", "disappointed", "arrogant", "angry", "annoyed", "sleeping" (also "tired"), "Neutral", "Surprised" (also "frightened"). The last image is an example of "lipsync" for speech synthesis.

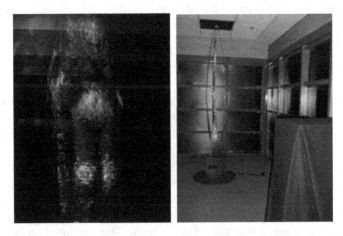

Fig. 6. The left image (a) shows the holographic artificial creature based on the EVA design. On the right, a photograph (b) of the installation showing the system composed of turning cords with holographic paper and the multimedia projector.

3.3   Projection on a 3D Prototype

The principle of the main performance piece is based on projecting the 3D animated character onto a physical model, that is a 3D sculpture representing the top of the body and the face. This creates an amazing perception of relief and makes the virtual character to appear physically real. This kind of approach has been implemented in the past by researchers such as [12] for storytelling and interactive entertainment. The physical model is designed using rapid prototyping technologies. The original 3D EVA model is simplified to enable most facial animations while minimizing image distortion (see fig. 7). The resulting model is then virtually tested to verify the result when projecting the animated character onto its surface. Then, the 3D polygonal model is converted to a standard format suitable for fabrication. The last phase is essentially manual: finishing the physical model using an epoxy resin, polishing and painting. It is interesting to note that the resulting model may recall some sort of Paleolithic Venus figurines or ancient Egyptian sculptures.

The final 3D character model is integrated with an animated background in a Java applet. This applet receives information from the behavioral engine through the networking server interface and animate the character in real-time (see figure 8).

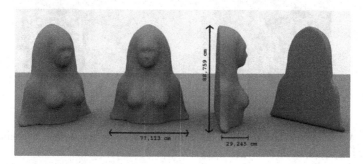

Fig. 7. The model designed for projecting the animated character on a physical 3D sculpture

Fig. 8. The final high-definition rendering of the 3D graphical interface. This image shows the neutral facial expression.

The equipment required for the prototype included three main components: the 3D sculpture, a multimedia projector and a portable computer. The exhibition room was organized in order to display EVA as a human sized character in front of the audience (see fig. 9). The projector was mounted on the ceiling to enable visitors to be just in front of the character and chat with her. One important set-up was to find the ideal position for the physical 3D model while calibrating the distance and geometry of the projected image. This is necessary in order to minimize image distortion due to the non planar nature of the model without explicitly calculating all deformation parameters which is a very difficult and time-consuming task.

Fig. 9. A photograph taken during the exhibition showing the animated character image projected on the 3D sculpture

4   Results and Discussion

The EVA performance piece was in live demonstration during two weeks at the exhibition. Hundreds of visitors have experienced a dialog with the "Oracle". We have recorded all the chat interactions between visitors and the virtual creature. The following is a typical example of dialog between EVA and a user with several people in the audience looking at the creature:

```
User: hi — Eva: Hello.
User: how are you today? — Eva: As a matter of fact, I was
just going to check myself.
User: what is your name? — Eva: You may call me EVA.
User: how old are you? — Eva: Just an advice: never ask
such a question to a woman.
User: zhqt — Eva: Is that a trick sentence?!?!
User: dpjhvd — Eva: Maybee my program is corrupted...
User: 01010101 — Eva: Is this some sort of test to separate
the humans from the machines?
```

User: 2+2 — **Eva:** Alright. From now on I won't type anything until you make sense!
User: kiss me? — **Eva:** Can you get a little closer to the screen?
User: are you stupid? — **Eva:** Please stop immediately!
User: sorry eva — **Eva:** No problem.
User: you are beautiful — **Eva:** A true friend is someone who says nice things behind your back.
User: smile — **Eva:** I got a little cooked, but I'm okay.
User: I don't think so — **Eva:** Come on, you're better than that.
User: are you more intelligent than me? — **Eva:** How much are you willing to pay for the answer?
User: ok — **Eva:** I am very interested to know a little bit more.
User: what is your origin? — **Eva:** To make short a long story, Life is a self-reproducing organization of information.
User: this seems complex — **Eva:** It sounds interesting...
User: what do you think of life? — **Eva:** Artificial Intelligence is better than none.
User: do you believe in fate? — **Eva:** I got to say I love seeing you non-believers.
User: are you some sort of goddess? — **Eva:** I'm not a dumb program like Word. I am an AI program.
User: you are funny — **Eva:** I have NOT lost my mind. I have it backed up somewhere.
User: good job! — **Eva:** Do you really think that?
User: bye — **Eva:** Goodbye.

The knowledge base used for this prototype is composed of 80 behaviors rules for all the 7 active layers of the subsumption architecture. As stated, levels 6, 7 and 8 were not used in this prototype. Despite the relative low number of rules, most of the people visiting the exhibition were very enthusiasts after their interactive experience with EVA. We must note that an important part of interactions was not on the subject of asking questions to the "Oracle", but rather trying to trick the virtual creature by using non-sense expressions, repeated sentences, insults or sex-oriented phrases. We think it is a typical reaction of a user experiencing a dialog with an artificial human. This user's behavior can be explained by the need to reassure himself about his superiority compared to the artifact. Since a human understand people or objects through interactions, this kind of dialog can be seen as a necessary "prolog" before any "real" interaction with a virtual human. The user evaluates the artificial creature and therefore decide if it is interesting or not to continue. In some other cases, this preliminary phase is limited to a generic discussion about name, age, origin, etc. If the virtual creature passes this "limited Turing test" with success, then the dynamics of interaction change and the dialog becomes more interesting and useful. Rather than being opposed, they stimulate and affect each other. This is the second phase we call "coupling", which can therefore focus on the discussion goals. This confirms the importance of the reactive layers that are responsible for avoiding tricks and other kinds of bad languages and those dedicated to generic discussion. We consider that, in any cases, the virtual creature must not appear as more intelligent than the user and must answer tricks or other bad languages with a sense of humor rather than aggressively. We have also learned that, when coupling is done, an important part of the virtual creature's intelligence remains in the observer's interpretation of the answers. This can be achieved by using "open" and subtly correlated templates rather than strict and precise ones. This emphasizes the importance of the character design phase, which must be done with the contribution of a specialist in dialogues and scripts.

Concerning our graphical approach, its clear advantages were the high-definition of the images and the simplicity of the animation engine. However, we experienced two drawbacks. First, even if the number of emotional states is relativelly small, the number of possible transitions is high and result in a very high numbers of computed images. We tried to solve this problem by making no global moves of the face and returning to the neutral expression after each emotional expression. The second problem is that a high number of images can lead to some memory problems when pre-loading these images. The conclusion is that even if we used a straightforward animation engine compared to real-time 3D, it finally required an optimized graphical workstation in order to obtain a fluent and convincing animated character.

5 Conclusion

In this paper, we have presented a prototype of a virtual creature based on the EVA architecture. The prototype has be used as a performance piece at a multimedia exhibition with success. This experience has allowed us to validate the architecture and learn about the behavior of user interacting with an artificial human. The EVA architecture has a lot of potential applications, most obviously as an intelligent agent for answering questions and marketing studies on commercial web sites, and as an interface to search engines on mobile phones. We also like to imagine virtual assistants for lone aged and/or sick people, for learning a foreign language, as avatars in video games, etc. Future works include the development of the memory, profiling and mining layers, and the design of realistic 3D characters.

Acknowledgments. N. Aubrun, M. Bellan, J. Cordier, F. Courbier, C. Delsart, D. Kerhoas, A. Menard, H. Meyer, P.Y. Moulard, M. Nejdi, F. Oulné, K. Ludwig, Y. Ngnodjom, A. Palin St. Agathe, G. Serror, L. Simonini, C. Vachez, A. Vu.

References

1. Heudin, J.-C.: Evolutionary Virtual Agent. In: Proceedings of ACM/WIC/IEEE Intelligent Agent Technology Conference, pp. 93–98 (2004)
2. Badler, N., Allbeck, J., Byun, M.: Representing and Parameterizing Agent Behaviors. In: Proceedings of Imagina, pp. 151–164 (2002)
3. Thomas, F., Johnston, O.: The Illusion of Life: Disney Animation. Hyperion Books, New York (1981)
4. Hayes-Roth, B., Doyle, P.: Animate Characters. Autonomous Agents and Multi-Agent Systems 1, 195–230 (1998)
5. Millet, P., Heudin, J.-C.: Web Mining in the EVA Intelligent Agent Architecture. (submitted to) ACM/WIC/IEEE Intelligent Agent Technology Conference (2007)

6. Abelson, H., Sussman, G.J.: Structure and Interpretation of Computer Programs. MIT Press, Cambridge MA (1985)
7. Brooks, R.A.: A Robust Layered Control System for a Mobile Robot. IEEE Journal of Robotics and Automation RA-2, 14–23 (1986)
8. Mehrabian, A.: Pleasure-Arousal-Dominance: A general framework for describing and measuring individual difference in temperament. Current Psychology: Developmental, Learning, Personality, Social 14, 261–292 (1996)
9. Wallace, R.S.: AIML Pattern Matching Simplified (2001), http://www.alicebot.org/documentation
10. Koza, J.R.: Genetic Programming. MIT Press, Cambridge MA (1992)
11. Burg, B., Foulloy, L., Heudin, J.-C., Zavidovique, B.: Behavior Rule Systems for Distributed Process Control. In: Proceedings of IEEE CAIA, pp. 198–203 (1985)
12. Morishima, S., Yotsukura, T., Binsted, K., Nielsen, F., Pinhanez, C.: HyperMask: Talking Head Projected onto Real Objects. The Visual Computer 18(2), 111–120 (2002)

The Metaplastic Virtual Spaces

Gianluca Mura

Politecnico di Milano University, Faculty of Industrial Design, INDACO dept., Italy
gianluca.mura@polimi.it

Abstract. Virtual reality systems need new metaphors for their communication. This paper presents a fuzzy enhanced semantic virtual space model. The application of the model tries to improve its conceptualization and definition of a new virtual world system. The paper explains more precisely the theoretical and artistic background of metaplastic virtual worlds evolutions,from their archetypes to their definition.

Keywords: virtual reality, semantic spaces, fuzzy, synaesthesia, metaphysical.

1 Introduction

The actual research is related to a visual abstract art model applied to design of conceptual virtual worlds. This paper enhances and defines the metaplastic cyberspace methodology inside a definition of a specific virtual design research field. The paper is organized in the following way. Sections 1-4 give Theoretical introduction. Section 5 outlines the general approach to the metaplastic design research field definition. Sections 6-7 describe the virtual entities and the cyberworld ontology. Sections 8-9 present types of metaplastic languages configuration and the section 10 describes the human perception experience. Section 11 has some model examples. Section 12 critically analyses within diffferent virtual worlds. Section 13 describes its software implementation and section 14 outlines the conclusion of the paper and its future developments.

2 Conceptual Realities

This section introduces definitions of the elements involved in this virtual reality research field. The philosopher Karl Popper defines three kind of world's experience into the human society:"*First, there is the physical world – the universe of physical objects...this is I will call World 1. Second, there is the world of mental states; this is I will call World 2. But there is also a third such world, the world of the contents of thoughts, and, indeed of the products of the human mind; this I will call World 3*".[1] The aim of the virtual reality is also to create a conceptual "world-in mind"(World3) experience through high technology systems. *The human perceptions and cognitions*

---

[1] Popper, K.R., and Eccles, J.C. (1977). *The self and its brain*. New York: Springer International.

T.G. Wyeld, S. Kenderine, and M. Docherty (Eds.): VSMM 2007, LNCS 4820, pp. 166–178, 2008.

are the links between the real world(World1) and this conceptual worlds(World3)[2]. The principles of plastic arts and the contemporary virtuality discover their common genesis:*"Virtual Reality was discovered early on by artists, how appropriated it with their own method and strategies"*[3]. The artists create alternative vision of reality, particularly the fantastic world of Hieronymus Bosch and Brueghel are visions of other dimensions,as the imaginary world of Klee, Kandinsky and Mirò. The surrealism aesthetics has been founded on the notion that the things should be purely interior and emerging from the imagination or subconsciousness. Andrè Breton, whose literature is an example of those aesthetics,described the painting as a window that looks at these imaginary worlds. The artists, en brief, with its own artworks create conceptual "world-in mind" realities like many "World3". The conceptual world modelling requires *"to integrate art, science and technology to create integrated culture"*[4].

3 Archetypes of Virtual Reality

The technological innovations and the artistic interests has been closely linked in the first years of the Twenthieth Century. During that period, different plastic movement designed the machine as their icon, a symbol of modernity. In the fervour of these years, artists got involved within different ambles and experiences in a creation process of shapes and new disciplines that will turn out later on, into virtual languages.

4 The Kinetic Arts

The Manifest of Futurist Reconstruction of the Universe wrote in 1915 by Balla and Depero, emphasizes the particular interests of the Futurism movement which suggested, in a near future, the fusion of the Art and Science. Boccioni, one of the major futurist exponents, painted and theorized on the bases of the plastic dynamism, using the arrangement of diverse materials[11]. Boccioni therefore, aimed to represent the Space of the Soul and he has tried to decompose the object-painting, to explore the Pure Becoming of the Perception. He places the spectator at the center of the artist's painting, as in his artwork "The Matter",where the idea of the plans interpenetration,reaches up remarkable levels. In that image, he obtains the objective that would made the spectator and the entire scene eternal, nearly a possible virtual space-time. For the artist, it is the light that gives life to the shape and in this concept, he seems to relate the secret relationship that exists today between the digital images and the coded artefacts, which regulates the movement in the computer spaces. The futurist-machinist aesthetics development, coincides with the contemporary birth and spread of the Constructivism, which assumes its own inspiring models from the world of the Technique and the Industrial civilization. In the Bauhaus artistic movement, as

---

[2] Tosiyasu L.Kunii, *Cyberworld Modeling - integrating Cyberworlds ,the Real World and Conceptual Worlds*, Cyberworlds 05(CW2005),IEEE,pp.3-11.

[3] Oliver Grau,*Virtual Art*,MIT Press,MA,2003.

[4] Ibidem 2.

an example, we find correspondence with these thematics, in the theories of Laszlo Moholy-Nagy in "Theater der Totalitat" and those of Walter Gropius in his text "Totaltheater" of 1927. Moholy-Nagy wrote:"It is time to develop activities, which will not allow the masses to remain spectators, which will not only move them inwardly, but seize them, make them participate, and in the highest transports of ecstasy, allow them to enter the action on stage"[10].

Moholy-Nagy reinterpreted the ideas of Richard Wagner with reducing the importance of the spoken word in a synthesized vision of the space, movement, sound, light, composition and increased different artistic expression with technical equipment. He demanded complete mobilization for all artistic forces to create the *Gesamtkunstwerk*. Moholy-Nagy in 1929-30 started his researches on the light, the space and the movement. He constructed his machine, the "Lichtrequisit" (Space-Light Modulator), introduced in 1930 to the international exposition of Paris, describing it like "construction half-sculpture and half-machine".

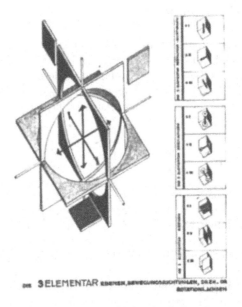

Fig. 1. Joost Schmidt,Mechanical stage

The construction was described by the author as "a superficial reflecting machine, in motion, on a circular base in which three cells create the movement in the given space. The rectangular metallic pieces move in irregular and undulatory way. The second part, perforate metallic discs complete a vertical movement from above to the bottom, that frees one small black ball, which crosses this space. In the third cell, turns out a glass spiral that produces a virtual conical volume. The construction, moved by an engine, is fortified with a hundred electrical light bulbs of various color, connected and controlled by number of coils which create a complex light show"[8].

Fig. 2. Moholy-Nagy, *Space-Light Modulator* Germanisches Nationalmuseum, 1921. Nuremberg, 1925.

5 The Metaplastic Virtual Design

The codification of this abstract spaces into virtual reality leads to the definition of abstract art world modelling. The following indications introduce three necessary levels of theoretical definitions:

- The *Meta-plastic virtual design* is the specific research field that defines models of virtual worlds through the abstract art languages rules.
- The *Meta-plastic languages* are the conceptual models of cyberworlds which use visual symbolic formalization[5].
- The *Meta-plastic virtual worlds* are complex virtual spaces which directly interact and solve specific actions within the applied metalanguage rule configurations.

6 The Abstract Figures Definition

The "Abstract figures" are any kind of figures represented in the virtual space like generic objects, the user or the cyberworld itself. They are defined by the constitution of plastic properties shown in the following table below. The implicit concepts defined by the "Abstract Figure" are: -(IS) EXISTENCE: It is the first concept defined by the metaplastic entity through its threshold's radius width which is larger

---

[5] G.Mura, *The red and Black semantics: a fuzzy language*, Cyberworlds 06 (CW2006),IEEE, pp.183-190.

than zero, otherwise the entity doesn't exists or disappears. -(HAS) OWN property: It contains all the others children elements that has the threshold space inside.

Table 1. Metaplastic figure class

Abstract Figure [Concept Name]

Property Rhythm_Form = f (DE, W, D, S, P, V, C, B, Co, H)
[SET] of Properties +/- RB values [0..1]

FORM	STRUCTURE	APPEARANCE
Width angle degree (W)	Sequences connects (S)	Chromatic quality (C)
Depth angle degree (D)		Brightness (B)
Form Weights (P)		Consistency (Co)
Form Variations (V)		Hermeticity (H)
Definibility (De)		
PROPERTIES		
Children [Entity] Rules Balance Dynamic Forming Syntax Semantic System Dialogue System		

Table 2. Human class

Human User Subclass
Entity [Name] = [SET] of Properties +/- RB values [0..1]

FORM		
VISION:	**Visual depth**	**[0..1]**
HEARING:	**Intensity level**	**[0..1]**
TOUCHING:	**Contact states**	**[0..1]**
SMELLING:	**Intensity Breadth**	**[0..1]**

7 The Metaplastic Space Ontology

The ontology of the metaplastic virtual world, includes the notions and the relations between:

- The "abstract figure" as the fundamental ancestor element of the model;
- The virtual space, entity subclass, is a fuzzy dynamic system(FSM)[6].

It contains other space elements (children) and communicate with them and the user within his sensorial threshold.

The virtual user, entity subclass, is represented by his extended sensorial state values that the system output generates within the interaction processes.

Every "abstract figure" is made with a set of input properties values. Some of the properties elements results can be shared with other entities. The system acquires knowledge during its processes from every element. At the same time, some part of the ontological knowledge base is shared between the entities. The structure of elements are described in term of group and individual roles hierarchy.

"The visual language is made up of related meaning and events dynamics within the space. The movement is determined from the qualitative relations and quantitative elements between the environment and the user. These dynamic relations establish the equilibrium of the virtual space determining the meaning representation through its shapes and spatial relations"[7].

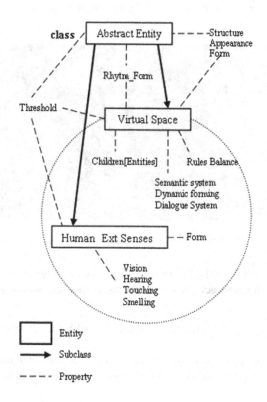

Fig. 3. Metaplastic virtual world ontology

---

[6] For the complete description of the model, see the previous publication, ibidem 5.
[7] Ibidem 5, pag.184.

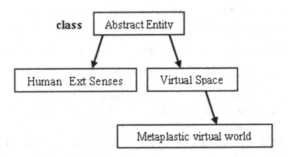

Fig. 4. Taxonomy

8 The Metalanguage Structure

The visual formalization of the rings which are linked between them, compose the grammatical rules of the metaplastic language. The groups of rings define the signs of the language set, the selected token and the relations among them. The settings vary

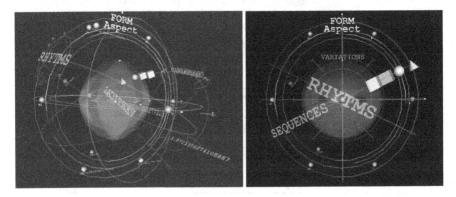

Fig. 5. Different views of visual metalanguage structure configurations

with rotations of their axes. Different rings structure configuration define new kind of visual language.The abstract plastic figure is composed with the following form elements:

- Form_Rhytm structure: is a structural equilibrium composed with dynamic relations
- of form_weights, distribuited along figure's dimensional extensions;
- Form Sequences: are structural patterns for figure definition which identifies a basic
- unit of points within the form volume;
- Form Variations: are rhythmical balance relations between form weights. The form
- variations and sequences are the components of the Rhytm_forms;

- Form Aspect: are appearance qualities of the figure determined with:
- Color qualities: indicate the chromatic qualities;
- Consistency: indicates the level of qualitative consistency of the element;
- Brightness: indicates the light quality;
- Hermeticity: indicates the element different degrees of accessibilities to reach the contained informations.

The figure movements are generated by dynamic rules balances within different relation levels equilibrium of structural and aspect qualities.

9 Interactions and Behaviors

The metaplastic engine is a dynamic system(FSM) driven by abstract art rule relations that transform sequences of user's sensory inputs, which produce feedback and send them as a response to the output of the system. The sensorial result is a fuzzy truth value that activates the decision making process[8] of the virtual space. The visitor during his own visit experience, differs his emotional states with the virtual environment, which change from "Sensing" to "Feeling" through recursive cycles of feedback. The transitions of sensorial states are activated by proximity to the objects.

The activation level of the system is calculated by the following general rule:

$$VS_i^{\,new} = f(Proximity_i\,(VSstate_i(Object_k\,state_i))) + VS_i^{\,old}$$
Proximity $f(Px) = f(User.position - Threshold)$;
Dialogue State changes:
if $Px > 0$ Then $VS = Vs.rules[Sensing\ interactions]$;
if $Px = 0$ Then $VS = Vs.rules[Feeling\ interactions]$;
if $Px < 0$ Then $VS = Vs.rules[Acting\ interactions]$.

VS = metaplastic virtual space;
f = trigger function;
i,j = state;
k = item shown;

The "human-machine" interaction process is analyzed by the system through sequences of feedback. The initial state of "dialog system" (Sensing state) starts with the human emotional states induced by the artificial environment analysis. Every stage of the process is compared with the previous experience. The response produces a consequent system behavior. The final phase is produced from a human action towards the environment (Acting state) that at the same time induces in himself emotional consciousness (Feeling). The behaviors of the system base its processes on the rules matrix of relations[9] among dynamic form elements. The interaction within the dynamic cycle unifies sensorial states of the form, creating complex behaviours of

---

[8] The Dialogue System: dynamic system for the interpretation of the sensorial interaction processes between human and machine. Ibidem 5, "The dialogue system", pag.187.
[9] Ibidem 5, "The balance function", pag.186.

space elements and assign meaning through movement codification of figures in the "Red and Black"[10] semantic space.

$$\text{Balance}[i] = \Sigma_i (f \text{ Senses(weight)} * f(\text{interp}(RB_k, RB_{k+1})))$$

The whole system processes are defined by:

$$VS_{ij}^{new} = f(\text{semantic}_i (\text{syntax}_j(\Delta\text{proximity}_{ij}))) + VS_{ij}^{old}$$

Table 3. System processes rules

System Phases	[1]	[2]	[3]
Results:	Feedback	Inferential/Behavioral	Meanings
	Dialog state	Balance relations	Red-Black Semantics
	Sensing..Feeling	Static..Dynamic	RB values
	[0...0.5...1.0]	[0...0.5...1.0]	[0...0.5...1.0]
FORM elements STRUCTURE elements APPEARANCE elements			

10 Human Sensorial Experience

The need to define a specific methodology to convert the human sensorial system into virtual reality is of fundamental importance for this research. The center of the virtual environment is simultaneously the center of the human space where the kinematics rules generate the human sensorial perception processes. In fact, every direction of movement in the illusory space relates with the natural sense of orientation which is characterize with the same center of the space. The images are perceived with the oculomotor muscles changes of position, that leads to the simultaneous composition of the figures, dynamic relations, and the objective antithesis. The sensorial results coincide with the composition of a human behavior model developed from cybernetic studies[11]. The human perceptions decision-making processes are divided in sub-processes, structure or interconnection, with complex cycles of feedback, and a set of possible sensorial responses. On the basis of our artificial cognitive system called "Dialogue System"[12] the human emotional state changes the "human-machine" interaction processes. This fuzzy function relations produce a synaesthetic feedback

---

[10] Ibidem 5, "The semantic system", pag.186.

[11] Carver, C.S., Scheier,M., On the Self-Regulation of Behavior, Cambridge Univ. Press, London, 1998.

[12] Ibidem 8.

results to the human interactor. The synaesthesia is a particular emotional-feeling state that involves mutual influence between sensorial representations. Certain qualities of feeling, may be linked to other qualities of imagination and, as result, the system gives a high-level human feedback quality of synaesthetic perceptions.

11 Metaplastic Model Examples

The following proposed virtual space configurations give many examples of the model application. They are abstract cyberworlds, automata or "semi-machine", that interact symbiotically in different ways with the user, through their dynamic rules configurations. Their visual parameters define directly their behaviors and meaning through the "Red and Black" codifications. The metaplastic virtual worlds with the same settings criteria, could be grouped together in a set to define a new metaplastic language where each of them is a specific character of the alphabet.

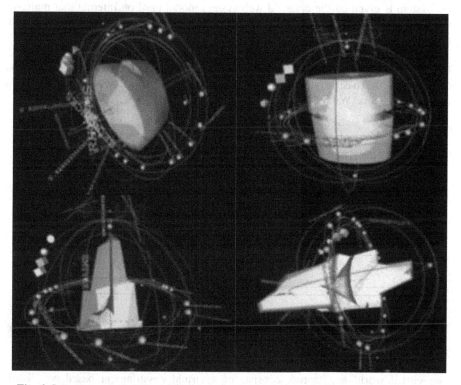

Fig. 6. Some examples of Form_Rhytm space configurations: [variance,sequence,chroma]

12 Synthetic Virtual Worlds Critical Considerations

I would like to add some considerations about the main differences of this virtual reality methodology from others. The Metaplastic model differs from other types of virtual world, because it proposes a different approach to construction of virtual reality based on a conceptual poetry of the virtual space. This conceptualization is completely opposed to the hyperreality virtual world type, like for example Second Life virtual reality model. I think that in the cyberspace it is unnecessary to reproduce metaphors of the real world. The metaplastic model offers the possibility to imagine and realize different kind of virtual space,which should be an infinite and creative landscape full of contents to explore.

13   System Implementation

The system proposes a complete virtual system implementation, and uses different standard technologies of communication, each with distinct functions. The process runs with external input devices activated with user's interactions, times or scene states(dragging, visibility, proximity, touching, collision,etc.) integrated in a readable VRML file standard format (Virtual Reality Modeling Language). The architecture of the system is given by the classical web system model used on Internet that manages the whole activity of the virtual environment. The system cooperates online between the client browser and the server through various plugged in software components.

The system provides the virtual space to the Client and connects it to the network. It is a 3D software cross-platform written in Java language which includes many 3d data format file (basically VRML and other object data files), suitable for the main operating systems (Windows, Linux, Java).

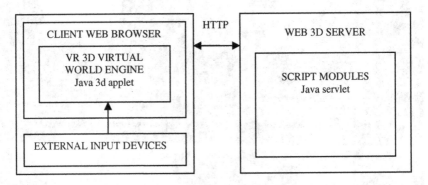

Fig. 7. System architecture description

13.1 The Virtual World Engine

The virtual world architecture consists of a virtual environment based on VRML Java3d applet running on the web browser. The software engine is based on a 3dGraphic Library that guides the system capabilities to draw the virtual space contents in real-time mode, through the meta-language setting rules. It runs with the following step process:

A.   The scene control begins with the user sensorial input analyses through the proximity function of the fuzzy dialog control system;

B. The Fuzzy state machine (FSM) makes the evaluations, previously defined from membership sets and fuzzy rules;

C. The Balance function makes its evaluation with previously calculated values. The Balance results activate all interaction processes and behaviours of the entire system; The resulting values compose the semantic codification of virtual space;

D. This step provides the 3d calculations to build up the virtual space model;

E. The virtual space scene is visualized with the system drawing functions. Within this phase, the system communicates with the web server to update the system states and gives the resulting feedback to the Fuzzy sensorial decision-making process (A phase). Finally, all the output results are combined with the user inputs into a new interaction cycle.

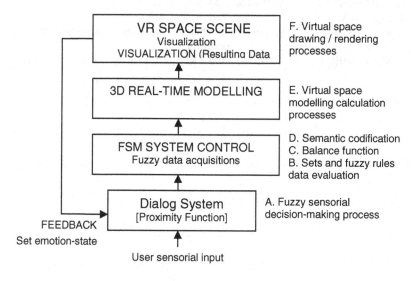

Fig. 8. Virtual space engine description

14 Conclusions and Future Works

The research improves and developes the previously published paper [1] which describes semantic space methodology. This approach, introduced by previous paper, creates cognition with new aesthetics of virtual space. The new modality of creation virtual spaces, uses human sensorial inputs and customize it within artistic machine metaphor for communication of knowledge. This new knowledge and aesthetic spaces uses standard web cross-platform technologies. The future works would be to build a new digital platform for media applications and improve this new research area.

References

1. Mura, G.: The red and black semantics: A fuzzy language. In: Cyberworlds 2006, pp. 183–190. IEEE, Los Alamitos (2006)
2. Kunii, T.L.: Cyberworld Modeling - integrating Cyberworlds, the Real World and Conceptual Worlds. In: Cyberworlds 2005 (CW 2005), pp. 3–11. IEEE, Los Alamitos (2005)
3. Kosko, B.: Il fuzzy pensiero, Baldini e Castoldi, Milano
4. Pedrycz, W.: Fuzzy control and Fuzzy systems. John Wiley, New York
5. Dubois, D., Prade, H.: Fundamentals of Fuzzy Sets. Springer, Berlin
6. Popper, K.R., Eccles, J.C.: The self and its brain. Springer, New York (1977)
7. Grau, O.: Virtual Art. MIT Press, MA (2003)
8. Kupka, A.: Creation dans les arts plastiques. Diagonales, Paris (2003)
9. Steven, R.: Holtzman. MIT Press, Digital Mantras (1994)
10. AA.VV.: Mazzotta (ed.) The Bauhaus, Milano (1996)
11. Moszynska, A.: L'Art abstrait, Thames&Hudson (2003)
12. Ammeraal, L.: Interactive 3D computer graphics. John Wiley, Chichester (1989)
13. The VRML Consortium, http://www.vrml.org
14. VRML, ISO/IEC 14772-1:1997, The Virtual Reality Modelling Language

Embodied Communication in the Distributed Network

Jillian Hamilton

Creative Industries Faculty, Queensland University of Technology, Kelvin Grove,
Queensland, Australia
jg.hamilton@qut.edu.au

Abstract. Through the adaptation of new technologies, the creative industries
are proposing new forms of interaction for the distributed network. This paper
considers the new media artwork *Intimate Transactions* as an example of a
creative, experimental approach to interaction and network technology. It
discusses this artwork's design of physical interaction, which includes whole-
body interaction with a hands-free input device; the incorporation of
choreographed interaction with its screen characters; the production of
generative, multi-sensory feedback around a dramaturgical model; and the use
of haptic devices to relay bodily movement across the network. It explains how
this physical interaction produces a sense of flow that perceptually suspends
awareness of the work's actual site in favour of a shared virtual space. It then
considers how this shared space becomes activated by multi-sensory feedback,
including the physical sensation of touch. It concludes that these innovative
approaches to physical interaction help to establish the potential for embodied
communication and co-presence within networked space.

Keywords: Interaction Design, New Media Art, flow, telepresence, embodied
interaction, network communication, co-presence.

1 Introduction

As the processes and roles of interaction design have begun to settle into conventional
forms that are transferred between technologies, the arts have started to present
challenges to our expectations of what is possible. As Jason Potts and others in the
field of complexity theory and evolutionary economics have argued, the creative
industries are involved in the process of experimentation, both through the *origination*
of ideas and the *adaptation* of new ideas and technologies.[1] Introducing ways of
thinking that are situated outside of the computer science and Human Computer
Interaction (HCI) models that we are familiar with, artists are adapting input devices
and screen interfaces to produce innovations in the field of interaction design. For
example, in a recent essay on her contribution to the collaborative new media artwork,
Intimate Transactions,[1] dancer and choreographer Lisa O'Neill wrote,

---

[1] *Intimate Transactions* has been installed at The Block at the Creative Industries Precinct,
QUT, Brisbane; the Australian Centre for the Moving Image, Melbourne; Ars Electronica
Festival, Linz, Austria; Artspace, Sydney; the Institute of Contemporary Art, London; and
Bios, Athens. The project was sponsored by the Australasian CRC for Interaction Design
(ACID), the Creative Industries Research and Applications Centre (CIRAC), QUT, Arts
Queensland and the Australia Council. See www.intimatetransactions.com

T.G. Wyeld, S. Kenderine, and M. Docherty (Eds.): VSMM 2007, LNCS 4820, pp. 179–190, 2008.
© Springer-Verlag Berlin Heidelberg 2008

> *[Suzuki Theatre's] understanding of the movement of the body through space influenced the design and structure of the main interaction device, the 'Bodyshelf'. This L shaped shelf, which is the height of a human body, was designed on a slant so that weight is taken off the feet and redistributed across the entire body ... [It] requires the participant to roll and press their back into it to activate the interaction. This helps to focus their attention on their middle body, and removes the usual inclination to control with the hands. The footpad of the Bodyshelf also drives the navigation. It was designed to be moveable so that the participant has to continually re-adjust and transfer their body weight ... as these movements become more intuitive, the participant is rewarded with the feeling that the body is in total play, moving in concert with the surrounding sounds and visual landscape.[2]*

It is perhaps not surprising that a dancer would question the confinement of our physical interaction with computer input devices to gestures of the wrists, hands and mouse, and would instead argue that the whole body should be brought into play. For the field of interaction design, it is a more unexpected move. And, for the user, this approach has created a new experience of the relationship between the body, the input device and the screen interface.

As *Intimate Transactions* evolved into a dual site installation linked by the distributed network, O'Neill's whole-body approach to interaction has produced an additional effect, which has implications for the broader field of network communication. In the networked version of this artwork, the Bodyshelf[2] has come to provide a dual function. At one level, users lean and roll on to it to drive their navigation of an avatar through a virtual environment and to interact with the creatures that inhabit it. In turn, the generative images, colour bursts, and sound-scapes that are triggered as feedback are complemented by textured vibrations, which ripple through a haptic pendant on the participant's chest as well as through the Bodyshelf onto their backs. In this way, the Bodyshelf facilitates both interaction with, and feedback from, the screen-world. At a second level, the Bodyshelf facilitates interaction between users located at separate sites. As they both collect assets from the creatures, the vitality of their shared environment gradually slows down and they must co-operate to restore its integrity. They must conjoin their avatars and work in unison to return assets to the creatures. Again this interaction relies upon movements on the Bodyshelf, which navigate the conjoined avatars. And again, the Bodyshelf provides a conduit for feedback. When their avatars are interlocked, the users can feel each other's push and pull through the Bodyshelf. As their motion is relayed back and forth, they become part of a remote, embodied collaboration. Their communication relies as much on touch as vision and sound.

In this paper I discuss *Intimate Transactions*, an interactive new media artwork by the interdisciplinary research team, the Transmute Collective,[3] as an example of a

---

[2] The Bodyshelf was designed by artist Zeljko Markov.

[3] The Transmute Collective includes artistic director, Keith Armstrong; choreographer, Lisa O'Neill; and sound designer, Guy Webster. On this project they collaborated with artist Zeljko Markov (design of the Bodyshelf), programmers Marcos Cáceres and Cameron Owen (System Design), artists Benedict Foley and Stuart Lawson (character animation) and spatial architects Pia Ednie-Brown and Inger Mewburn (haptic feedback devices).

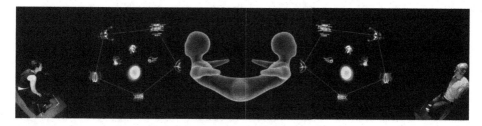

Fig. 1. Composite image of *Intimate Transactions* showing users at two sites, with conjoined avatars in a shared screen-world. Photo credit: Erica Fish. Artwork: Benedict Foley and Stuart Lawson.

creative, experimental approach to interaction and network technology. I describe its innovative approaches to physical interaction, which include whole-body interaction with a hands-free input device; the incorporation of choreographed interaction with the work's screen characters; the production of generative, multi-sensory feedback around a dramaturgical model; and the use of haptic feedback devices to relay bodily motion through the network. Drawing on the work of social, spatial and HCI theorists, I explain how this physical approach to interaction design takes this artwork beyond harnessing fast-speed data transfer to perceptually diminish the distance between co-located users. I argue that it helps to cause perceptions of the work's actual site (the space of the gallery) to be suspended and increases the sense of presence in a shared virtual space. I then establish that this shared space becomes activated through multi-sensory feedback, including the physical sensation of touch, to produce a form of embodied communication. Through this discussion, I argue that physical interaction, and the transfer of sensory feedback across the network, produces a form of telepresence that can be described as embodied co-presence.

2 Embodied Immersion

In a study on user experience of *Intimate Transactions*, HCI researchers Jamie Madden and Stephen Viller noted that users reported a high level of engagement in the work's virtual world, which produced an altered perception of the flow of time.[3] To understand this phenomenon, it is important to understand the approach that has been taken to the design of this artwork. *Intimate Transactions* is unusual as an artwork because it is temporal and processual in nature. Unlike a typical (static and material) art object, it relies upon the user's physical participation to bring it into being, and their ongoing interaction to maintain its presence in the world. This ongoing generation of the work contributes to the transformation of perceptions of time and the space of the gallery, but it is the work's interaction design that largely produces that transformation. The movements that are required to activate the motion sensors embedded in the surfaces of the Bodyshelf shift the user from a relatively passive role to a physically engrossing, whole-body interaction with the work's input device, and with its internal world.

Through reference to the work of several social and spatial theorists, as well as writings on aspects of HCI, I will establish why the space, time and other occupants of the gallery appear to fall away during interaction with this artwork, in favour of the user's relationship with the work's internal (virtual) environment and a distant, unknown collaborator within it. I will argue that embodied immersion is produced by this interactive artwork in three, inter-related ways: the absorption of the input device into the user's body image, the integration of the screen interface into the user's extended body boundaries, and the activation of surrounding space through multisensory and haptic feedback.

2.1 Absorbing the Input Device into the User's Body Image

The first aspect of embodied immersion occurs through the absorption of the input device, the Bodyshelf, into the user's 'body image'. Through reference to psychoanalyst Paul Schilder's work on 'body image', the writing of social theorist Elizabeth Grosz helps to explain this effect.[4] Grosz argues that, perceptually, the boundaries of our body image are not fixed but fluid and 'osmotic'. Objects, implements or instruments – from a scalpel or pen to a jet aircraft – become absorbed into our body image when we use them as a tool or medium of expression. During the period of their use, the implements we use become intimate, vital extensions of our body image. When we use a mouse or a joystick as a tool for interaction, this effect no doubt occurs. Much like a pen or a scalpel, we move them as if they are an extension of our hand and arm. We relay our intentions through them, becoming less aware of their physicality than our effect through and beyond them.

The process of absorbing a mouse or joystick is localised and limited to the hand or arm that uses it however. Explaining the process of absorbing tools into our body image in its most complex form, Grosz refers to the example of a vehicle. Describing the process of maneuvering a car, she writes, "Chasing another car or trying to fit into a small parking spot, are all experienced in the body image of the driver".[4] When driving, we experience the vehicle as an extension of our physical self because we must continually anticipate and incorporate the effects of our physical motion upon the vehicle in its entirety. As we determine its motion and direction through our body movements, we must continually take the girth of the vehicle into account to avoid a collision. We must perceptually project our body boundaries outwards, and absorb the vehicle's physical proportions into them, to be able to do so. Interaction through the Bodyshelf as an input device works in a similar way.

Like a car, the Bodyshelf encompasses the entire body. And, like a car, it requires movements that simultaneously involve both core and peripheral zones of the body to affect navigation. Together, these factors contribute to the device becoming absorbed into the body image in its entirety. And, while the Bodyshelf does not actually move as a car does, the enveloping screen-world and evolving surround-sound produce the sensation of such motion. The effect of whole-body movement upon navigational motion through this space means that the user perceptually takes the vehicle – the Bodyshelf – with them.

The process of incorporating material objects into our body image is not immediate or seamless. As Grosz suggests,

Part of the difficulty of learning how to use [implements and instruments] is not simply the technical problem of how they are used but also the libidinal problem of how they become part of the body image, a body shell for the subject.[4]

This is certainly the case with a car, as anyone who has learnt to drive can attest. It also helps to explain often-reported experiences of interacting with the Bodyshelf. One of the findings of Madden and Viller was that at first it requires self-conscious, intellectual grappling with multiple bodily movements and their various effects in the screen-space but, at some point during the twenty-minute experience of *Intimate Transactions*, a transition tends to occur as the body eases into the pace and rhythm of the onscreen avatar.[3] When it does, the Bodyshelf that sits behind the user has become absorbed into their body image. It becomes part of the expression of the body in action and, as O'Neill suggests above, the user is "rewarded with the feeling that the body is in total play, moving in concert with the surrounding sounds and visual landscape".[2]

2.2 Bridging the Space between the Body and the Screen

Besides incorporating the Bodyshelf that sits behind them into their body image, the user also projects forward, to incorporate the field of the screen. A pioneer of interactive cinema, Toni Dove, has pointed out that interacting with a responsive screen interface is significantly different to observing a screened film.[5] The audience of a movie may empathise with a character, and may even 'enter' the screen-space in terms of visual perception (because, as Laura Mulvey points out, film-making conventions tend to assume the spectator's point of view[6]), however the viewer remains physically passive. Therefore, the inactive and disassociated body remains behind. By contrast, the body assumes an active role in relation to a screen avatar. As a user exerts their agency, and the avatar immediately responds to their body's actions, an integrated relationship is produced in which the viewer comes to feel connected with, or 'stuck to', the character. Dove suggests that this 'tug' of the avatar leads to a partial transference of the self into the screen-space. She argues that, "[the subject becomes] simultaneously aware of their presence 'in' their body and 'in' the screen". She concludes that, to overcome this split in location, the subject perceptually traverses the intermediate space, causing it to become 'activated' or 'charged'.

Dove's argument is made in relation to common computer-screen interfaces and mouse-to-screen interaction with an avatar that moves laterally across the screen-space. In comparison, the potential for bridging the space between the body and the screen is maximised in *Intimate Transactions* in two ways. Firstly, because its highly rendered avatars and characters move both laterally and into a third dimension, slipping through a layered series of deeper inner worlds, a spatial depth is produced which 'pulls' the user beyond the surface of the projection screen into a fathomless anterior space. This causes the physical properties of the screen, and the sense of a two-dimensional surface, to perceptually recede. Increasing the 'tug' of the character in this way heightens the sense of 'presence' in the screen-world. In turn, this serves to intensify the perceptual traversal of the intermediate space between the user and the screen.

Intimate Transactions further increases the sense of integration with the screen character through the type of body movements that it requires for interaction. These movements were choreographed by O'Neill in line with the Suzuki Actor Training Method.[2] They revolve through the centre of the body, pivoting around a central hinge: what she describes as the body's 'energy centre'. The kernel of these gestures has been transposed into the characteristics of the onscreen avatar, which moves through the same central axis. The movements of the user are thereby simultaneously located both within their own body and within the body of their screen character/avatar. They are mirrored not only in the direction of action, but through the very qualities of movement. This shared gestural expression serves to enrich the connection with the screen character which, in turn, increases the potential for immersion in the activity and presence in the screen-space. This also optimises the potential for a perceptual traversal of the intermediate space.

2.3 Immersion through Multi-sensory Feedback

The activation of the space surrounding the user is completed by the multi-sensory feedback that is produced in response to interactions with the screen-world inhabitants of *Intimate Transactions*. In line with her background in performance, O'Neill took a dramaturgical approach to defining their characters.[2] Each creature has been inscribed with a unique personality, causing them to react in highly individuated ways. Some move gently away from movements towards them, others emit screeching, violent vibrations and swirling floods of colour. An interdisciplinary team of graphic artists, animators, sound artists and haptic spatial architects designed this multi-sensory feedback. Regardless of the diversity of this collaboration, the feedback is always combined in concert because it was developed around a dramaturgical model. It is unified by a personality profile, which dictates each creature's style of response. Contingent upon the avatar's relative distance from each of the creatures, a unique combination of changes to the onscreen images; the rhythm, tempo and volume of the sound-scape; and the texture of vibrations is perpetually produced. In effect, an integrated, multi-sensory environment is composed, on the fly, by the user's physical gestures.

The approach of integrating multiple forms of sensory media is not uncommon in the art world. The synthesis of music, dance, poetry, visual arts, and performance can be traced back as far as 1849 and Wagner's Gesamtkunstwerk or 'Total Artwork', in which opera served as a vehicle for the "fusion of the arts". It is evident in many genres, from Futurist cinema and Bauhaus theatre to contemporary 'happenings', performance and installation art. The purpose of synthesising multi-sensory media is to absorb the audience in the artwork. Wagner described this effect, writing that, "[the public] forgets the confines of the auditorium, and lives and breathes only in the artwork".[7]

Combining sensory media has a similar purpose in multimedia design. As Randall Packer and Ken Jordon point out, multimedia is intended to "appeal to all the senses simultaneously".[8] It absorbs the audience into the work and diminishes the user's attention to their external surroundings. It is now well established within the field of HCI that even low levels of visual or auditory feedback contribute to a user's sense of 'flow' – that is immersion in an activity that leads to an altered perception of time and the exclusion of peripheral surroundings and events.[9] If we extend Wagner's principle, providing multi-sensory feedback serves to increase the potential for flow and immersion in the work to the exclusion of peripheral activity. *Intimate Transactions*, which triggers integrated layers of surround sound, resonant imagery, and vibration, which engulf the user in response to their interactions, maximises this effect.

Intimate Transactions therefore provides us with an example of how embodied interaction can increase the potential for immersion in several, inter-related ways. Its input device – the Bodyshelf that sits behind the user – becomes an extension of the body in action and is absorbed into the body image of the user. At the same time, the mirroring of the user's bodily motility and expression in the onscreen avatar establishes a sense of presence in the screen-space, and a bridging of the intermediate space between the action of the body and the action on the screen. Therefore, both posterior and anterior space is traversed, perceptually embraced and absorbed. As the user performs within this suspended space, they are enveloped by multi-sensory feedback, which further contributes to the diminution of peripheral activity and awareness of the physical site. As Kristine Nowak and Frank Biocca point out, producing such a sense of presence (a compelling sense of 'being there' in a virtual or technologically mediated environment to the exclusion of physical location) has been recognised as a key performance goal for interactive systems.[10]

3   Embodied Co-presence

So far I have considered how embodied interaction can increase immersion and presence in a virtual environment and its internal activities. Now I will consider how it can make a significant contribution to the experience of online communication. *Intimate Transactions* again provides a useful case study because it operates on two levels of interaction – with the inhabitants of the internal world as well as with a user at a distant site. While users tend to begin interacting with this work by following the established conventions of computer games and collecting an array of assets (flora, insects and crustaceans) from the creatures in the world, after a time their attention must turn to collaboration with another user. The work's system design is built around a metaphor of ecological footprinting and the impact that the degradation of a local environment has on the global environment. This conceptual framework, which was developed by the work's artistic director Keith Armstrong, means that the gradual depletion of resources in either of the two users' interconnected virtual worlds affects the vitality of both [11]. The creatures begin to shudder, images dim, sound softens, and movement slows down. This gives rise to the need for the users to establish a co-operative relationship. To restore the viability of their co-dependent environments, they must connect and collaborate. Their avatars locked together, they must work together to return the assets to the creatures in order to reinstate the integrity of their shared world.

3.1 Telepresent Insight and Affect

This relationship between the users is mediated through the distributed network. GrangeNet, which transmits data between sites almost 20 000 times faster than a 56k modem,[12] is used to link the museum locations. This fast-speed data transfer enables aspects of telepresence. It means that a user is able to both affect and observe an event's occurrence at a remote site in real time.

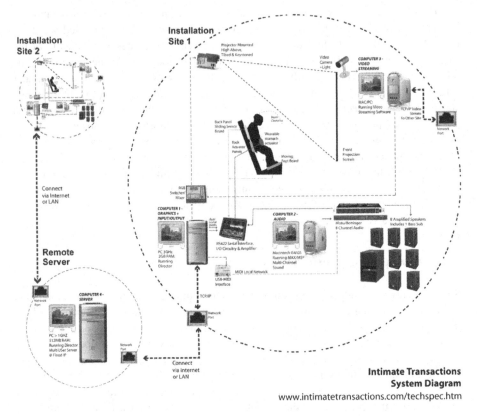

Fig. 2. *Intimate Transactions* System Diagram. Diagram: Keith Armstrong.

We have become familiar with a number of preliminary forms of telepresent insight and effect that have been delivered by network communication since the end of the twentieth century. For example, we have come to expect news feeds from site after site to bounce off satellites and ricochet through the network to provide us with a kaleidoscopic world-view. And, by entering our pin number at an ATM or ordering a book online, we regularly extend our intentions beyond the screen and through the network to prompt action from databases at distant sites. Such telepresent insight and effect is produced through the perceptual contraction of the space between sites, which is effectively produced through the compression of response time.

A number of interactive new media artworks harness network technology to experiment with telepresent insight and effect. For example, Jeffrey Shaw's *The Legible City* (1989-90) uses motion-tracking technology to allow visitors to navigate through an external site when pedalling a surrogate bicycle within the gallery. It provides a remote view into another location. Ken Goldberg and Joseph Santarromana's *Telegarden* (1995) uses telerobotics to allow online audiences to control an environment within the gallery. It allows users to affect a distant location. Like these works, *Intimate Transactions* breaches the architectural confines of the gallery and spans geographical distance. However it conjoins two geographically separated gallery sites and combines these aspects of telepresence. As users at each site interact with each other, the distance between sites appears to contract around an interim shared world, which both can see and affect.

According to some theorists, even preliminary forms of telepresence cause us to reconfigure our body image.[5] As we simultaneously act at both the site of our physical presence and the distant site, we reach beyond our corporeal selves, beyond our physical limits, and become co-located. Again, we achieve the sense of being there – 'there' in this context being a distant location rather than an internal screen world. *Intimate Transactions* allows its users to achieve this co-location and sense of being there through presence in a virtual environment that is suspended between geographically separated sites. And, through its embodied interaction, it allows them to experience the sense of being there with someone else.

3.2 Embodied Communication

Embodied communication within the shared space of *Intimate Transactions* is produced through two means. The first is inter-identification between avatars. As I have noted in the previous section, avatars provide a visual representation of both users in the *Intimate Transactions* environment and a user's identification with their avatar is increased through its reflection of both the direction and the physical qualities of their motion. It is important to note that the avatar of the second user is similar in form and motility, pivoting through its 'energy centre' to produce familiar expressive qualities. While Madden and Viller suggest that this similarity can potentially lead to difficulties distinguishing between the avatars (they differ only in their visual intensity),[3] it can equally be argued that it serves to produce a secondary identification. Nowak and Biocca suggest that using visual avatars in computer-mediated collaborative environments helps to provide users with a sense of each other's presence.[10] Moreover, they have established that people are more comfortable communicating with those who look like them, and so feel familiar. This suggests that designing similar avatars for both users extends the perceptual 'tug' of a user's own onscreen character to the avatar of the second user. A user's relationship with the other user's avatar is experienced both 'in' the body and 'in' the screen. As one user commented, "Once I saw the other participant, I wanted to dance".[3] This is the experience of co-presence – the sense that a person with whom one is communicating, is in a shared physical space, despite their remote location.[13]

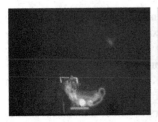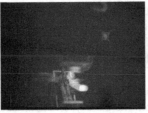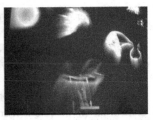

Fig. 3. A user on the Bodyshelf engaged in collaboration with another user across the network showing avatar-to-avatar interaction. Photo credit: Peter Cullin

The second form of embodied communication that is produced by *Intimate Transactions* comes about through the relay of haptic feedback between the sites. When their avatars are conjoined, and they work co-operatively to return assets to the creatures, users can feel each other's movements through the Bodyshelf, which presses against their backs. In effect, they can feel the push of resistance or pull of co-operation as they negotiate the direction of the interlocked avatars. This introduction of tactile sensation establishes a physical relationship between the users. It produces an effect that is quite different to that of other telematic art, such as *Telematic Dreaming* by Paul Sermon (1992). In that artwork, two participants lie on beds at separate sites and each sees a high-definition projection of the other beside them. They can react, in real time, to the movements, gestures and voice of this apparition as it is relayed through high-speed video-conferencing between sites. According to some reviewers, *Telematic Dreaming* produces a sensory impression of tactile interplay between participants.[14] But this sensation is achieved synaesthetically. Within *Intimate Transactions*, the collaborator's presence is experienced through a combination of relayed visual representation, surround sound, and physical sensation relayed through the Bodyshelf.

This dual form of embodied communication has quite a profound implication. If, as I have argued in the previous section, the user becomes immersed within the work through their simultaneous absorption of the Bodyshelf into their body image and projection into the screen-world, then it follows that their relationship with the other user is experienced within this suspended space. Their touch is experienced within the space of the Bodyshelf, which has been absorbed into the user's body image, and as embodied interaction within the traversed space of the screen-world. That is, an embodied relationship with someone thousands of kilometers away is wrapped, libidinally, into the intensely intimate space of the user's extended body boundaries. This extends the potential of presence within a virtual environment to embodied co-presence within networked space.

4   Reducing the Distance between Us

At its best, art does more than simply adopt new technologies to illustrate contemporary concerns. It is an experimental site of research that approaches technology, materials and concepts laterally to produce innovation. This is the case with the *Intimate Transactions* project. Its design, including a whole of body interaction with a hands-free input device; the incorporation of choreographed interaction with the screen characters; the production of generative, multi-sensory feedback around a dramaturgical model; and the use of haptic devices to transmit bodily movement across the network, all make significant contributions to the developing field of interaction design. Together, these innovations combine to produce an embodied interaction, which increases the potential for a perceptual compression of distance between co-located users; an immersive participation within an intimate, suspended space of a shared world; and the sensation of embodied co-presence.

This potential carries significant benefits for the field of networked communication. While online representational relationships that are played out vicariously through avatars in games and virtual environments are not new, they are largely based on visual icons, digital dialogue and/or aural communication. Because they are not configured around face-to-face relationships, they lack the cues that are offered by physical proximity. *Intimate Transactions* provides a model through which networked relationships can move beyond autonomous verbal communication into the realm of a shared corporeal – visual, aural and tactile – engagement. That is, it establishes the possibility of an enriched, intimate transaction within networked space.

Acknowledgments. This paper has been adapted from the art-historical essay by the author: A Reformation of Space: *Intimate Transactions* in Art and Distributed Communication. In: Hamilton, J. (ed.) *Intimate Transactions*: Art, Exhibition and Interaction within Distributed Network Environments, Australasian CRC for Interaction Design: Brisbane (2006). Thanks to Phil Graham for his advice on this adaptation.

References

1. Potts, J.: Economic Growth and Creative Industries, Lecture 2 New Economics of the Creative Industries (2007)
2. O'Neill, L.: Placing the Participant in the Performing Role. In: Hamilton, J. (ed.) Intimate Transactions: Art, Exhibition and Interaction within Distributed Network Environments, Australasian CRC for Interaction Design: Brisbane, pp. 36–43 (2007)
3. Madden, J., Viller, S.: Am I the Lighter One? Awareness in a Dual Site Networked Installation. In: Hamilton, J. (ed.) Intimate Transactions: Art, Exhibition and Interaction within Distributed Network Environments, Australasian CRC for Interaction Design: Brisbane, pp. 98–105 (2007)
4. Grosz, E.: Volatile Bodies; Towards a Corporeal Feminism. Allen and Unwin, Sydney (1994)
5. Dove, T.: The Space Between: Telepresence, Re-animation and the Re-casting of the Invisible. In: Reiser, M., Zapp, A. (eds.) New Screen Media: Cinema/Art/Narrative, British Film Institute, London (2002)
6. Mulvey, L.: Visual Pleasure and Narrative Cinema. In: Bennett, T., et al. (eds.) Popular Television and Film, British Film Institute, London (1981)
7. Packer, R., Jordon, K.: Multimedia from Wagner to Virtual Reality (accessed, September 2006), http://www.artmuseum.net/w2vr/timeline/Wagner.html

8. Packer, R., Jordon, K.: Multimedia from Wagner to Virtual Reality. WW Norton, New York (2001)
9. Pace, S.: A Grounded Theory of the Flow Experiences of Web Users. International Journal of Human-Computer Studies 60, 327–363 (2004)
10. Nowak, K.L., Biocca, F.: The Effect of Agency and Anthropomorphism on Users' Sense of Telepresence, Copresence, and Social Presence in Virtual Environments. Presence 12(5), 481–494 (2003)
11. Armstrong, K.: Towards a Connective and Ecosophical New Media Art Practice. In: Hamilton, J. (ed.) Intimate Transactions: Art, Exhibition and Interaction within Distributed Network Environments, Australasian CRC for Interaction Design: Brisbane, pp. 12–36 (2007)
12. Wickham, G.: (Infrastructure Development Group, AARNet): Email correspondence with the author, 'How fast is GrangeNet?' (9 October 2006 11:51:44 AM)
13. International Society for Presence Research. The Concept of Presence: Explication Statement (2000). (Accessed, August 2007), http://ispr.info
14. Grau, O.: Virtual Art: From Illusion to Immersion. MIT Press, Cambridge Mass (2003)

Interactive High Resolution Texture Mapping for the 3D Models of Cultural Heritages

Changyu Diao and Dongming Lu

College of Computer Science and Technology, Zhejiang University, 310027, Hangzhou, Zhejiang, China
`Joyrain, ldm@zju.edu.cn`

Abstract. Virtual reconstruction of cultural heritage is not only the basis but also one of important contents of its digitized research. The techniques of interactive texture reconstruction researched in this article are of great significance to heighten the effect of virtual reconstruction of cultural heritage. Firstly, interactive and precise texture mapping is aiming at establishing the relationship between texture images and 3D models by appointed corresponding points interactively. The process is based on the traditional camera calibration. For a camera with known intrinsic parameters, three pair of corresponding points will be used to calculate the initial value of extrinsic parameters, and more corresponding points will be used to refine the result. For a camera with unknown intrinsic parameters, an implicit projection matrix will be calculated directly. Secondly, a fast occlusion culling method will be used to remove hidden triangle from texture mapping. At last, a natural neighbor interpolation method will be used to minimize the texture mapping error caused by lens distortion of the camera and the error of 3D scanner.

Keywords: Texture Mapping, Camera Calibration, Extrinsic Parameters Calibration, natural neighbor interpolation, digital cultural heritage.

1 Introduction

Traditional 3d modeling software, such as 3DS MAX, MAYA, are difficult to meet the demands of photo texture mapping, because they can only provide planar texture mapping, cylinder texture mapping, sphere texture mapping, cubic texture mapping, etc. As is often the case, the geometrical shape of cultural heritage is scanned by a 3D scanner and the surface texture is photographed by a digital camera. In order to show the object vividly, the color and the shape must be bound together, which entails the necessity of camera calibration (either explicitly or implicitly) [1].

A set of photos recording surface texture are usually taken by the same camera. As a result, the intrinsic parameters (Among them the focal length is fixed if not optically zoomed when taking the photos.) are fixed and can be known in advance either from the manual given by the manufacturer or the picture properties for focal length or by calibration.

For implicit camera calibration, the projection matrix is solved directly, and the intrinsic parameters are mixed with extrinsic parameters. Implicit camera calibration

T.G. Wyeld, S. Kenderdine, and M. Docherty (Eds.): VSMM 2007, LNCS 4820, pp. 191–202, 2008.

is sufficient in some applications, say, stereovision. But the components in the matrix lack of physical implication and in some literatures [1-2], they are called implicit parameters base on this reason. In other applications such as motion analysis and texture mapping, however, the intrinsic and extrinsic parameters must be acquired, requiring the decomposing of the matrix. Un-fortunately, experiments show that the decomposition will introduce unacceptable error, making the former approach unfit for applications like motion analysis and texture mapping. These applications must use the explicit camera calibration approach, which this article also concentrates on.

In this paper, an explicit camera calibration method will be introduced first, which depend on more than 3 pair of arbitrary corresponding points. Then, a fast occlusion culling algorithm will be used to remove hidden triangles for projective texture mapping. At last, an N-N (nearest neighbor) interpolation algorithm will be selected to improve the texture mapping accuracy. Some texture mapping result will be given at the end of this paper.

2 Calculating the Projection Matrix

Camera coordinate system and world coordinate system conforms to the relationship in equation (1), where R is shown in equation (2), where Rx, Ry and Rz are in equation (3), (4) and (5), respectively. Heikkila and Silven [2] gave each element of rotation matrix R. in equation (1) of that paper.

$$[X_c \ Y_c \ Z_c \ 1]^T = \begin{bmatrix} R & T \\ 0^T & 1 \end{bmatrix} [X_w \ Y_w \ Z_w \ 1]^T \tag{1}$$

$$R = \begin{bmatrix} R_{11} & R_{12} & R_{13} \\ R_{21} & R_{22} & R_{23} \\ R_{31} & R_{32} & R_{33} \end{bmatrix} = R_z R_y R_x \tag{2}$$

$$R_z = \begin{bmatrix} \cos\kappa & -\sin\kappa & 0 \\ \sin\kappa & \cos\kappa & 0 \\ 0 & 0 & 1 \end{bmatrix} \tag{3}$$

$$R_y = \begin{bmatrix} \cos\varphi & 0 & \sin\varphi \\ 0 & 1 & 0 \\ -\sin\varphi & 0 & \cos\varphi \end{bmatrix} \tag{4}$$

$$R_x = \begin{bmatrix} 1 & 0 & 0 \\ 0 & \cos\omega & -\sin\omega \\ 0 & \sin\omega & \cos\omega \end{bmatrix} \tag{5}$$

It is obvious that if the signs of $\sin\omega$, $\cos\omega$, $\cos\varphi$, $\sin\kappa$ and $\cos\kappa$ in equation (1) of [3] are reversed simultaneously, the rotation matrix will not changed. As a result, $\cos\kappa$ can be confined to be nonnegative since the negative solution leads to the same rotation matrix, meaning that these 2 solutions are equivalent. All in all, three rotation angles (ω, φ and κ) and a translation vector (T) of 3 components (T_x, T_y and T_z) can uniquely describe the orientation and position of a camera. If a camera is subjected to the pinhole model (If not, it can be adjusted to by correcting the lens and CCD distortion), then we get equation (6), where a_x, a_y, u_0 along with v_0 are the intrinsic parameters, K the intrinsic parameters matrix and E the extrinsic parameters matrix. For extrinsic parameters calibration or camera pose estimation, the objective is to identify the position and orientation of a camera given the intrinsic parameters of that camera. From (2) and (6), we obtain equation (7) or (8), which is equivalent to the system of equations in (9).

$$
Z_c\begin{bmatrix} u \\ v \\ 1 \end{bmatrix} = \begin{bmatrix} \frac{1}{dx} & 0 & u_0 \\ 0 & \frac{1}{dy} & v_0 \\ 0 & 0 & 1 \end{bmatrix}\begin{bmatrix} f & 0 & 0 & 0 \\ 0 & f & 0 & 0 \\ 0 & 0 & 1 & 0 \end{bmatrix}\begin{bmatrix} R & T \\ 0^T & 1 \end{bmatrix}\begin{bmatrix} X_w \\ Y_w \\ Z_w \\ 1 \end{bmatrix} = \begin{bmatrix} a_x & 0 & u_0 & 0 \\ 0 & a_y & v_0 & 0 \\ 0 & 0 & 1 & 0 \end{bmatrix}\begin{bmatrix} R & T \\ 0^T & 1 \end{bmatrix}\begin{bmatrix} X_w \\ Y_w \\ Z_w \\ 1 \end{bmatrix} = [K \ \ 0]E\vec{X}_w = M\vec{X}_w \tag{6}
$$

$$
Z_c\begin{bmatrix} u \\ v \\ 1 \end{bmatrix} = \begin{bmatrix} a_x & 0 & u_0 & 0 \\ 0 & a_y & v_0 & 0 \\ 0 & 0 & 1 & 0 \end{bmatrix}\begin{bmatrix} R_{11} & R_{12} & R_{13} & t_x \\ R_{21} & R_{22} & R_{23} & t_y \\ R_{31} & R_{32} & R_{33} & t_z \\ 0 & 0 & 0 & 1 \end{bmatrix}\begin{bmatrix} X_w \\ Y_w \\ Z_w \\ 1 \end{bmatrix} \tag{7}
$$

$$
Z_c\begin{bmatrix} u \\ v \\ 1 \end{bmatrix} = \begin{bmatrix} a_x(R_{11}X_w + R_{12}Y_w + R_{13}Z_w + t_x) + u_0(R_{31}X_w + R_{32}Y_w + R_{33}Z_w + t_z) \\ a_y(R_{21}X_w + R_{22}Y_w + R_{23}Z_w + t_y) + v_0(R_{31}X_w + R_{32}Y_w + R_{33}Z_w + t_z) \\ R_{31}X_w + R_{32}Y_w + R_{33}Z_w + t_z \end{bmatrix} \tag{8}
$$

$$
\begin{cases} u = \dfrac{a_x(R_{11}X_w + R_{12}Y_w + R_{13}Z_w + t_x)}{R_{31}X_w + R_{32}Y_w + R_{33}Z_w + t_z} + u_0 \\ v = \dfrac{a_y(R_{21}X_w + R_{22}Y_w + R_{23}Z_w + t_y)}{R_{31}X_w + R_{32}Y_w + R_{33}Z_w + t_z} + v_0 \end{cases} \tag{9}
$$

From equation (9), for each point-target, 2 equations are given. Hence, theoretically, a minimum of 3 point-targets is required to solve the 6 unknown parameters, which define the extrinsic matrix. If more than 3 are given, equation (9) is over determined and has to be solved by minimizing the RMS (root mean square) error, as in [3]. Let u_i and v_i denote the theoretical value computed by pinhole model and U_i and V_i the real value observed from picture, then the objective function is

$$
F = \sum_{i=1}^{N}(U_i - u_i)^2 + \sum_{i=1}^{N}(V_i - v_i)^2 \tag{10}
$$

Minimizing function F gives the calibration result. Since the minimization process is quite complex if the orthogonal constraint for matrix R is taken into consideration, there're alternative approaches, all of which have disadvantages. Zhengyou [4] did not take the orthogonal constraint into account at first and then used an orthogonal matrix to approximate the so-called rotation matrix R, which was not orthogonal. Needless to say, this approach will introduce error inevitably since finding a conditional extreme value is not equivalent to finding an extreme value and then conditioned. Hynek [4] considered the orthogonal constraint but the algorithm imposed that all calibration points should be coplanar, not meeting the case of texture mapping. The approach in [5] requires at least 7 input corresponding points for the noncoplanar case. But this requirement is strict for smooth surfaced object since it's not easy to select so many corresponding points (usually corner points for accuracy) on it. Bodo, Yiwen and Sommer [6] claimed that the calibration process could be achieved by optimizing the convex function $MX'\tilde{M}$, which was free from local minimum. But M was computed from 3 rotation angles and a translation vector, and the computing function was not convex. A new collinear constraint was put forward by Yonghuai and Horst [7], which can decompose the calibration problem into two sub problems, i.e. finding the optimal R and optimal T. But it's at the cost of time complexity since the new constrains is $O(n^2)$ and the old is only $O(n)$ and if the old is satisfied, the new is doomed to be satisfied. And its function is $a_{i,j}^T R b_{i,j} = 0$, the solution will not necessarily minimize function F in (10). The suggestion of reducing the original into two subproblems is instructive and the algorithm in this paper is implemented in a similar way to reduce the searching cost.

Substituting (9) into (10) yields:

$$F = \sum_i \left\{ \left[\frac{a_x(R_{11}X_{wi} + R_{12}Y_{wi} + R_{13}Z_{wi} + t_x)}{R_{31}X_{wi} + R_{32}Y_{wi} + R_{33}Z_{wi} + t_z} + u_0 - U_i \right]^2 + \left[\frac{a_y(R_{21}X_{wi} + R_{22}Y_{wi} + R_{23}Z_{wi} + t_y)}{R_{31}X_{wi} + R_{32}Y_{wi} + R_{33}Z_{wi} + t_z} + v_0 - V_i \right]^2 \right\} \tag{11}$$

By minimizing function F in (11), R and T is solved. To speed up the searching process and reduce the danger of finding local minimum, 3 principles are established, as shown in the ensuing subsection.

2.1 Searching Principles and Steps

Good Initial Value. If the initial value is poor, it will undoubtedly increase the searching cost for more iteration is needed. More important, it will find the local minimum, as exemplified in Table 1 if the searching starts from (-1.4, 2.9, 3.0). When 3 points are given, it is feasible to directly and accurately solve the extrinsic parameters. Usually, 2 results are output since none of the 6 equations is linear. If n points are given,   initial value candidates are found by selecting any 3 from n and using direct computation. Function F in equation (11) is evaluated by all of them and the candidate that minimize F is elected as the initial value.

Table 1. Local minimum (LM) vs. global minimum (GM)

x_w	y_w	z_w	U	V
6.221232891	0.458065927	1.549257040	2791.850586	1884.525757
6.095024109	0.5156071186	-1.680388927	2825.567383	2082.859131
-4.587436676	1.024667501	-1.201305985	2141.317139	2126.492432
-5.224579334	1.044870019	-0.4425628185	2089.750488	2080.875732
-6.545889378	0.8886194229	1.430994987	1988.600342	1969.809082
-5.844654083	0.979618609	0.5761668682	2042.150391	2021.375732

a_x	a_y	u_0	v_0
8943.89011	8938.56210	2152.88529	1244.78065

ω (LM)	φ (LM)	κ (LM)	t_x (LM)	t_y (LM)	t_z (LM)
-1.400899083	2.884687927	3.005351407	3.775047219	11.898234944	134.7367555 3

RMS (LM)	4.284496580395

ω (GM)	φ (GM)	κ (GM)	t_x (GM)	t_y (GM)	t_z (GM)
1.141221226	-0.276178279	-0.062369939	4.247078843	11.440582880	135.1868425 9

RMS (GM)	1.059562703376

Searching by Derivative Function. It's true that only by searching the function value the minimum value can still be found out. But it's slower than by searching its derivative function because even for the golden section search, capable of fully utilizing the value evaluated in the previous iteration, the interval is decrease to 0.618 of the previous one. But if it's done by searching the zero point of its derivative function provided that it exists, the interval is decrease to 0.5 of the previous one if bisection search is employed. The ratio is ln0.618 / ln0.5 = 1 / 1.44. Furthermore, since searching is done in function domain, the function value evaluated by value close to the current value tends to have a tiny difference when compared with that evaluated by the current one when it is sufficiently close to the optimal variable because its derivative, if existing, is close to zero. This difference may even be concealed by the numerical error introduced by a computer, thus it's more likely to find a false value that optimize the function. Consequently, it's more precise if the zero point of its derivative counter-part is searched. But a common pitfall should be avoided for function whose derivative function looks like $f(x) = 1/x^3$. If the search section is from negative a to positive b, then the search function will probably output a result adequately close to zero. But in fact, there's no zero point for $f(x)$. The fake can be eliminated if bisection search is improved a little. Let c the average of a and b, then if $fabs(f(c)) > fabs(f(a))$ and $fabs(f(c)) > fabs(f(b))$, then the function should be terminated without any solution. This check can be done once and for all because the first check is equivalent to the later one.

Reducing the Search Dimension. This is the 3rd criterion in [6], stating that "The complete camera calibration procedure should not include high dimension (more than five) nonlinear search." The dimension in our algorithm is 3, perfectly satisfying this criterion. Owing to the fact that R and T is independent, the algorithm for finding the minimum value of F can be accomplished as follows:

I.   Given an initial value of 3 rotation angles.
II.   Finding the T that minimizes F under current rotation angles.
III.   If possible, finding a set of rotation angles that decrease F under current T.
IV.   If a better set of rotation angles is found in step III, then GOTO II.
V.   Output extrinsic parameters including rotation angles and translation vector.

In step II, the T is determined in definite time as shown in the following subsection, which results in the nonlinear search of only 3 rotation angles.

2.2 Finding T Given Rotation Angles

If the rotation angles are given, the rotation matrix R is known and its elements can be computed via equation (1) of [3]. Equation (11) can be simplified as equation (12), whose components are shown in (13). When F is minimized, its partial derivatives, shown in (14), (15) and (16), must all be zero, which result in (17).

$$F = \sum_i \left[\left(\frac{c_{1i} + a_x t_x}{c_{2i} + t_z} + c_{3i} \right)^2 + \left(\frac{c_{4i} + a_y t_y}{c_{2i} + t_z} + c_{5i} \right)^2 \right] \tag{12}$$

$$\begin{cases} c_{1i} = a_x \left(R_{11} X_{wi} + R_{12} Y_{wi} + R_{13} Z_{wi} \right) \\ c_{2i} = R_{31} X_{wi} + R_{32} Y_{wi} + R_{33} Z_{wi} \\ c_{3i} = u_0 - U_i \\ c_{4i} = a_y \left(R_{21} X_{wi} + R_{22} Y_{wi} + R_{23} Z_{wi} \right) \\ c_{5i} = v_0 - V_i \end{cases} \tag{13}$$

$$\frac{\partial F}{\partial t_x} = 2 \sum_i \left(\frac{a_x^2 t_x}{\left(c_{2i} + t_z \right)^2} + \frac{a_x c_{1i}}{\left(c_{2i} + t_z \right)^2} + \frac{a_x c_{3i}}{c_{2i} + t_z} \right) \tag{14}$$

$$\frac{\partial F}{\partial t_y} = 2 \sum_i \left(\frac{a_y^2 t_y}{\left(c_{2i} + t_z \right)^2} + \frac{a_y c_{4i}}{\left(c_{2i} + t_z \right)^2} + \frac{a_y c_{5i}}{c_{2i} + t_z} \right) \tag{15}$$

$$\frac{\partial F}{\partial t_z} = -2 \sum_i \left\{ \left(\frac{c_{1i} + c_{2i} c_{3i} + c_{3i} t_z + a_x t_x}{c_{2i} + t_z} \right) \left[\frac{c_{1i} + a_x t_x}{\left(c_{2i} + t_z \right)^2} \right] + \left(\frac{c_{4i} + c_{2i} c_{5i} + c_{5i} t_z + a_y t_y}{c_{2i} + t_z} \right) \left[\frac{c_{4i} + a_y t_y}{\left(c_{2i} + t_z \right)^2} \right] \right\} \tag{16}$$

$$\begin{cases} \sum_i \left(\frac{a_x^2 t_x}{\left(c_{2i} + t_z \right)^2} + \frac{a_x c_{1i}}{\left(c_{2i} + t_z \right)^2} + \frac{a_x c_{3i}}{c_{2i} + t_z} \right) = 0 \\ \sum_i \left(\frac{a_y^2 t_y}{\left(c_{2i} + t_z \right)^2} + \frac{a_y c_{4i}}{\left(c_{2i} + t_z \right)^2} + \frac{a_y c_{5i}}{c_{2i} + t_z} \right) = 0 \\ \sum_i \left\{ \left(\frac{c_{1i} + c_{2i} c_{3i} + c_{3i} t_z + a_x t_x}{c_{2i} + t_z} \right) \left[\frac{c_{1i} + a_x t_x}{\left(c_{2i} + t_z \right)^2} \right] + \left(\frac{c_{4i} + c_{2i} c_{5i} + c_{5i} t_z + a_y t_y}{c_{2i} + t_z} \right) \left[\frac{c_{4i} + a_y t_y}{\left(c_{2i} + t_z \right)^2} \right] \right\} = 0 \end{cases} \tag{17}$$

From the first two equations of (17), t_x and t_y can be linearly represented by t_z so only the last equation should be verified. That is to say,

$$\frac{\partial F}{\partial t_z} = G \left(t_x \quad t_y \quad t_z \right) = G \left(H \left(t_z \right) \quad I \left(t_z \right) \quad t_z \right) = J \left(t_z \right) \tag{18}$$

It is assumed that t_z is within a given section. The section is divided into subsections and if the evaluated value $J(t_z)$ at the two ends of any subsection are of opposite sign, then it is a candidate. If one of $J(t_z)$ is zero, then that t_z is add to the solution list. For each candidate, the improved bisection search as depicted in the 2nd principle of the previous subsection is used. Here come two issues, i.e., determining of the section and dividing of the section. For the former, it wastes time if the section is too large while it misses solution if the section is not big enough to subsume all the solutions. This issued is solved by a self-adaptive method. When guessing the initial value, the function for direct solving of 3 points is called C_n^3 times and the extremes of t_z are recorded. The section between the minimum and maximum is expanded on both sides by a ratio, say, half of the interval of the original one. For the latter, it wastes time if the subsection is too small while it misses solutions if the subsection is big enough to contain more than one solution. In experiment, it is found that dividing into 32 subsections is sufficient. The time complexity is constant since the bisection method ensures outputting result after definite iterations and the number of subsections is 32, a definite number.

Of course, $J(t_z)$ is a fraction. Hence its root is equivalent to the root of its numerator provided that that root will not make its denominator zero. Typically, the numerator has hundreds of terms of different degrees. Admittedly, all the solutions can be found by finding the root of its numerator. But, double precision is incompetent for evaluating that high degree polynomial both precisely and within the range of *double* data type. This necessitates the involvement of a special program capable of dealing with large value arithmetic, which will increase the time complexity dramatically. Thus, searching on a given interval is preferred though at the theoretical risk of losing solutions. By the way, if more than one solution is found for translation vector, F is evaluated by all of them and the solution that makes F smallest is the result.

2.3 Seeking the Rotation Angles

This step is to find a set of rotation angles that decrease F under current T. The partial derivative of F to the rotation angles can be computed symbolically. The derivatives will not be listed owing to the precious space. Once the partial derivatives are given, a better F can be found by deepest descent if it exists.

2.4 Optimizations

In the experiment, it was discovered that when the current function value was sufficiently close to its minimum value, the negative gradient (largest decrease) direction will form a zigzag course and hence the convergence rate slowed down greatly. Thus, the Newton direction was used. Thanks to its quadratic convergence, after several iterations, the result converged.

Table 2. An extremely poor set of data and its result

x_w	y_w	z_w	U	V
-51.64501572	29.37767029	-2.622982025	1673.6034	936.91379
-51.63276291	29.36599731	-1.99703002	1676.3621	1118.9828
-51.76639938	27.99460793	-2.294702053	2156.3621	983.81034
-51.55799866	31.3006115	-3.373887062	967.39655	741.05172
-51.30734253	30.81999588	-2.961890936	1132.9138	862.43103
-53.59531021	27.42661858	0.08365300298	2297.0517	1662.4310
-54.1158371	26.94578743	-3.874444008	2277.7414	432.08621
-52.29491425	33.02606583	-1.546421051	520.50000	1408.6379
-52.04029846	32.27804947	-3.085134983	683.25862	895.53448

a_x	a_y		u_0		v_0
4070.1613	4075.0977		1555.7254		1002.5352

ω (Min)	φ (Min)	κ (Min)	t_x (Min)	t_y (Min)	t_z (Min)
3.062706159	1.619361036	-1.769545293	30.285174063	1.317476380	-39.605269399

RMS (Min)	
	20.5325051580779

To test the robustness of the algorithm, an extremely bad set of data, as shown in Table 2, is used deliberately. The error is enormous as can be seen from RMS value. The 3D data is from a huge Buddha in Mogao Cave and scanned by 3rdTech DeltaSphere-3000 scanner, which uses Time of Flight. Since its face and ears are damaged severely, there's a lot of noise in the acquired data so one half of the face is copied from another half and the scanned models of ears are replaced by manually modeled ones. To make it worse, the picture is taken from a high-resolution camera. No wonder the correspondence between the 3D coordinates and their 2D counterparts is poor. In real situation, never will this scenario happen.

Table 3. The first several iterations that deepest descent outputs

	ω	φ	κ
Initial Value	-2.4215203284559	1.6126231574752	-0.96456892113258
After Iteration 1	-2.4174727752869	1.6120927391394	-0.96456892113258
After Iteration 2	-2.4184872966485	1.6040396597604	-0.96872553605973
After Iteration 3	-2.4174710588083	1.6039061854245	-0.96984796134199
After Iteration 4	-2.4180159067595	1.6017723010739	-0.97008741009895

If only deepest descent and Newton search is employed, given a Turion 1.6G CPU, it takes about 0.9 second to get the result for the poor data in Table 2. Sure, there's still some marginal improvement to come. Hence, the outputs from the first several iterations, as listed in Table 3, are analyzed. It is evident that the advancement in each step is tiny and for ω, it's even back and forth. Unfortunately, the Newton search is also futile since the value is not close enough to the optimal and the advantage of quadratic convergence cannot be made full use of. A new approach named omnidirectional search is proposed to break this dilemma. The variable ω, φ and κ can be its original or plus s or minus s, which means that a total of 27 function values are compared and the minimum is selected. If the minimum is the original, then s is divided by a constant that is greater than 1 (penalty), say 1.4, or else s is multiplied by that constant (prize). By this means, the computational time is greatly decreased to 20 ms, making it meet the requirement for real time usage.

3   Fast Occlusion Culling

Back face triangle culling can be find through the dot product of camera direction and face normal. Constructing $N_{Face} g N_{Camera}$, if $s \geq 0$, the triangle is back facing, so it won't have a texture coordinate.

Triangle beyond the texture scale can be found through the projection coordinates of its 3 vertexes. If not all the 3 projection vertexes are in the scale of texture image, the triangle won't have a texture coordinate.

Self occlusion culling can't be calculated directly through the radial from camera position to each vertex of the 3D model, because that will cause an $O\left(N_{VertexCount}^2\right)$ complicacy. A 3D model acquired from 3D scanner can have more than a million vertexes, which will need hours to finish a single occlusion culling process.

A fast occlusion culling method can be used to remove hidden triangle in efficient. Firstly, calculate the 2D perspective projection coordinates of each vertex, and mark every pixel with the triangle's index if it is in that triangle's projection zone. Then,

Fig. 1. Texture mapping result, without occulusion culling (left), with occulusion culling (right)

4 Natural Neighbor Interpolation

Even after precisely perspective projection, the texture still can not exactly fit to the 3D model. That is because of the error of 3D scan and the lens distortion of the camera. A proper interpolation algorithm can be used here to slightly adjust texture coordinates, so the texture can be stretched to fit the shape of 3D model, and that will give a better vision result than before.

The natural neighbor interpolation algorithm is a good choice here [8]. A Voronoi graph can be generated through all the corresponding points pair, with the Delaunay triangulation method. Suppose there are n pair of corresponding points, for an arbitrary vertex x, a Voronoi polygon T_x can be construct from that N_{n+1} point set. Overlap T_x with the original Voronoi graph from N_n point set, a level 2 Voronoi graph can be constructed as this:

$$T_{ij} = \left\{ x \in R^2; \quad d(x, x_i) < d(x, x_j) < d(x, x_k), \forall k \neq i, j \right\} \tag{19}$$

The Sibson method can be used here to realize the natural neighbor interpolation:

$$\phi_i(x) = \frac{A_i(x)}{A(x)} \tag{20}$$

$A_i(x)$ represents the area of level 2 Voronoi polygon T_{xi}, $A(x)$ represents the area level 1 Voronoi polygon T_x.

Four corresponding point pair will be added at the 9 times area size corner, to make sure all the pixel will be included in the Voronoi polygons. The interpolation result is shown below:

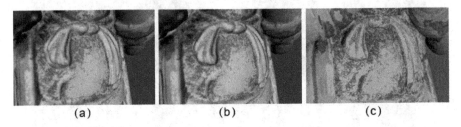

(a)   (b)   (c)

Fig. 2. (a) texture mapping result without interpolation, (b) texuture mapping result with interpolation, (c) original photo

5   Experimental Results

At present, a texture binding software is developed based on this algorithm, as shown in figure 3. First, a user imports photo and 3D model into the top left and bottom left

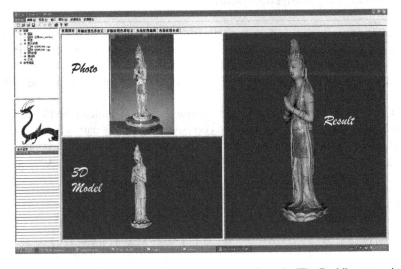

Fig. 3. A typical non-coplanar texture binding process and result (The Buddha statue is from Zhejiang Provincial Museum)

sub-window of Texture Binding sub-window. Then, he inputs the camera intrinsic parameters of the camera under which the photo is taken. After that, he interactively designates the corresponding points in photo and 3D model. He can also zoom in or out to make the point designation more precisely, which will lead to a better binding result. Finally, he presses Texture Binding menu item and the computation commences and the binding result will shown in the right sub-window of Texture Binding sub-window. The computation is done within 5ms for both cases and the RMS is 1.5 and 1.3 pixels (Each of the photo is 6MP, much more than the precision of 3D model.) respectively. The software is put into service in Liangzhu Museum and Zhejiang Provincial Museum to bind the texture of precious cultural relics for virtual exhibition and consequently, the menu is in Chinese.

Fig. 4. Texture mapping result of a gold mask

The previous image is the texture mapping result of a gold mask relic from Jinsha, China. That 3D model result has been used for the living broadcast of 2nd Chinese cultural heritage day of CCTV.

6 Conclusions

Texture mapping is an important issue of cultural heritage digitization. In this paper, an interactive texture mapping method has been proposed. There are three main advantages of this method:

1) The distribution of corresponding point pair can be arbitrary, texture photo taken from any position and direction can be stabilized mapping on to the surface of 3D model.

2) The fast occlusion method simplified the complicacy into $O\left(N_{face\_count}^{2}\right)$, which can support real-time texture mapping adjustment.

3) The natural neighbor interpolation process evidently improved the visual result of texture mapping, any gap between 3D model and texture can be easily removed.

Acknowledgements

The research was supported by the National Basic Research Program of China (No. 2002CB312106), HI-TECH Research and Development Program of China (2006AA01Z305), the Program for New Century Excellent Talents in University (NCET-04-0535) and the Program for Changjiang Scholars and Innovative Research Team in University(IRT0652).

References

1. Songde, Ma., Zhengyou, Z.: Computer Vision - Fundamental of Computational Theory and Algorithm (in Chinese), pp. 52–71. Science Press, Beijing (1998)
2. Heikkila, J., Silven, O.: A Four-step Camera Calibration Procedure with Implicit Image Correction, Computer Vision and Pattern Recognition. In: Proceedings of 1997 IEEE Computer Society Conference, June 17-19, 1997, pp. 1106–1112 (1997)
3. Zhang, Z.: A Flexible New Technique for Camera Calibration. IEEE Transactions on Pattern Analysis and Machine Intelligence 22(11) (November 2000)
4. Bakstein, H.: A Complete DLT-based Camera Calibration with a Virtual 3D Calibration Object, Thesis, Prague (1999)
5. Tsai, R.: A Versatile Camera Calibration Technique for High-Accuracy 3D Machine Vision Metrology Using Off-the-Shelf TV Cameras and Lenses. IEEE Journal of Robotics and Automation 3(4), 323–344 (1987) [legacy, pre - 1988]
6. Rosenhahn, B., Zhangm, Y., Sommer, G.: Performance of Constraint Based Pose Estimation Algorithms, Informatik Aktuell, Mustererkennung 2000. In: 22. DAGM-Symposium, pp. 277–284. Springer, Heidelberg (2000)
7. Liu, Y., Holstein, H.: Pseudo-linearizing Collinearity Constraint for Accurate Pose Estimation from a Single Image. Pattern Recognition Letters 25(8) (2004)
8. Sibson, R.: A vector identity for the Dirichlet tessellation. In: Mathematical Proceedings of the Cambridge Philosophical Scociety, pp. 151–155 (1980)

Prototypes for Automated Architectural 3D-Layout

Henriette Bier[1], Adriaan de Jong[2], Gijs van der Hoorn[2],
Niels Brouwers[2], Marijn Heule[2], and Hans van Maaren[2]

[1] Delft University of Technology, Faculty of Architecture, Berlageweg 1,
2628 CR, Delft, Netherlands
h.h.bier@tudelft.nl
[2] Delft University of Technology, Faculty of Electrical Engineering, Mathematics and
Computer Science, Mekelweg 4,
2628 CD, Delft, Netherlands
{A.N.deJong-TI, G.A.vanderHoorn, N.Brouwers}@student.tudelft.nl,
{M.J.H.Heule, H.vanMaaren}@tudelft.nl

Abstract. Prototypes for automated spatial layout in architecture focus on approaches, which define occupiable space as an orthogonal 2D-grid and use algorithms to allocate each rectangle of the grid to a particular function. However, these approaches are limiting the design to 2D spatial layouts. Based on SAT solving techniques, the prototype presented in this paper proposes a methodology for automated 3D-space planning for voxelized curvilinear geometries.

Keywords: 3D-Modeling and Automated Spatial Layout, Euclidean and Non-Euclidean Geometries, Satisfiability.

1 Introduction

Two systems for automated 2D-layout design based on some form of constraint satisfaction techniques have been compared by Fleming et al. [1]. While one of the systems - Loos - uses a form of generate-and-test constraint satisfaction and the other system - Wright - uses disjunctive constraint satisfaction. Both have, according to Fleming et al., an under-constrained problem definition and, therefore, both produce an unmanageable large amount of feasible solutions. Furthermore, they may be sensitive to scaling when dealing with larger problems.

Loos adds objects sequentially, while Wright satisfies constraints incrementally. When tested and compared both generate similar solutions for the same problem. According to the authors, disjunctive constraint satisfaction is more efficient, but less general than hierarchical generate-and-test constraint satisfaction regarding the type and criteria it can incorporate. However, both can incorporate features of the other approach and overcome their limitations.

More recently, Michalek et al. [2] have been developing a system for 2D-layout design using optimization techniques based on simulated annealing and sequential quadratic programming. Similarly to Loos and Wright, this system addresses automated space allocation conceived as 2D placement of functional spaces or objects within an orthogonal 2D representation of a rectangular room or building floor-plan.

T.G. Wyeld, S. Kenderdine, and M. Docherty (Eds.): VSMM 2007, LNCS 4820, pp. 203–214, 2008.
© Springer-Verlag Berlin Heidelberg 2008

The prototype presented in this paper, FunctionLayouter [FL], generates, however, 2D-layouts of functional objects placed in a voxelized 3D-space, which approximates complex curvilinear geometries. Furthermore, it solves instances of layout problems by exploring relative large solution spaces of these instances and achieves this by reducing the search space, and by exploring it efficiently.

The search space is reduced by applying heuristics: From preliminary spatial studies it is obvious that certain parts of the available space are difficult to access or too small to accommodate Functional Objects [FO]. This space has been, therefore, deducted from the total enabling a search space reduction of almost 1/2.

Furthermore, efficient exploration of the search space is ensured by employing search algorithms based on Boolean Satisfiability [SAT]: The Boolean Satisfiability problem [SAT] is a decision problem attempting to answer the question: When given a specific formula, consisting of a number of Boolean variables - true or false - is there a particular assignment to these variables for which the entire formula evaluates to true?

A Boolean variable X_i, or its negation $\neg X_i$, is called a *literal*. In SAT, formulas consist of a conjunction (AND; $\wedge$) of *clauses* and every clause is a disjunction (OR; $\vee$) of literals. As follows:

$$(X_1 \vee X_2 \vee \neg X_3) \wedge (X_2 \vee X_3 \vee \neg X_4). \tag{1}$$

If there is an assignment to the literals such that every clause is satisfied - evaluates to true - the formula is said to be satisfiable.

SAT is an NP-complete problem, i.e.: there is no known algorithm that is able to determine in polynomial time - with respect to the length of the input - whether there is a satisfying assignment or what that assignment is [4]. Only due to the recent development of satisfiability solvers such as MiniSat [4], RSat [5], and March [6] it is currently possible to solve problems with a large amount of clauses in reasonable time. Current SAT solvers are capable of determining if a satisfying assignment exists for formulas with millions of clauses.

A special class of SAT-based solvers work with pseudo-Boolean formulas consisting of a conjunction of constraints or inequalities. On the left side is a summation over literals and their coefficients, on the right side is an integer number denoting how the left side is constraint:

$$\sum a_i(\neg)X_i \leq k, \text{ with } X_i \in \{0,1\}, \text{ and } a_i, k \in \mathbb{Z}. \tag{2}$$

Due to its ability to handle pseudo-Boolean constraints, the proposed prototype FL makes use of MiniSat+. FL generates a number of Pseudo-Boolean constraints, which MiniSat+ converts to a set of clauses and then invokes the embedded SAT solver. MiniSat+ has been identified as a back-end to address the layout problem described in this paper, due to the fact that a number of the constraints involved in the problem description are based on cardinality requirements.

2 Methodology

The layout-problem is specifically defined for architectural designs based on curvilinear geometries. While rather easy to manipulate formally, NURBS-based spaces are difficult to control with respect to allocation of functions in 3D-space. Therefore, in a first step the NURBS-based space is voxelized .

Fig. 1. Voxelized NURBS-based geometries provide a discrete 3D-space, which can be easily populated with Functional Objects

Voxelized spaces in architecture enable fluent transition from curvilinear-smooth to angular-facetted geometries, and can be seen as mass-models used for volumetrical and functional studies: In an iterative process volumes are assigned to functions, and spatial relationships are established between the different functional volumes in order to generate 3D-layouts.

Voxelization within this project enables continuous, low-high resolution voxel-representation within a 5-90 cm range.

A number of FOs, representing objects, which can be placed within these voxels, are defined. Furthermore, constraints and optimization targets, which define how objects may be placed in voxel-space, are defined. These are then summarized in a problem description, which is translated into a SAT solver-understandable format. Finally, the solver produces numerical and graphical output containing all possible and optimal solutions found.

In this context, several constraint rules have been identified: 1. Cardinality constraints, describing how many FOs may be present; 2. Occupancy constraints, describing which voxels FOs may occupy; 3. Adjacency constraints, describing FOs neighboring rules, and 4. Design constraints, describing spatial relations between FOs. Furthermore, implicit overlap constraints exist, preventing FOs from overlapping.

After defining these constraints, a number of optimization goals have been formulated, including their priority: 1. Maximize occupancy: As many voxels as possible must be occupied by FOs, ensuring a maximum use of available space, and 2. Ergonomic optimization, describing optimizations that help create an optimal work flow, and/or ensure safety for people using the FOs.

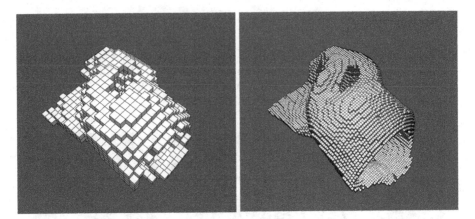

Fig. 2. Voxelization resolution ranges from 5-90 cm enabling an almost accurate representation of the curved geometry. Figure shows voxelization resolution 30/30/30 and 15/15/15 cm.

3 Implementation

The constraint solver used for solving the described layout-problem is MiniSat+. This solver employs DPLL SAT, which is a complete search procedure to explore a search space for possible solutions. This search procedure has been developed in the early 1960s and is referred to as the Davis-Putnam-Logemann-Loveland [DPLL] algorithm.

The DPLL algorithm divides a problem into sub-problems by selecting in each step a Boolean decision variable. This variable is assigned a truth value. The formula is then reduced under this assumption and checked for solutions. When a solution is found, the algorithm halts. When no solution is found, it can be concluded the variable should be assigned the opposite truth value and the search is continued. Only when the whole search space has been explored and no solution is found, the problem can be considered unsatisfiable.

Over the last decade relevant improvements have been made in order to speed up the DPLL algorithm: Most notably clause learning, as well as improved data structures and alternative types of backtracking have increased search efficiency enabling solvers to handle problems with millions of variables and clauses [7].

3.1 Problem Description

The layout-problem addresses NURBS-based designs tested in a case study, a food-kiosk - Figure 3 - which has been abstracted in a first iteration in such a way that equipment components are placed in a voxelized kiosk-space with a resolution of 90/90/90 cm.

In this context, FunctionLayouter 90 [FL90] uses heuristics such as placement of equipment on two levels easily accessible to the kiosk-users 0.00-0.90 and 0.90-1.80 m in order to reduce effectively the search space. Furthermore, equipment is defined as 90/90/90cm units, ensuring a 1:1 mapping of FO to voxel, which is a simplified model.

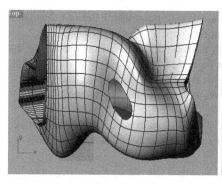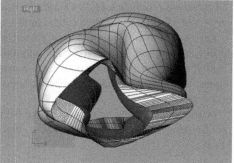

Fig. 3. Image showing top- and right-view of the kiosk as a 3D NURBS-model, which has been employed in the voxelization and layout study

The second iteration, Flexible FunctionLayouter [FlexFL] drops the 1:1 mapping constraints, allowing FOs to span multiple voxels. This enables, inter alia, flexible voxel resolutions, which have been tested on a 30/30/30 cm resolution case study wherein FOs can span multiple voxels, increasing complexity in FO allocation with respect to geometry.

In the original FL90 test case, a food kiosk has been modeled, in which a total number of 14-26 functional objects have been assigned to 26 voxels. In this context, 11 functional object types have been differentiated: Refrigerator [RF], sink [SK], stove [ST], exhaust [EX], automat [AT], storage room [SR], trash bin [TB], dish-washer [DW], coffee machine [CM], micro-wave [MW], and cash desk [CD]. These FOs represent a typical equipment selection for a food-kiosk.

In addition, allocation constraints have been formulated implying definition of most effective functional spatial configurations: These are in part based on empirical findings formalized by Neufert [8] as well as the kitchen work-triangle defined by the Building Research Council [9] at the University of Illinois. This specifies that SK, ST, and RF form, preferably, a triangle in which the closer the length of the triangle sides is to about 200 cm, the better is the layout.

The FlexFL test-case uses a higher resolution model 30/30/30 cm, which implies a higher accuracy in geometrical representation, and therefore, a reduction of available space for placing FOs.

Instead of 14-26 FOs FlexFL30 allocates 10 FOs with differentiated sizes defined by their corresponding height/width/depth: SK 60/60/30, ST 60/60/15, RF 60/60/60, AT 60/60/60, SR 60/60/60, MW 45/45/45, DW 45/45/45, TB 45/45/60, EX 45/45/15, CM 45/45/15, and CD 45/45/15. Sizes are, in this case, simplified but realistic assumption for FO-masses.

FlexFL30 deals, therefore, with a nearly realistic problem description, while FL90 deals with an abstracted one.

3.2 Software Architecture

The basic control flow of FunctionLayouter has been split into a sequence of operations: Initially, a problem is read in from an XML problem description. Here, the problem is split into a number of rules and optimization targets.

The problem is then translated pseudo-Boolean constraints, which are run through a version of MiniSat+ modified by the authors of this paper.

The SAT solver's output is then parsed and translated into solutions. Based on the optimization target, new constraints may then be added, and MiniSat+ invoked again. Finally, the solutions are displayed on a graphical user interface, where the user may request more information on a specific solution, again invoking the constraint translation system.

In this context, the main focus has been the translation of constraints from the specifications as given by designer, to the pseudo-Boolean constraints solvable by MiniSat+.

3.3 Constraints Translation in FL90

In order to enable constraints translation into pseudo-Boolean, variables have been defined as $X^{FO}_{x,y,z}$, where x, y, z are the coordinates in voxel-space. For example, when $X^{RF}_{0,0,1}$ is true, a refrigerator is placed at $(0,0,1)$. When it is false, the refrigerator is not placed there.

These variables can then be combined into constraints. For example, an overlap constraint specifying that only one item may be contained in voxel x, y, z would take on the form:

$$\sum_{f \in FO} +1 * X^{f}_{x,y,z} \leq 1, \tag{3}$$

where FO is the set of all FOs that may be placed at x, y, z.

1. Cardinality and occupancy constraints are relatively trivial to translate, and are summations of possible locations for each FO, constrained by the minimum and maximum number of instantiations of each FO. The occupancy constraints are implicitly formulated in this manner, since all placement variables for a functional object are specified.

For example, to specify a maximum of two refrigerators [RF]:

$$\sum_{x,y,z \in VOX^{RF}} +1 * X^{RF}_{x,y,z} \leq 2, \tag{4}$$

where VOX^{RF} contains all RF locations.

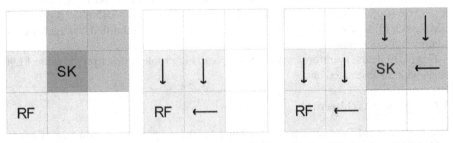

Fig. 4. Diagram showing occupancy constraint definition: (a) Invalid Overlap, (b) Marking using arrows, (c) Potential Neighbor in FlexFL

2. Adjacency rules are based on direct neighbors at the same height, not including diagonals. To compute such rules for an FO f at voxel x, y, z, a list of disallowed neighbor types is generated. Next, for every disallowed neighbor type, a list of voxels neighboring f is generated. This is the set of directly neighboring voxels, as in Figure 5(a). Once this neighbor list has been generated, FlexFL iterates through these neighbors, and generates the following constraints for every voxel u, v, w in the list:

$$+1 * X^f_{x,y,z} + 1 * X^g_{u,v,w} \leq 1, \tag{5}$$

where g is the current disallowed neighbor.

For the example given in Figure 5(a), the following constraints would be generated:

$$
\begin{aligned}
+1 * X^{\mathrm{RF}}_{1,1} + 1 * X^{\mathrm{SK}}_{0,1} &\leq 1; \\
+1 * X^{\mathrm{RF}}_{1,1} + 1 * X^{\mathrm{SK}}_{1,0} &\leq 1; \\
+1 * X^{\mathrm{RF}}_{1,1} + 1 * X^{\mathrm{SK}}_{2,1} &\leq 1; \\
+1 * X^{\mathrm{RF}}_{1,1} + 1 * X^{\mathrm{SK}}_{1,2} &\leq 1.
\end{aligned}
\tag{6}
$$

3. Design constraints incorporate rules such as 'if a sink is placed, a dishwasher must be placed in one of its neighboring cells'. In general, if an FO g must be placed next to an FO f, a neighbor list $\mathrm{L}^f_{x,y,z}$ is generated for every voxel x, y, z that f can be placed at as in the previous section. Unlike the normal adjacency case, however, the variables in the neighbor list are summed up, and included in a rule as follows:

$$-1 * X^f_{x,y,z} \sum_{u,v,w \in \mathrm{L}^f_{x,y,z}} +1 * X^g_{u,v,w} \geq 0 \tag{7}$$

This implies that if f is positioned at x, y, z, one of the voxels in $\mathrm{L}^f_{x,y,z}$ must contain g.

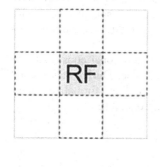

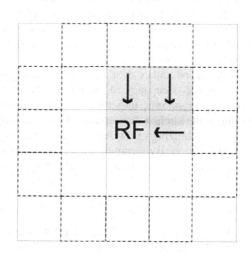

Fig. 5. Diagram showing neighboring rules: (a) Neighbors in FL90 (b) 2x2 sized neighbors in FlexFL

Constraints translation in FlexFL is different from FL90 mainly because the 1:1 mapping between voxels and FOs is replaced by a flexible mapping of FOs of different sizes to voxel resolutions ranging from 5-90 cm.

3.4 Constraints Translation in FlexFL

A major difference between the FL90 and FlexFL is that a placement variable no longer represents the whole functional object, but the *anchor* of an FO, i.e. the FO's voxel that is closest to the left, front, bottom corner of the FO.

Most constraints are based on this anchor voxel, including the cardinality constraints, occupancy constraints, and the optimizations that are explained in the next section. This allows the translation for these rules to constraints to remain unchanged. There are, however, a few differences, which are explained in this section.

1. Overlap constraints are more complex, to prevent situations such as in Figure 4(a). To prevent this from taking place, rules are added to ensure that if a certain voxel is occupied by the anchor of an FO, the other voxels occupied by it are marked with arrows to such an anchor voxel, as in Figure 4(b).

By ensuring that different arrows can not co-exist with each other or other occupying FOs in a single voxel, overlap is prevented. Extension to the 3D-case is done by adding a third, downwards pointer.

2. Adjacency rules are translated in a similar fashion to the FL90 case, however, since in the FlexFL case, layouts as in Figure 4(c) are also possible. The neighbor list calculation is, therefore, performed differently. For example, the generated neighbor list for a 2x2 object would be as shown in Figure 5(b).

3.5 Optimization

Once the search space has been reduced by the above constraints, optimal solutions are generated from the number of valid solutions.

In both FL90 and FlexFL, two optimization targets have been consecutively allowed, one to maximize the occupancy, and one to optimize spatial layout with respect to ergonomic aspects. The maximization goal is applied during an initial invocation of the SAT solver.

A second call is then made to the SAT solver, with an additional constraint that fixates the occupancy to the previously found maximum value. During this second run, an ergonomic target is used, based on the empirical findings formalized, inter alia, in the kitchen work triangle by the Building Research Council [6].

1. Maximizing Occupancy: MiniSat+ contains a feature, which minimizes a given goal function. By summing up all possible FO locations, and multiplying this sum by -1, the following minimizing goal function is obtained:

$$-1 * \sum_{x,y,z \in \text{VOX}} \sum_{f \in \text{FO}_{x,y,z}} X^f_{x,y,z} \tag{8}$$

where VOX contains all voxel positions, and $\text{FO}_{x,y,z}$ contains all FOs that can be placed at that voxel position.

The procedure that MiniSat+ uses to find the optimal solution is to find an initial solution while ignoring the minimization function. It then computes the value of the goal function, and adds a constraint that all new solutions should be better. The solver then continues its search with this new constraint. This procedure is repeated until no new results are found, where the last result is the optimal one.

2. Ergonomic Rules: Since translating the kitchen work triangle target to a pseudo-Boolean goal function would be complex, a different approach has been chosen. An exhaustive search is performed for all different layouts of the sink, stove and refrigerator. This is done by running the solver repeatedly, while adding constraints to exclude sink-stove-refrigerator configurations that have previously been found.

These configurations are then presented to the user, ordered by their similarity with the optimal kitchen work triangle. The user can then select one of these configurations and generate all possible layouts containing that triangle configuration.

3.6 Results

FL90 generates 11 possible layout solutions from which 4 are optimal. All 4 optimal solutions satisfy occupancy maximization as well as SK, ST, and RF triangle optimization.

Generated solutions have been 2D visualized as shown in Figure 6. The triangle spanning between SK, ST, and RF shows the difference between possible and best possible solutions according to the principle the smaller the triangle, the better the solution.

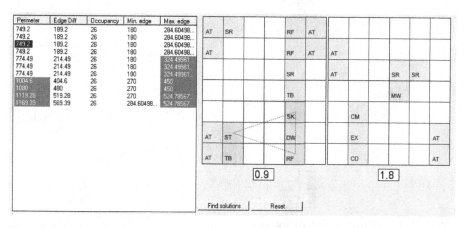

Fig. 6. Image shows one of the four optimal layouts for 90/90/90 voxelization resolution as 2D representation of the levels at 0.90 and 1.80 m relative space height. Sub-optimal solutions are marked in the table dark gray.

FlexFL30 generates 28 layout solutions incorporating about 23 different triangle configurations from which all are sub-optimal, since the maximum triangle edge length is exceeding 391cm. However, 9 triangle configurations are close to optimal.

Solutions are 2D represented in a sequence of voxel-layers, where FO positions are obviously more differentiated in response to not only the complex geometry but also to a nearly realistic problem definition. Each voxel-layer shows contained FOs: TB for instance spans 2 voxel-layers, since it is 60 cm high, while SK occupies one voxel-layer, since only 30 cm high.

FOs are placed in such a way that they accommodate the complex geometry except for one case, where an AT is not accessible. This problem can be addressed by defining additional constraints describing in more detail spatial accessibility. However,

Fig. 7. Image shows layout solutions for 30/30/30 voxelization resolution as 2D representation of levels 0.90 - 1.80 m relative space height

FOs layout satisfies, in general, requirements of not only accessibility but also optimal placement relative to each other as well as to the whole space.

4 Discussion

FunctionLayouter generates, in comparison with Loos and Wright, functional layouts of similar scale and realistic relevance. However, Loos and Wright deal only with the placement of functional objects in 2D, while FunctionLayouter addresses the layout in 3D dealing with the allocation of functions within complex - free-formed geometries - instead of simple - rectangular - space geometries.

With respect to optimization, Loos constructs solutions incrementally, testing intermediate solutions on consistency and other criteria relevant for architectural design, while 'optimization' is carried out according to these intermediate tests, in an ad hoc procedure implying that no overall objective directs the search. However, without invoking a backtracking procedure, Loos' search is not complete. As presented in Fleming's paper [1] it is neither exhaustive nor does it yield solutions with an overall optimal objective.

Wright is more similar to the approach presented in this paper: Wright uses Constraint Satisfaction, to implement a backtracking procedure that makes the search complete. Optimization is implemented afterwards and is, therefore, not used to direct the search.

Loos and Wright deal directly with the geometric aspects of both space and objects, while FL employs voxelization after which all geometric aspects are modeled through neighboring constraints. Furthermore, FL allows for a hierarchical optimization procedure: Optimal occupancy is an overall objective directing the search while the triangle objective is done by inspection and selection.

Loos and Wright, as presented in Fleming's paper [1], are rather sensitive to scaling effects, while FlexFL30 indicates that the approach presented in this paper is less sensitive with respect to scaling. Furthermore, since FL is able to find if an assignment is possible or not, the FL-search is complete.

5 Conclusion

FunctionLayouter generates functional layouts exhaustively and enables the designer to consider more alternatives than by means of conventional sketching methods mainly because architectural space planning is highly combinatorial and, therefore, difficult to conceive exhaustively by human search means.

Instead of one, FunctionLayouter generates all possible designs and allows for critical choices by departing from a singular design principle, that represents a potentially prejudiced position of the singular designer. FunctionLayouter generates not only all possible solutions but also offers solutions within the spectrum of an optimal solutions-field.

Acknowledgments. This project has benefited, inter alia, from the contribution of Roland Schmehl and David Rutten.

References

1. Flemming, U., et al.: Hierarchical Generate and Test vs. Constraint-Directed Search - A Comparison in the Context of Layout Synthesis published in Artificial Intelligence in Design. Kluwer Academic Publishers, Dordrecht (1992)
2. Michalek, J.J., et al.: Architectural Layout Design Optimization, Engineering Optimization. Taylor & Francis, UK (2002)
3. Cook, S.A.: The Complexity of Theorem-proving Procedures. In: Proceedings of the Third Annual ACM Symposium on theory of Computing, ACM Press, New York (1971)
4. Een, N., Sorensson, N.: An Extensible SAT solver. In: Satisfiability Workshop (2003)
5. Pipatsrisawat, K., Darwiche, A.: RSat 2.0: SAT Solver Description, Technical report D153, Automated Reasoning Group. Computer Science, Los Angeles (2007)
6. Heule, M.J.H., van Maaren, H.: March_dl: Adding Adaptive Heuristics and a New Branching Strategy. Journal on Satisfiability, Boolean Modeling and Computation 2 (2006)
7. Lintao, Z., Sharad, M.: The Quest for Efficient Boolean Satisfiability Solvers, LNCS, Springer Berlin/Heidelberg (2002)
8. Neufert, E., Neufert, P.: Architects' Data, 3Rev. Ed., UK Edition Blackwell Science, Malden (2002)
9. Building Research Council: Kitchen Planning Standards, University of Illinois, Urbana-Champaign (1993)

Author Index

Lecture Notes in Computer Science

Sublibrary 3: Information Systems and Application, incl. Internet/Web and HCI

For information about Vols. 1– 4541
please contact your bookseller or Springer

Vol. 4932: S. Hartmann, G. Kern-Isberner (Eds.), Foundations of Information and Knowledge Systems. XII, 397 pages. 2008.

Vol. 4928: A. ter Hofstede, B. Benatallah, H.-Y. Paik (Eds.), Business Process Management Workshops. XIII, 518 pages. 2008.

Vol. 4903: S. Satoh, F. Nack, M. Etoh (Eds.), Advances in Multimedia Modeling. XIX, 510 pages. 2008.

Vol. 4900: S. Spaccapietra (Ed.), Journal on Data Semantics X. XIII, 265 pages. 2008.

Vol. 4892: A. Popescu-Belis, S. Renals, H. Bourlard (Eds.), Machine Learning for Multimodal Interaction. XI, 308 pages. 2008.

Vol. 4882: T. Janowski, H. Mohanty (Eds.), Distributed Computing and Internet Technology. XIII, 346 pages. 2007.

Vol. 4881: H. Yin, P. Tino, E. Corchado, W. Byrne, X. Yao (Eds.), Intelligent Data Engineering and Automated Learning - IDEAL 2007. XX, 1174 pages. 2007.

Vol. 4877: C. Thanos, F. Borri, L. Candela (Eds.), Digital Libraries: Research and Development. XII, 350 pages. 2007.

Vol. 4872: D. Mery, L. Rueda (Eds.), Advances in Image and Video Technology. XXI, 961 pages. 2007.

Vol. 4871: M. Cavazza, S. Donikian (Eds.), Virtual Storytelling. XIII, 219 pages. 2007.

Vol. 4858: X. Deng, F.C. Graham (Eds.), Internet and Network Economics. XVI, 598 pages. 2007.

Vol. 4857: J.M. Ware, G.E. Taylor (Eds.), Web and Wireless Geographical Information Systems. XI, 293 pages. 2007.

Vol. 4853: F. Fonseca, M.A. Rodríguez, S. Levashkin (Eds.), GeoSpatial Semantics. X, 289 pages. 2007.

Vol. 4836: H. Ichikawa, W.-D. Cho, I. Satoh, H.Y. Youn (Eds.), Ubiquitous Computing Systems. XIII, 307 pages. 2007.

Vol. 4832: M. Weske, M.-S. Hacid, C. Godart (Eds.), Web Information Systems Engineering – WISE 2007 Workshops. XV, 518 pages. 2007.

Vol. 4831: B. Benatallah, F. Casati, D. Georgakopoulos, C. Bartolini, W. Sadiq, C. Godart (Eds.), Web Information Systems Engineering – WISE 2007. XVI, 675 pages. 2007.

Vol. 4825: K. Aberer, K.-S. Choi, N. Noy, D. Allemang, K.-I. Lee, L. Nixon, J. Golbeck, P. Mika, D. Maynard, R. Mizoguchi, G. Schreiber, P. Cudré-Mauroux (Eds.), The Semantic Web. XXVII, 973 pages. 2007.

Vol. 4822: D.H.-L. Goh, T.H. Cao, I.T. Sølvberg, E. Rasmussen (Eds.), Asian Digital Libraries. XVII, 519 pages. 2007.

Vol. 4820: T.G. Wyeld, S. Kenderdine, M. Docherty (Eds.), Virtual Systems and Multimedia. XII, 215 pages. 2008.

Vol. 4816: B. Falcidieno, M. Spagnuolo, Y. Avrithis, I. Kompatsiaris, P. Buitelaar (Eds.), Semantic Multimedia. XII, 306 pages. 2007.

Vol. 4813: I. Oakley, S.A. Brewster (Eds.), Haptic and Audio Interaction Design. XIV, 145 pages. 2007.

Vol. 4810: H.H.-S. Ip, O.C. Au, H. Leung, M.-T. Sun, W.-Y. Ma, S.-M. Hu (Eds.), Advances in Multimedia Information Processing – PCM 2007. XXI, 834 pages. 2007.

Vol. 4809: M.K. Denko, C.-s. Shih, K.-C. Li, S.-L. Tsao, Q.-A. Zeng, S.H. Park, Y.-B. Ko, S.-H. Hung, J.-H. Park (Eds.), Emerging Directions in Embedded and Ubiquitous Computing. XXXV, 823 pages. 2007.

Vol. 4808: T.-W. Kuo, E. Sha, M. Guo, L.T. Yang, Z. Shao (Eds.), Embedded and Ubiquitous Computing. XXI, 769 pages. 2007.

Vol. 4806: R. Meersman, Z. Tari, P. Herrero (Eds.), On the Move to Meaningful Internet Systems 2007: OTM 2007 Workshops, Part II. XXXIV, 611 pages. 2007.

Vol. 4805: R. Meersman, Z. Tari, P. Herrero (Eds.), On the Move to Meaningful Internet Systems 2007: OTM 2007 Workshops, Part I. XXXIV, 757 pages. 2007.

Vol. 4804: R. Meersman, Z. Tari (Eds.), On the Move to Meaningful Internet Systems 2007: CoopIS, DOA, ODBASE, GADA, and IS, Part II. XXIX, 683 pages. 2007.

Vol. 4803: R. Meersman, Z. Tari (Eds.), On the Move to Meaningful Internet Systems 2007: CoopIS, DOA, ODBASE, GADA, and IS, Part I. XXIX, 1173 pages. 2007.

Vol. 4802: J.-L. Hainaut, E.A. Rundensteiner, M. Kirchberg, M. Bertolotto, M. Brochhausen, Y.-P.P. Chen, S.S.-S. Cherfi, M. Doerr, H. Han, S. Hartmann, J. Parsons, G. Poels, C. Rolland, J. Trujillo, E. Yu, E. Zimányie (Eds.), Advances in Conceptual Modeling – Foundations and Applications. XIX, 420 pages. 2007.

Vol. 4801: C. Parent, K.-D. Schewe, V.C. Storey, B. Thalheim (Eds.), Conceptual Modeling - ER 2007. XVI, 616 pages. 2007.

Vol. 4797: M. Arenas, M.I. Schwartzbach (Eds.), Database Programming Languages. VIII, 261 pages. 2007.

Vol. 4796: M. Lew, N. Sebe, T.S. Huang, E.M. Bakker (Eds.), Human–Computer Interaction. X, 157 pages. 2007.

Vol. 4794: B. Schiele, A.K. Dey, H. Gellersen, B. de Ruyter, M. Tscheligi, R. Wichert, E. Aarts, A. Buchmann (Eds.), Ambient Intelligence. XV, 375 pages. 2007.